...ornia

...ss the Arctic circle.

Ben has presented numerous programmes, including the BBC's *Animal Park, Countryfile, Wild in Africa, Wild on the West Coast, Crufts, One Man and His Dog* and *Swimming with Crocodiles*. He is an ambassador for WWF, TUSK, the PDSA and Hearing Dogs for Deaf People, a Fellow of the Royal Geographical Society, the President of the Campaign for National Parks and President of the Hedgehog Preservation Society.

He lives in London with his wife Marina, their children Ludo and Iona, and their dog Maggi. He is currently preparing to swim across the Atlantic.

For more information on Ben Fogle and his books, see his website at www.benfogle.com

Also by Ben Fogle

THE ACCIDENTAL ADVENTURER
THE TEATIME ISLAND
OFFSHORE
THE CROSSING (with James Cracknell)
RACE TO THE POLE (with James Cracknell)

THE ACCIDENTAL NATURALIST

My Wild Years

BEN FOGLE

CORGI BOOKS

TRANSWORLD PUBLISHERS
61–63 Uxbridge Road, London W5 5SA
A Random House Group Company
www.transworldbooks.co.uk

**THE ACCIDENTAL NATURALIST
A CORGI BOOK: 9780552165808**

First published in Great Britain
in 2012 by Bantam Press
an imprint of Transworld Publishers
Corgi edition published 2013

Addresses for Random House Group Ltd companies outside the UK
can be found at: www.randomhouse.co.uk
The Random House Group Ltd Reg. No. 954009

The Random House Group Limited supports The Forest Stewardship Council
(FSC®), the leading international forest-certification organization. Our books
carrying the FSC label are printed on FSC®-certified paper. FSC is the
only forest-certification scheme endorsed by the leading environmental
organizations, including Greenpeace. Our paper-procurement
policy can be found at www.randomhouse.co.uk/environment

Typeset in 11/14.5pt Minion by Falcon Oast Graphic Art Ltd.
Printed and bound by CPI Group (UK) Ltd, Croydon, CR0 4YY.

2 4 6 8 10 9 7 5 3 1

To Inca, and all the animals
I have known (and eaten)

Contents

THE ACCIDENTAL
NATURALIST

Introduction
Crocodile Tears

'Haw, haw, haw . . . hawwwwwww.'
   It sounded like an old man laughing.
'Haw, haw, hawww.'
The deep, loud bass reverberated across the inky river. A slight chill had descended with the darkness and the moon was just beginning its spectacular rise. A rich orange glow appeared on the horizon, dancing like distant flames, the optical illusion making the moon look twice its normal size. The calm waters reflected its light and cast long shadows to the shore, leaves and grasses turning silver as we gently paddled along.

I jumped each time a fish leapt out of the darkness and crashed back into the river. Mosquitoes buzzed around my head. I swatted them away and stared closely at the water as a powerful beam of light swept back and forth. A chorus of cicadas and frogs sent a wave of music dancing from shore to shore. Nature's orchestra can be breathtakingly beautiful.

Sitting at the front of the boat, I pulled my fleece close to my neck as I stared, mesmerized, at the beam of light ahead.

'Haw, haw, haw.'

They were close. Very close.

A couple of bats swept low over the water, their silhouettes caught in the eye of the moon. We all remained deadly silent, eyes fixed on the beam of light. Watching. Waiting. Wanting.

Back and forth, the light swept from bank to bank like the beam of a lighthouse, as hundreds of flies, insects and moths converged within it.

Then the light settled on a bright white reflection close to the shore. My heart leapt. This was what we were after.

'It's a spider,' said Clive, continuing the sweep.

We were in the Caprivi Strip, a long, thin tentacle of land in northern Namibia that borders Angola and Botswana. This was the real Africa – a green, watery world of forest and river rich in wildlife.

I was on the river with a team of scientists and a BBC film crew in search of Nile crocodiles. It was my big break into natural history presenting and this was my moment to catch a crocodile with my bare hands at night. We were all pumped with adrenaline. There is something so uniquely exciting about the African night, and here we were, in search of one of the continent's most feared predators.

But as we drifted down the river it wasn't the crocodiles that were our main concern. It was another African animal that is feared in equal measure and, debatably, is responsible for even more deaths.

'Haw, haw, hawwwww' – the unmistakable grunt and

snort of the hippos that float on the surface of the water like angry icebergs.

Hippos get out of the wrong side of bed every day. I'm not sure why they are so grumpy, but they need anger-management classes more than any other African animal. Pessimistic, cantankerous and cranky sums them up. Their perpetual bad mood makes them incredibly dangerous. Hippos take no prisoners.

Now the hippos added to the drama of the night as we continued our search. We had been out for several hours under the magical African night, quietly sharing our wildlife encounters from across the globe: tales of hungry hyena and soaring condors. I had just finished recounting my favourite campfire tale about the night of the turtles (you'll have to wait for that story) when we spotted our first croc.

The red reflection from the creature's eyes confirmed that this was indeed what we were after. It was crucial that Clive estimated the size of the animal. Too big and I'd become its dinner.

We held our breath as the boat crept towards the un-suspecting crocodile. The torchlight remained on its eyes, blinding it to our approach.

'It's about a two-footer,' he whispered.

On the shore, a two-foot crocodile had sounded a little disappointing. 'Can't we go for something a little larger?' I had implored.

'Wait till we're on the river,' smiled Clive. 'It might seem a little bigger then.'

And right now, a two-foot crocodile sounded like a gargantuan dinosaur.

'If you're happy, you can try for it,' said Clive.

I could feel my heart pounding.

'Hang low over the front of the boat. When you can see its neck, grab it hard behind the eyes,' he advised, 'and hang on.'

It seemed slightly ludicrous that I was about to hang over the side of a boat on an African river teeming with hippos – to catch a crocodile with my bare hands . . .

But this was no dream. This was the real deal and I had a TV crew in tow to record every breathless moment for millions to see.

'Focus, Ben,' I said to myself under my breath. 'Breathe deeply.'

Carefully, I moved to the front of the boat and gently eased my body over the edge. I stared at the red eyes reflecting just a few metres away.

Limbering up, I practised a fast snatch with my hands. Suddenly I wished I'd paid more attention in all those lessons at Lord's cricket ground in London, where my mother had sent me as a boy in the hope that I would become the next Ian Botham. I was always terrible with my hands, but now my very fingers depended on them. If I miscalculated my snatch, I risked plunging my hands into the croc's mouth. I didn't need reminding that a two-foot croc could do serious damage to a pair of pinkies.

The universe around me narrowed as I focused on those two eyes. I didn't dare blink. I held my breath. It was as if the world had stopped. No noise. No smell. Just me and the croc.

I wriggled my fingers gently for fear they would cramp with terror. I had to do this. My pride and my career were at stake.

The croc was just a metre away. I could make out its body under the surface; it looked huge. It was facing head on to the boat. The torchlight held on firmly to its eyes, giving me a clear chance to strike.

'Go,' whispered Clive. 'Go!'

I can still remember as a child being frozen with fear at the edge of a small cliff.

'Jump!' hollered my sister Emily. 'Jump, you wuss.'

It was only about 20 feet, but I stood there, rooted like a plant. I was physically frozen with fear.

'*Jump!*' came the cry from the water.

Why couldn't I jump? It was like a physical barrier. I knew it was safe, but the longer I waited the worse the paralysis became. Several times I edged towards the cliff, but each time I hit an invisible wall. I could see my skin physically moving above my heart.

'*Jump!*'

The more my sister implored, and the longer I procrastinated, the worse it became.

Five minutes. Ten minutes. Fifteen minutes. By now there were other people behind me waiting to jump.

I gave up, and with my tail between my legs I gently clambered down. Pride dented, it was an early lesson in the dangers of procrastination and the art of immediate action. Here on an African river, I knew I had to act at once or risk failure.

I stared at the neck of the croc, lifted my hands slightly to gain more leverage – and swiped.

My hands dipped into the tepid waters and I felt the tough, scaly skin as I made contact with the crocodile. I felt it struggle against my grip and locked my hands tight. In the commotion I wasn't sure where I had grabbed it, but I had the croc in my grasp. As I lifted my arms from the water I could see its head just beyond my hands.

Adrenaline coursed through my body as I hauled the creature on to the boat. I couldn't believe I had done it. I had actually caught a crocodile with my bare hands. I was puffed with pride and excitement.

'Whoaaaa!' I squealed to the camera.

'Look at this turtle!' I said with excitement. 'I have caught this turtle with my bare hands!'

Where had that come from? Why had I called it a turtle? It was a crocodile. I knew that. Everyone knew that.

'Idiot – idiot!' I berated myself silently. *Why had I called it a turtle?*

I had been talking about turtles, but this wasn't a turtle. I have sometimes wondered whether I have a form of verbal dyslexia. I have often confused and mixed words over the years, but there were no excuses. This was my chance as a wildlife presenter and I'd just ruined it. My dreams and aspirations of becoming a naturalist began to fizzle and fade.

A little like that descent of shame down the cliff face as a child, I returned to our Namibian lodge humiliated and dejected.

One of the hardest parts of this book was not the writing, nor the recollection of the events themselves, but the title. I can't tell you how many sleepless nights I have had worrying about it. 'Who am I to call myself a naturalist?' I would berate myself.

16

A naturalist is defined in the dictionary as someone with an interest in nature and the environment, which in my case is true. The inescapable reality is that, whatever I am, I happened by accident. I never intended to work with nature and wildlife; as with so much in my life, it just sort of happened.

In a way it isn't surprising. Animals have always been a big part of my life. As a young boy I would spend all my summers out on Lake Chemong in Canada, where my grandparents had built a wooden cottage. I loved to paddle out on to the lake and fish, but my late grandfather, Morris, would only allow me to take part on the understanding that I ate anything big enough to keep. I hated fish, but decided it was worth a few unpleasant mouthfuls in return for the hours of pleasure it gave me. I would sit in my little wooden rowing boat and watch as muskrats porpoised in the water while Canadian loons glided by. I loved being so close to nature and wanted to understand more about it.

Like Gerald Durrell, I really can refer to 'my family and other animals'. Animals are part of my DNA. My father, Dr Bruce Fogle, a veterinary surgeon, is a world authority on animal behaviour and has written dozens of books on the subject. I always longed to follow in his footsteps. I grew up watching *All Creatures Great and Small, Lassie, Flipper* and *Gentle Ben* and they only added fuel to my pursuit of animal medicine.

I can remember watching in awe as Sir David Attenborough was tumbled around on the jungle floor by a silverback gorilla, and who can forget the elephant pooing on the *Blue Peter* studio floor? I admired both Michaela

Strachan and Terry Nutkins on *The Really Wild Show* and dreamed of one day doing the same.

Sadly, my brain never quite matched my aspirations and a couple of failed A-levels soon put paid to any lingering hopes of becoming a vet. But my love of animals and fascination with the natural world have never waned; indeed, throughout my life my curiosity to discover more has only been fuelled.

Dogs in particular helped inspire my interest in the animal world. From the day I was born, they have been a constant for me. Our four-legged friends have helped bend and shape my life, and I'd argue that one black dog in particular has been responsible for finding me a career, a wife and a family. The dogs in my early life offered me a tiny window into the animal kingdom and fuelled my curiosity about the natural world. How can a small chihuahua be related to a wolf? I still wonder. What evolutionary quirk created the elephant and how can whales navigate across vast oceans?

My life in animals has been as colourful as it has been varied and over the years I have had more than my fair share of adventures and misadventures with creatures great and small. I have travelled to some of the furthest regions of the globe in search of wildlife. I have been chased by bull elephant seals in the Falkland Islands and enchanted by penguins in the Galapagos. I have watched great white sharks hunting off San Francisco and washed an elephant in a river. I've translocated rhino and helped operate on a cheetah. I've been bitten by parrots in Wiltshire and been diving with wild saltwater crocodiles in northern Australia. From turtles in

Honduras to condors in California, over the years I have built up a wealth of experiences from my encounters that have instilled wonder and fear in me in equal measure. I have learnt to love the environment through my understanding of the planet's fragile ecosystem.

As a society we tend to group animals into different categories, essentially creating a rating system in the same way we classify celebrities from A list to D list. I am always appalled to see celebrities romping around the Australian bush for ITV's *I'm a Celebrity . . . Get Me Out of Here!*, eating live insects and torturing spiders and eels. 'Why,' I ask myself each year, 'does society permit such wanton cruelty to any creature?' Just because it has eight legs and no spine doesn't mean it is any different from an animal that has two and vertebrae. What has always upset me is that the programme is symbolic of our relationship with animals. The programme makers take precautions not to hurt the animals and deny that any excessive harm is caused, but what kind of message does it give to young people when they see such cruel acts inflicted on rats and snakes?

Every creature, great and small, has a role in the carefully balanced ecosystem of the planet, and I have always thought it wrong to categorize animals according to their importance. We are all living, breathing creatures – doesn't that make us essentially the same? The answer is, I don't know.

The reason I don't know, and the reason that I must also regard myself as a bit of a hypocrite, is that I too will eat beef, lamb and pork but will turn up my nose at rabbit or horse. It is not because I don't like the taste, but because I don't like the thought of it. For me, horses and rabbits are pets, not dinner. But why is it that we have chosen to live with dogs, eat pigs and wear cows? How is it that one nation's dinner is another nation's pet? How can two different cultures revere and deride the same animal? These are questions that have intrigued me since I was a child.

I have also always been intrigued by man's power to 'harness' wildlife. But are we 'harnessing' it at all, or are we working with it? Perhaps it is merely working with us. I have always been fascinated by the theory that dogs are the most intelligent 'parasites' on earth, merely using their affections and cute puppy looks to get closer and closer to man before taking over the world. From being wild, they have slowly worked their way into our lives until they are not only in our homes but also in our beds.

Keeping animals in captivity has always been a highly emotive subject. However, I would argue that it has become key to the conservation of wildlife. The irony is, of course, that even though we might object to it, we have brought it on ourselves through the destruction of habitat. It is a deeply sad vicious circle of our own making.

Animals stir some of mankind's greatest questions but also answer some of our key concerns. Our relationship with them is symbolic of our attitudes towards nature and our effect on the natural world in general. Wildlife has become our litmus paper, an advanced warning of our impact on the planet and how it will eventually affect us too. Climate change has become a highly contentious issue in itself. While I agree the planet is going through a natural cycle of evolutionary climatic change, it seems impossible to deny our own effect on the environment.

Over the years I have seen first hand the changing conditions in the Arctic Circle and the effect that has on the polar bear. I have seen the effects of deforestation in the Amazon Basin and the 'plasticization' of the oceans. I, like most of us, have become a helpless spectator, but I have also become desperate to do something. Determined to make a change.

Although I didn't follow my earliest ambition to become a vet, a series of misadventures, dogged determination, fighting against all odds, and some remarkable events and encounters have colluded to help me in my lifelong dream to become a sort of naturalist anyway. This is the story of my life in animals and a tale of hope – hope for nature, the planet, mankind, and my own hope in the pursuit of becoming a naturalist.

Part One

The Bark

1

Jaws, Sea Monkeys and Other Pets

She gazed up at me with her hazel eyes as I ran my fingers through her thick black hair. It was instant love as she stared longingly back at me. I nuzzled my nose behind her ear and inhaled her scent. I had always been told that I'd find her, and now I really had found 'the one'. Life can work in strange ways with its twists and turns, and they always say momentous things happen when you least expect them. I certainly never thought it would be here, in a semi-rural farm next to Heathrow airport, that our lives would collide.

'She's taken,' shrugged the woman in charge.

'What do you mean she's taken?' I was heartbroken.

She pointed to a small blue pen mark in her ear. 'She was bought this morning.'

I was devastated. I was in love and had already envisaged our life together. Now I was being told I couldn't have her.

'What about this one?' she suggested.

She picked up a rather scrawny-looking thing. She was small and had a large swollen eye.

'Wasp sting,' the woman explained.

I held her close to me and examined her carefully.

'No, thanks,' I said rather heartlessly, handing her back.

'Are you sure?' asked the woman. 'She's the last one.'

In retrospect, I don't know how or even why I could have rejected her, but I did.

As I pulled away from the yard, I caught a glimpse of her sad, dark eyes. Little did I realize I was walking away from one of the most important things in my life.

I stared into the rearview mirror at the tiny black Labrador with her swollen eye. Why was I turning my back on this lone little puppy? Suddenly I wasn't sure – but just as with love, I wanted to be certain. How would I know she was the one?

For more than a week my father and I had toured the country looking at litter after litter. Too thin, too fat, too noisy, too boisterous. None was quite right. The final litter was up in Scotland. We set off early in the morning for the long drive north.

There was something rather special about this search. Father and son on a journey together. I had always dreamed of having my own dog and now the time was right. The stars were aligned and this was the moment I had been waiting for.

Dogs have always been an important part of the Fogle family. My father had grown up with two Yorkshire terriers which had helped shape and direct his life. My mother had grown up with a beagle before getting a dog of her own – Honey, a golden retriever. It was she who was destined to bring my parents' worlds together.

My dad had graduated in veterinary medicine from the University of Guelph in Canada and shortly afterwards was given a placement at London Zoo. He packed his bags and crossed the Atlantic, little realizing he would never return. He spent a year at the zoo, then went to work with a London vet called Mr Singleton. At the same time my mother, Julia, was in her acting prime. She had received plaudits for her roles in *Alfie* and *Half a Sixpence*, and was currently treading the boards as Lulu. Then one day her dog Honey swallowed a balloon and my mother rushed her to the vet . . . and met my father. They married less than three years later.

In turn, my life too was shaped by the dogs and other animals that passed through our home. As a child, Honey was my best friend. I loved that dog. She was old by the time I was a little boy and I can remember her greying muzzle and all her lumps and smelly breath. I loved everything about her – the soothing snore, the tear marks around her eyes.

We all have moments from our childhood that remain etched for ever in our consciousness and I shall never forget the day my father had to put Honey down. She lay in her wicker basket in my parents' room with her old toys around her, an elderly dog suffering from old age. It is one of the hardest decisions for any dog-owner – when to let go. For many it is hard to distinguish between saving a dog for itself or for yourself.

'Come and say goodbye,' said my mother. I crawled into

Honey's bed and held her close to me, listening to her shallow breaths. I ran my hand through her fur and across her lumpy belly. I kissed her head and her nose and felt her silky ears.

'Bye.'

Away from our eyes, my father gave her an injection from which she never woke.

I remember taking one final look at her lifeless body in that basket at the foot of my parents' bed. For sixteen years she had been my mother's best friend. They had shared their life together and she had even helped my parents fall in love; and now she was gone. She left a large void in all our lives.

I lay in my bed and wept. I had never known pain like it. I had lost my best friend.

But life is full of surprises for a seven-year-old and, just when I didn't think my heart would ever recover, along came Liberty. Liberty Olympia Sweetpea Chewingdog Fogle, to be exact. Liberty bounded into my life and it wasn't long before she had stolen all of our hearts . . . and all of our socks . . . and pants . . . and teddy bears. Dogs have an ability to gnaw their way into your affections. Sometimes you don't even see it happening, but before you know it they have become part of the furniture.

I loved Liberty, and even after she was joined by a lively young upstart called Lexington I remained loyal to Lib, as she became known. I never sat on a sofa or a chair. I was always on the floor with Lib. I used to watch telly using her haunch as a pillow. In the car she would lay her head on my lap and at night my parents would allow her to sleep on my bed. Nightmares became a thing of the past with my canine protection. She would lie stretched out along my side, her back to me, with her paws dipping over the side of the bed. She would grumble if she heard a sound and I would fall asleep to the melancholic rumble of her snore. To this day I love the sound of snoring. It is my comforter, my white noise; it soothes, calms, reminds. The sound of a dog snoring makes me regress to my childhood and the wonderful animals that shared our home.

We used to live in a tall Georgian house on Seymour Street in the middle of London. From my bedroom window I could see Marble Arch. Our nearest shop was Selfridges and there was a busy police station opposite. It was as urban as you could get. But it was still full of animals.

My father ran his veterinary surgery, Portman Veterinary Clinic, from the first few floors of our house. To get to our home, you had to walk past reception, up a steep flight of stairs and past my father's consulting room, then up another flight of stairs into our living room. It meant that his clinic, the nurses and of course the patients were all very much part of the family.

It was a very busy house. As well as my sisters, dogs and parrots, we had a live-in nanny and one of the nurses also had her own little apartment at the back of the house. There was never a dull moment at Seymour Street – always people or animals coming and going, seven days a week. I sometimes describe my childhood as like something from Dr Dolittle. That is probably a little bit of poetic licence and retrospective fantasy, but it was certainly filled with a lot of animals. Often my father would bring a sick dog up to our house rather than leave it in the creepy kennels overnight.

The kennels and the operating theatre were in the basement of the building. I was terrified of the basement. It was down a steep set of stairs into the bowels of the house, below the pavement. Some dirty glass bricks allowed a small pool of natural light to get in, but as a child I found it a very creepy place. During the day it was all right; it was busy with nurses and I would often sit in the operating theatre while my father performed surgery. But in the evening it was different.

I used to supplement my pocket money by cleaning the cages. They were simple kennels lined with newspaper and my job was to remove the used paper, disinfect the kennel, then replace the paper and refill the water bowls. My heart would start to race as I descended the steep stairs and I can still remember the creak of the door at the bottom and the blind struggle to find the light switch. A single bare bulb cast a small pool of light near the foot of the stairs, while the rest of the basement remained in shadow. I never knew how many dogs or cats were in the kennels, and to an eleven-year-old their noises sounded like monsters in the gloom. Like most London basements, it smelt slightly damp and musty. Now I don't want you to get the wrong idea about the conditions in the kennels or the clinic – it was an amazing state-of-the-art place and the dogs that were kept in overnight lived in relative luxury, but to a young boy it was a very, very eerie place.

I would walk past the darkened operating theatre with its dozens of scalpels, machines and tools hanging on the wall. Even once I was in the company of the overnight patients, I still found it incredibly scary down there. It was a race to clean the kennels before I frightened myself to death. Every noise seemed amplified, and to a child's rather active imagination all sorts of ghouls and ghosts lived in the cellar. I spent several years doing this job each night and it never got any easier.

When I grew out of cleaning the kennels I became my father's 'sometime' nurse. Each Christmas he would give the nurses the whole period between Christmas and the New Year off, but accidents happen whatever the date and my dad would open the clinic for that week, with me as nurse. I loved those weeks. True, my job was largely restricted to answering the phone and holding dogs while he injected them, but it was as close as I was ever going to get to being a real-life James Herriot, or his nurse at any rate.

Dad used to have a tiny little camper van which he called his 'mobile animal clinic'. It had a green flashing light and was about as near as you can get to an animal ambulance. It had an operating table and oxygen and he would use it to make house calls. Sometimes I would go with him, and of all the trips on which I accompanied him there is one that stands out a mile. The day we went to the Sanctuary in Covent Garden.

The Sanctuary is a women-only health club. It still exists, but I've never been back – because I am a man – but on this particular day my father had been called out on emergency because they had a problem with their Japanese koi carp. As I remember – and it may have changed – the whole centre of the club was made up of a vast pool filled with the exotic fish, hundreds of them, and they were ill.

In those days women wandered around the club naked, but they were warned that a male vet would be coming into the club and so they should cover up. My father and I remember the story differently – he doesn't recall any naked women. Well, I can assure you I lost my visual virginity that day. I was a red-blooded thirteen-year-old and my eyes stood out on stalks. Perhaps my father didn't notice because he was so engrossed in the task in hand. He had to collect, anaesthetize and treat every single koi. It took us the best part of the day.

No one believed me when I went to school the next day, but it only strengthened my resolve to spend my life working with animals.

Around this time, my father was dipping his toe into the world of TV. He had already written a number of books and he was being courted by several of the national broadcasters. His first show was a live series for the BBC called *Pet Watch*, which was made from BBC Bristol. It was a Sunday night studio show all about animals and if I was lucky I was allowed to go and watch it being recorded. One time I met Terry Nutkins' sea lion splashing around in a child's paddling pool, but the highlight was when Lib and Lex made an appearance. Not long after, Mum and Dad made a series for Thames Television called *Paws Across London*. It was based on a book my father had written and involved my parents walking the dogs through every green space in London. I was so proud of Lib. Next Dad became the resident vet on an ITV morning show for two new TV hosts, Richard and Judy.

* * *

Almost every aspect of my childhood seemed to encompass animals and wildlife. Even our dentist worked with them. One day my father saw a cat who needed some root canal work done on its teeth. He wasn't sure how to do it, so he hopped in a cab to Bond Street in London and asked our dentist, Peter Kertesz, if he had any ideas.

Peter looked through his tools and, placing the cat on the chair, performed what is arguably one of the earliest root canal operations on a cat. A trickle of animal patients began and soon increased, and Peter found himself summoned to zoos and safari parks. One of the little joys of going to the dentist as a child was the 'Our Fridays' book, which was a journal of photos of all the animals Peter and his nurses worked on each Friday.

It wasn't long before he was called overseas to work on elephants, lions and gorillas, but my favourite story was when he was asked to do root canal work on a killer whale. Peter needed a tool big enough for the job, so he got Rolls-Royce Precision Instruments to make him a set of implements that he could use on elephants and whales. But while an elephant could be sedated, a whale would need to be fully conscious, and what's more it would need to open its mouth for him. For two months before Peter's house call, the whale's trainers taught it to come to the side of the pool and open its mouth while they held a mock Black & Decker drill into its mouth, after which it would receive a fish and swim off.

The day came, and Peter and his team flew across the world with tons of equipment for this pioneering procedure. He set up all his tools at the side of the pool and the whale was summoned to the edge. On cue it arrived and opened its mouth. Peter was astonished. He found the rotten tooth and turned on his enormous whale drill – at which point the whale bolted. Someone had forgotten to warn 'Orca' about the noise and it took them a further two months to accustom him to it before Peter and his team could return.

My father sometimes joined Peter on his overseas missions. They once travelled to Greece together to work on some former dancing bears that had been rescued but needed urgent treatment on their rotten teeth.

I have always been mesmerized by my father's photographs and stories. Although he has spent the last forty years working with small animals, I think there is a part of him that hankers to work with large ones again.

Apart from the dogs, there were the parrots. Now neither my father nor I particularly approve of keeping exotic birds or parrots as pets, but the life of a vet takes many strange turns and we ended up with three: Bill, Clive and Humphrey.

Parrots have been kept as companions for as long as written records have existed. Pictures of parrots occur in ancient Egyptian hieroglyphs and Alexander the Great is said to have introduced them to Europe in 397 BC. Pliny the Elder, in his *Natural History*, offered a somewhat cruel account of how an owner of a parrot might teach it to speak: 'While being taught to speak it must be beaten on the head with an iron rod; its head is so hard that it will not feel lesser blows.'

Since those days parrots have continued to be kept as pets in Europe, but often only by the rich and famous. Christopher Columbus is said to have brought a pair of Cuban parrots for

Queen Isabella of Spain when he returned from discovering the Americas in 1493; and Henry VIII is said to have kept an African Grey parrot at Hampton Court Palace. Throughout their domestication parrots have been taught to speak. In 1876 Friedrich Engels wrote, 'Teach a parrot swear words in such a way that it gets an idea of their meaning (one of the great amusements of sailors returning from the tropics); tease it and you will soon discover that it knows how to use its swear words just as correctly as a Berlin costermonger.' By this time America had already learnt this lesson: in 1837 former President Andrew Jackson's pet parrot had to be removed from his funeral for swearing.

Today parrots remain a popular pet, with the small budgerigar, which has been bred domestically for 150 years, being the most popular of all. I can still remember my grandmother Aileen out in Canada at the cottage on the lake walking around with her budgerigar on her head. It was always perched there. Once it escaped and we had to wait for Grandma to return from the shops so that the little bird could be coaxed from the trees with the temptation of grandma's hair.

One of the most prized companion parrots is the African Grey, which is well known for its ability to learn large vocabularies and is considered to be one of the most intelligent breeds. It is believed that each year over 20 per cent of the wild African Greys are captured to be sold as pets. Another popular species is the macaw, which has been kept domestically since the twelfth century. And again, because of their popularity as pets, as well as deforestation in the twentieth century, almost all species of macaw are now endangered. The Spix's macaw is believed to be extinct in the wild, but continues to be bred in captivity.

Bill was our first feathery friend. A magnificent macaw, he came as a patient and stayed after he was never collected. I've never understood how someone could abandon their pet, but Bill soon became part of the furniture. He lived in the reception on the ground floor of the house. He had his own cage, but my father and the nurses always felt too guilty keeping him shut up, so his door was left ajar and he was allowed to wander around on the roof of his cage. He loved sitting on shoulders and gently nibbling ears. I would rush home from school in time for him to perch on my shoulder.

Bill spent a year with us before we felt too guilty about his incarcerated life and gave him to Sir John Gielgud, who had converted his orangery into an aviary. It was sad saying farewell, but even with my childhood sensitivities I knew he was off to a much happier life.

We were only bird-free for a few months before another parrot was dumped on us, this time an Amazon Green called Clive. He stayed for a short while before joining Bill.

The house wasn't quiet for long. Humphrey changed all our lives. An African Grey, he fluttered into our home, stole our hearts and never left. African Grey parrots can look rather splendid with their crimson tails and their red crowns, but Humphrey was all a little wrong. He didn't have much red on his tail or head; in fact, he looked like a rather bedraggled exotic pigeon. And maybe that was why we loved him so much. He was quite a personality. He too lived in the clinic, but it didn't take long for us to realize that he wasn't fond of women – in fact, he would allow only my father and

36

me anywhere near him. He would let us scratch his head and he even regurgitated food for my father as a sign of affection.

In his home in the reception area his favourite game was tormenting the canine and feline patients. He would climb down the side of his cage and pull the fur out of unwitting dogs' tails or even sometimes their heads. As if the vet's wasn't bad enough for most dogs, the presence of Humphrey made it unbearable and he was soon consigned to our house, where his trail of destruction began.

For some unfathomable reason, his previous owner had clipped his wings so that he couldn't fly. I remember thinking how mean it was to prevent a bird from doing the one thing it is made to do – fly. It was a little like cutting off a human's legs or a fish's fins. The only advantage for us was that he could live in and on his cage with his door open without fear of his destroying our house. That was until the day his wing feathers had grown back sufficiently for him to try flying again. We found him on a bookshelf where he had destroyed several valuable antique books by pecking and clawing, and had pooed over the rest.

For some reason, his new ability to fly didn't change our habit of leaving his door open. He never got very good at it, but he continued to fly clumsily around the house with great squawks of delight, flapping his wings uneasily and crashing into the bookcase, a window or, more often than not, crash-landing on to the floor. He would then make a beeline for the sofa, which he would duck down under and promptly get himself stuck, necessitating a highly complex rescue that invariably involved Dad or me, as we were the only people he would let near him.

Carefully we would have to lift the sofa, making sure we didn't squash him, then I would slowly creep up on him. He *hated* being handled. I don't blame him, to tell you the truth. The only way was to creep up with a nut or a grape. I would hold it out, offering it to his sharp beak. As he took it, I would throw my hands around his body to envelop his wings. He would drop the fruit and go to bite me, though I never minded; he often drew blood, but I always forgave him. I'm not sure why. He was the grumpiest parrot I ever met, but we all loved him, even my mother and sisters. Our nanny did too, until the day he bit her on the boob. After that she wasn't so sure.

When I changed the newspaper on the floor of his cage, he would take the new paper that I had carefully cut to fit the round bottom of the cage and tear it to shreds.

He was a cantankerous old bird and very, very fussy. He would only eat grapes that had been peeled for him so I used to spend hours with one of Dad's surgical scalpels, carefully removing the skins from a whole bunch. Humphrey would proceed to take a single bite from each grape before flinging it to the bottom of his cage. We would buy him mixed bird food containing sunflower seeds, nuts, peppers and seeds, which I would pour into his bowl – at which point he would clamber down the cage and push everything out of the bowl with his beak until there was just one sunflower seed left . . . which he would then eat.

He hated the peppers in his food. Correction: he hated the fiery seeds in the middle of the dried red chilli peppers. Loyal companion that I was, I would carefully prize the peppers apart and remove the seeds before returning them to his food bowl. I had to be incredibly careful where I put my fingers after the removal procedure. One time I picked my nose and my whole face swelled. It was a lesson I didn't forget. Humphrey never thanked me for it.

There was one game I used to play with Humphrey that, on the face of it, may sound a little cruel. Each night we would place an old sheet over his cage so that he could sleep in darkness and every night after doing this I would lift a finger and gently poke at the sheet. A second later, Humphrey would tear through the fabric sticking between the bars. I would wait a moment then do it again somewhere else. I would play this for hours until it became a game of Russian roulette. If Humphrey anticipated where I was going to stick my finger, which invariably he did, then he would grab it, giving me a well-deserved bite.

African Greys are famed for their ability to mimic noises and there was one passion that Humphrey and I shared: whistling. I loved it and he loved it even more. It must have driven my mother to distraction, but we would spend hours whistling to one another. I would whistle a tune which he would then copy, always adding something to the end which I would then repeat. This could go on for hours. I even taught him to wolf whistle whenever a girl walked into the room, and he learnt how to do an ear-splitting whistle that made everyone cover their ears.

Although Humphrey was a brilliant whistler, he couldn't talk for toffee. He could say 'Hello' and during his short time in the veterinary clinic waiting room he learnt to taunt the dogs by meowing like a cat, but apart from that he remained relatively mute when it came to words.

One year we began to feel sorry for Humphrey living without a companion. We had thought about giving him to Sir John's aviary where Bill and Clive were both spending their retirement, but we were all too in love with the grumpy old bird. Even the dogs had learnt to put up with him. Then Dad heard of another African Grey that was looking to be re-homed. He was called Rex and we thought that he and Humphrey might keep one another company and become the best of friends. We were advised to take Rex on a trial basis to see whether they got on. I don't think any of us ever really expected grumpy old Humph to get on with anybody, but it was worth a try, if only to lessen our own guilt at keeping a parrot as a pet.

Rex arrived one afternoon. He was a fine-looking bird. His tail was more crimson than Humphrey's and he looked more like a – well, more like a parrot. We began the introduction slowly. The first day, we set their cages at opposite ends of the room and slowly, over the course of a few days, we moved them closer and closer together. It was fascinating to watch their behaviour with one another. Before long their cages were touching, side by side.

One morning we caught them touching beaks and the decision was made to open their doors. Humphrey wandered straight out and on to Rex's cage. Rex didn't move. We watched them for the day and eventually decided to leave them for the night with their cage doors open to one another so they had access to each other.

We knew Humphrey could be mean-spirited and grumpy, but none of us could have predicted what he would do.

My mother came down the next morning and slowly

lifted the sheets off their cages. She screamed in horror at what she found. Humphrey was sitting on the perch in his cage looking as glum as ever, chewing on a nut. In the other cage, Rex was also sitting on his perch ... naked, bald, featherless. Humphrey had removed each and every one of Rex's feathers. It sounds horrifying, and it was. But for me it was also a fascinating insight into animal behaviour. What drove Humphrey to such a mindless act of aggression and hooliganism? Was he jealous? Angry? Perhaps it was a mis-guided display of affection? Humphrey had been born into captivity. He had never known freedom. He had learnt the lessons of life from us, his family. Whatever his intentions, this was a firm sign that he didn't want company.

For a long time I wondered what happened to Rex after we returned him. His owners must have got quite a shock. Several years ago I was making a short film for the BBC about *Chitty Chitty Bang Bang*. We had found Adrian Hall, the actor who played Caractacus Potts's son Jeremy in the film.

'You made our parrot bald,' he said as we met.

So that's where Rex went.

'Sorry,' I was finally able to say.

Humphrey had made it clear that he wanted to be alone, and he spent several more decades destroying our house and generally dominating the Fogle family with his ear-piercing shrieks, bloody bites and embarrassing wolf whistles. Even after we moved from Seymour Street to a new house in Notting Hill Gate he ruled the household. He used to fly from his cage to the front window, where he spent most of the day marching up and down the windowsill watching the world go by. Occasionally he escaped and we had to entice him back with some peeled grapes or apple. He became something of a fixture in Notting Hill, with passers-by admiring him in the window. There wasn't a bookshelf, book or surface that hadn't been chewed, scratched or pooed on.

There was one last unexpected turn in Humphrey's life. Several years ago my parents came down one morning and removed the sheet from his cage only to find an egg at the bottom of the cage. An egg? Humphrey continued nibbling at a nut while my parents looked at him in astonishment. He wasn't a male after all. Maybe it had been several decades of being mistaken for a boy that had created his grumpiness. Perhaps it explained his dislike of other females. Whatever the reason, we were suddenly faced with the realization that Humphrey wasn't a Humphrey after all; he was a Humphretta.

Even long after we had left home, he still played a key role in our lives. Whenever my parents went away my sister Tamara or I were tasked with looking after Humphrey. And while he remained his cantankerous self, we resorted to playing rock, paper, scissors to determine who would have him.

It became a standing joke in our family that, given some parrots have been recorded as living to over a hundred, Humphrey would be part of someone's inheritance. The prospect terrified Tamara, which makes his final days even more poignant. She was given Humphrey to look after one weekend and, as had been done thousands of times before, she placed the sheet carefully over his cage and put him to bed. Next morning she lifted the sheet off. There was no sign of Humphrey. Tamara opened the door and took a closer look inside. There on the bottom of the cage was Humphrey. Dead.

Now before we have any Monty Python Dead Parrot jokes, it's important to say that we were all genuinely sad. My poor sister was distraught that he had died on her watch, but, as my father pointed out, it was simply his time to go. We buried Humphrey, or should I say Humphretta, in my parents' garden in Notting Hill Gate. He had certainly entertained us during his life and he was an instrumental part of my own fascination with animal behaviour. It would be some years later before I would get to spend any time with parrots again, at Longleat in Wiltshire.

And then of course there was Jaws, my goldfish. I won him at a fairground and carried him home in his plastic bag. I was fascinated by him, as was Humphrey. Occasionally I would find Humph on the table next to Jaws's bowl, watching him like a cat.

As a young boy I was also fascinated by 'sea monkeys'. Now some of you will know exactly what I am talking about here, but some will think I have totally lost the plot. Culturally, I think sea monkeys were really more of a North American phenomenon that I discovered and then imported during one of my many summers in Canada. While the term 'sea monkey' may conjure up images of swimming primates, the reality was a little more dull, though none the less fascinating for a twelve-year-old boy. Sea monkeys came in a small packet and they hatched after you added them to water. Like some Frankensteinesque science experiment, you had to add a special chemical compound to the water and then let magic, or science, begin.

Soon tiny dots appeared and within days these had grown into centimetre-long creatures; before long my little aquarium was brimming with tiny sea monkeys that would swoop around their tank. I suspect the reason they never really took off in the UK was that the Trades Description Act may have had something to say, because they weren't monkeys at all, but tiny shrimps. It didn't hamper my passion or enthusiasm and my bedroom was filled with small tanks containing pet 'monkeys'. I had a little sea-monkey football pitch, complete with football, and even had names for them. I particularly remember a special large-nozzled syringe that allowed me to 'suck' individual sea monkeys from their main tank into a portable tank that I would take into school. None of my friends was ever really impressed – after all they were only shrimps – but I loved them, and they outlived Jaws, who committed suicide by leaping from his bowl one night. I have still never established whether goldfish can really jump.

And then there were cats. We had a fleeting affair with Milly the Maine Coon cat. My wife thinks I'm lying when I describe Milly as being the size of a puma, but in my memory she was huge. She skulked around the house terrifying the dogs, the bird, the fish and us. Cats are extra-ordinary creatures. They say that you own a dog, but a cat owns you. That was certainly true with Milly. Cats have always struck me as a little Machiavellian; they will use you when they need you, but then they turn on you for no apparent reason. Milly's behaviour was so different from that

44

of our dogs, who were always pleased to see us, that I struggled to understand her.

A year after getting her, however, I began to suffer wheezing attacks. A visit to the doctor concluded that I was highly allergic to cats.

'If I were you, I'd take the cat to the bottom of the garden and shoot it,' the doctor told my mother, with fantastic insensitivity given that my father's job was to make animals better.

But he was right in one sense. Milly had to go. To be honest, I wasn't sad to lose her. I had never formed a bond with her and found her erratic, schizophrenic behaviour difficult to read. It may be something to do with the asthma, which never fully left me, but I have always found it hard to enthuse about cats. I know, I know – all you cat lovers out there will be horrified to hear that, but I prefer the loyal constant of a dog.

I still suffer an allergic reaction, and occasionally asthma, whenever I am near to cats, both big and small. Interestingly, so does my father, although his allergy doesn't stop at cats – he is also allergic to rabbits, guinea pigs and horses. I have always marvelled at the selflessness of his career choice. My father has written forty books, but if and when he writes a veterinary memoir I think he should call it 'The Sneezing Vet'.

Luckily we found a wonderful new home for Milly around the corner and my mother used to visit her regularly. I actually think she was the only one of us who ever really missed her. To me, Milly will always be the cat the size of a puma who gave me asthma.

Humphrey may have been a large character, but it was still Lib and Lex who were my world. My childhood photo albums are groaning with photos of me with the dogs. They came everywhere with us.

A little like my life now, my childhood was full of yin and yang. I spent my weeks in the grey urban sprawl of London. Without a garden we would walk the dogs along the roadside gutter each evening. Indeed, one of my memories of Lib is of a black smudge on her head from the exhaust pipes of parked cars. We would walk the dogs in Hyde Park once a day. Then each weekend we would pack up our Toyota Space Cruiser with Mum, Dad, my sisters Emily and Tamara, Lib, Lex and Humphrey and we would trundle off to our little farmhouse cottage near Horsham in West Sussex. I would spend the weekend playing with the dogs, kicking a football round the garden, climbing in the haystacks and going for muddy walks through bluebell woods.

Our only separation came each summer when I disappeared off to Canada for eight weeks. I can still remember the excitement of our reunion at the end. It became a ritual for my mother to meet us at the airport . . . with Lib and Lex. Invariably they were the only dogs in the arrivals hall and they would jump all over us with excitement. I used to lie in bed recounting the tales of my summer to Lib. I realize it sounds ridiculous, but I know she was listening.

When I was fourteen I finally had to say goodbye to the dogs as I was packed off to boarding school. I was hopelessly homesick for the first year and, if I'm to be honest, it was mainly for the dogs. I missed them so much. I wept into my pillow each night, longing for my loyal Lib, and I carried a photograph of them around in my pocket. One of our teachers, Deej, had a black Labrador and I took some solace in stolen hugs, but it never made up for the enforced separation from my own dogs.

Lib was a naughty dog and chewed up more things than I care to remember. Her favourite trick was to hide my socks and pants, then greet any visitors with a pair of Spiderman Y-fronts in her mouth. I'd die with embarrassment. But pants were nothing compared to the day she swallowed my mother's diamond.

Lib loved kissing ears. I'm not sure why. I always felt she was trying to tell me something, but one day she jumped up at my mother and accidently yanked one of her very large diamond studs from her ear . . . and swallowed it.

Now this created a conundrum: how were we going to retrieve it? Liberty had a very expensive diamond inside her and my mother wanted it back. It's at times like this that it is very useful having a vet as a father. We were promptly instructed to collect every single poo in a bag, which would then be scanned under the X-ray machine for the missing booty. We still have the X-ray at home of a perfectly curled poo with a bright, shiny diamond in the middle . . . and my mother still wears those earrings. Never a dull moment.

Throughout all these escapades, I remained loyal to Liberty. I have written before about my childhood complexes so I don't want to go over old ground, but Liberty became my soul mate. It sounds a cliché, but she really was my best friend. Even up to my A-levels I was confiding in her. She was my loyal confidante on whom I could offload my fears and worries. I would whisper into her silky ears. How I loved those ears. I would spend hours with her on my lap. Have you ever seen a fully grown golden retriever sitting on someone's lap? It looks ridiculous, but I didn't mind and she didn't mind.

Some people refer to their dogs as pets, but our animals were always so much more than that. Sure, we may have been boss, but to all intents and purposes they were a part of the family. Dogs rely on us entirely and their love is absolute. It doesn't matter what you do or say, a dog will always love you. They rely on you, need you and want you. You are the leader of their pack. You catch their food (or open it in this case) and keep them safe. In return you get unending love. They are always pleased to see you. They bring happiness into your life.

But all good things have to come to an end, and the end of Liberty's life was incredibly painful for me. Animal bereavement is a complex thing. For those of you who have never had an animal, it is difficult to explain and harder to understand. The reality is that you never really have an animal. It has you. It dominates your life. Your every plan or action revolves around it. It is like being a full-time carer and therefore the bond, I would argue, is exceptionally strong.

And when the end comes it creates a large, yawning hole that is hard to fill. Liberty died when I was twenty-one years old. I was away being a ski guide in the French Alps when my mother called. 'Liberty has died,' she sobbed down the phone. I couldn't stop crying. My beloved Lib. I loved that dog so much. We buried her in her basket with her favourite toy. She left a huge hole in my life, even though I was at a stage of great transition, having left school and begun to travel the world. My parents were heartbroken, but they still had Lex.

I was on Taransay in the Outer Hebrides, making the TV series *Castaway*, when Lex died. I received a letter in the post. We were filming the letter-opening but my mother, anticipating such a thing, had written on the envelope, 'Please read this alone.' Did I pay attention to her advice? No. I opened the letter and read it aloud.

'Darling Ben, I am so sorry to tell you that Lex—' I ran from the room. Now this may seem like an overreaction from a twenty-six-year-old, but I hope it gives you an understanding of my deep-rooted love for the animal kingdom.

You never forget the loss of an animal. I have lost track of the number of tears I have seen over the years, from everyone from black-cab drivers to Hollywood A-list actresses who have lost their best friend. I can remember sitting next to Amanda Donohoe at the BAFTAs, her face tear-stained with mascara after she learnt her dog had passed away. She left early. I didn't blame her. The bereavement is something only a fellow dog-owner can really relate to.

The loss of Lex was far more than the loss of a dog or a pet. It was the end of my childhood. Those dogs had been the continuum in my life. Through puberty, exams, girls, boarding school, my travels in Latin America . . . they had always been there. My loyal friends, listening, loving. And suddenly I felt alone. I was marooned on a deserted island and I was hit by the realization that life had moved on.

My mother was distraught. For a long time she refused to get another dog for fear of losing it. The brutal, unfair reality of having a dog is that you *will* outlive it. They have a limited lifespan and the pain of losing a dog is the worst thing about having one.

Lex, of course, had been a family dog, loved by us all, but even before her death I had decided that the time had come to make the commitment of getting a dog of my own and carrying on that Fogle legacy of caring for an animal.

2

One Man and His Inca

In 1999 I had applied to be part of a ground-breaking social experiment that would see thirty-six people marooned on a deserted island in the Outer Hebrides for a year, beginning in January 2000. The project was to be filmed by the BBC and would later become one of the first reality shows to be broadcast in the UK.

In the meantime we had each been asked to choose a luxury item. One couple had chosen a bed; another asked for a piano. Ray Bowyer had chosen a home-brewing kit, and me – I'd settled on a puppy.

'No,' said the producer.

'Why not?' I asked.

'Because there will already be a dog coming with one of the families and we don't want too many.'

I resorted to writing a letter to the producer and the director, extolling the virtues of bringing a puppy. 'Think about how a puppy will bring the community together,' I implored. 'It will teach the children about life.'

'And it will be good for morale,' I continued.

'Stroking dogs has been proved to reduce stress and blood pressure,' I canvassed.

'And puppies are always a winner on TV,' I finished.

I'm not sure what sold it, but they finally relented and that was how I found myself on the road with my father in the winter of 1999.

Six hours after leaving the puppies near Heathrow, we pulled up at a farmhouse in Scotland where we met our next litter of dogs. They weren't quite right, so within an hour of arriving, after a cup of tea and a digestive, we were on our way back to London.

For the next few days I couldn't stop thinking about the lone little puppy with the puffy eye that I had rejected. It had been more than a week and I was certain that she'd be gone.

'She's still here,' said the woman down the phone.

The next day I drove back there with Tamara. We pulled up at the house and were led into the living room, where the puppy was alone. She had been weaned from her mother, which meant separating the dogs. Immediately she ran up to me and licked me on the face. The swelling on her eye had subsided and, away from her greedy siblings, she was now much rounder, with a bulging pink belly.

'Her name is Camilla,' said the woman, handing me the certificate.

Not for long, I thought.

I held her close to my chest as we went out into the crisp

winter night, but as we walked to the car I heard a small commotion in the background.

'Get back here!' cried a voice.

The puppy's mother had broken free and came bounding over. She jumped up at me and licked the little puppy clean across the face, then lifted her ear. I am not one to over-anthropomorphize our animals, but I swear she was wishing her luck. She was whispering something into that little dog's ear and I'd like to think she was telling her to look after me.

As quickly as she had appeared, my new puppy's mother disappeared back into the darkness. Her owner looked on in astonishment, a tear in her eye.

My sister drove, while the puppy sat on my lap.

'Inca.'

I had thought about all sorts of names and my first choice had been Tatty, but I had been rather smitten by a dog I once met in Costa Rica during my university placement there. I had become friends with a British expat, who lived in the jungle where she ran a macadamia nut farm and had a large black Great Dane called Inca. I always loved the name and, when I looked into my new puppy's dark eyes, I knew she was more of an Inca than a Tatty. She certainly wasn't a Camilla (although her certificate still says she is).

And so began a friendship that would change things for ever. Little did I realize then how much this little dog would form, shape, bend and create my life. She would change it in ways I never thought possible. The story of Inca is ultimately the story of me; of my love of the natural world and how I became an accidental naturalist.

Inca and I became inseparable. She coincided with my last

few weeks working for *Tatler* magazine in London and I would take her into work with me each day. I suddenly found myself much more popular with the girls. It's amazing the power a puppy has.

We travelled up and down the country to various meetings and training weekends in the lead-up to the year away on Taransay. Then on Boxing Day morning 1999 my parents drove me and my little dog to Victoria Coach Station, where we would embark on the journey of a lifetime. I waved at my parents as the bus pulled away. My mother was in tears again at another parting from her beloved son, but for the first time I didn't feel so sad saying goodbye, because I wasn't alone.

Inca enchanted everyone she met and it wasn't long before she had become an integral part of our island community. Having her there was not without its mishaps, I should say. Just a week into the project she had to be helicoptered off the island to the local vet, Hector Low in Stornoway, after cutting her foot open on a shard of glass. Then came the time she was caught *in flagrante* with a visiting shepherd dog and once again got helicoptered away for the morning-after pill. And finally there was the time she got bitten on the paw by an otter, necessitating a third chopper to whisk her to the vet. It was an expensive year for the production company, but I like to think they got their value out of Inca.

Dogs were a contentious issue on Taransay. For starters there were far more than had originally been planned. Trish Prater, who initially said she would be bringing only one dog, brought two and Ron Copsey also insisted on bringing his dog, and then there was Inca. Four dogs was quite a pack, particularly when some of the castaways didn't like dogs anyway.

But that wasn't all. Unbeknownst to Trish, one of her dogs had arrived on the island pregnant and just eight weeks into the project gave birth to a litter of seven. Suddenly there were eleven dogs on the island.

Crisis meetings were held and eventually the SSPCA agreed to help re-home the puppies, only by now both Julie Lowe and Ron had each fallen in love with a puppy and insisted on keeping them. Dogs suddenly dominated meetings. At one point several castaways threatened to leave if any of the dogs stayed.

In the meantime, Charlie, Ron's beloved sheepdog, passed away. It must have been a desperately sad time for Ron and not helped, from what I gathered, by the crew's handling of the situation. Subsequently, there was a breakdown in relations between one faction of castaways and the crew that would eventually become irreconcilable and would lead to the departure of Ron.

Inca and I largely kept to ourselves. Seeing the divisive effect dogs were having on the community, I wanted to keep Inca out of it. But things went from bad to worse. There were complaints about dog poo around the island, but the discovery of a mauled sheep was the last straw. There was an 'inquiry' to find the culprit dog, with all the owners denying their dogs' responsibility. I knew Inca would never do such a thing, but I felt guilty by association.

Without Inca, I'm not sure how well I would have fared for the whole year. She was my reason and excuse to go off and explore the island; indeed we rechristened one of the hills Inca Ra because she and I spent so much time there.

Marooned on the island, Inca made do with a rudimentary bed made of wood on stilts, and with sticks as toys. Her one treasured item was a plastic lemon that squeaked – 'Mr Lemon'. She loved that lemon and it was her devotion to it that got her into so much trouble.

Taransay is a relatively large island, but Inca never wandered far. I had taught her all her discipline myself. She would sit, stay and come; the only time she was naughty was when food was involved. She is a typical Labrador – she thinks with her stomach. She will eat anything and she will do almost anything to get it.

Her favourite thing was to sneak around the back of the steading and graze on the compost heap. One time I found her looking more like a barrel of whisky than a Labrador. She looked like Augustus Gloop in *Charlie and the Chocolate Factory*. She couldn't walk because she was so bloated. I practically had to roll her back to my pod.

One day I called a crisis meeting of castaways. 'Guys, I can't stop Inca eating. If any of you see her, will you please stop her?' I implored. There was a suppressed giggle and chuckle from the Robinsons. Through the window behind me was Inca, standing atop the compost heap with a mouthful of teabags.

Apart from her eating obsession, she was a good dog and everyone loved her. She never wandered far from our little settlement of Paible – until one day when she went missing.

For an hour I searched the whole village. Nothing. No one had seen her. I walked up Inca Ra. Still nothing. I went to all our favourite places. There was no sign of her. By now I was beginning to panic. She had been missing for several hours and darkness was falling.

A couple of castaways agreed to form a search party and we set out with torches into the Hebridean night.

'Inca!' I shouted. 'Inca! *INCA!*'

I was becoming more exasperated and worried with each passing hour. We scoured the island, but there was no sign of her anywhere. It seemed inconceivable that she would stray so far.

We had one final location: the bothy. It was an hour's walk from Paible and a popular place for us to meet at weekends. We worked our way across the boggy ground until we could see the little building in the distance. There was smoke coming from the chimney which meant someone was in.

Even though we were meant to be marooned alone, there is no rule of trespass in Scotland so people were free to come and go on the island at will and throughout the summer there was a steady stream of visitors who would stay in the desolate bothy, which was little more than a stone house.

As we got closer we could see the flicker of candlelight and hear the hubbub of talking. We approached and I peered through the window. Four people were sitting around the fire chatting and drinking – and there, sitting in front of them, was the unmistakable silhouette of Inca being fed ham.

I don't know if I wanted to laugh or scream. Ham. Ham! I longed for ham, and here was Inca being hand-fed.

We knocked on the door.

'Come in.'

The door creaked open and Inca ran into my arms with Mr Lemon in her mouth.

'We wondered when you'd come,' smiled a man. 'We assumed she belonged to you. We recognized her from the telly.'

'I think she came for her lemon,' he added.

Suddenly I remembered that we had forgotten it the last time we had visited. We had left it in the bothy and I had planned to collect it during our next visit. Inca, it seemed, had other plans.

She eventually lost that lemon. It floated out to sea, adrift somewhere in the North Atlantic, but shortly after leaving the island Inca appeared one day with Mr Lemon. I was mystified as to how on earth she had suddenly found it, but I later discovered that my friend and fellow castaway Tanya Cheadle had found another lemon in her local pet shop and had put it in the post. Inca had found the package on the doormat and torn it open to reveal her beloved Mr Lemon.

Castaway changed my life in many ways, but it also thrust me into the public eye. Stripped of my anonymity, I suddenly became a household name, but not without Inca. In many ways I would argue that Inca was instrumental in my success. While I never set out to create a career in the media, my time in the spotlight and the addition of a cute puppy undeniably helped cement my name into people's minds. We were a team.

I can still remember my absolute devastation and heartache when it came time to leave Taransay. It was like a bereavement. It wasn't just the loss, but also fear of the unknown. I've never been good with change and here I was, having just got used to life on Taransay, about to change it all again.

But what really worried me was how Inca was going to cope. She had spent the first year of her life in this wonderful environment. She hadn't ever worn a collar or been on a lead. She wouldn't remember what a car was or what it was like to live in a centrally heated house. For a whole year she had spent every day outside, whatever the weather, and suddenly she was facing an urban life indoors. She had adapted to Hebridean life. Her paws were toughened to the rock and bog, her coat was like a polar bear's, thick and curly to keep out the cold wind. She was a Hebridean dog, not a London one, and I was racked with guilt at dragging her away from this paradise.

There is a photograph that was used on the front of *The Times* on the day we left Taransay; I have a copy of it hanging in our bathroom. It is such a poignant photo. It is of me, Tanya, Toby, Tammy and Inca. I am opening a bottle of champagne while a helicopter hovers behind. It was the first time Inca had been in a collar and lead and she has contorted it so it pulls at her neck. It's a sad photo.

The first month after *Castaway* was a maelstrom of interviews and TV appearances, and Inca came to every single one. She was photographed for the cover of *Heat* magazine and she came on *BBC Breakfast* and *The Big Breakfast*. When I was asked to be a guest on *So Graham Norton*, Graham pleaded with me to bring Inca on the show. As promised, we turned up together only to discover that the other guest, Sophia Loren, was absolutely terrified of dogs so Inca was consigned to her own dressing room throughout.

Shortly after returning to London, I found myself an agent to help me deal with the tidal wave of media requests. They had a very smart office in Covent Garden and I used to take Inca in with me.

'Is that the famous Inca?' asked a pretty woman holding a young child's hand. 'Can I introduce my daughter?'

'Sure,' I replied with a smile. It was only a little later that Ginnette, my agent, pointed out that Inca had just been cuddled by Kate Winslet and her daughter. Not bad going for a castaway dog.

Soon after this I met with the then controller of the BBC, Lorraine Heggessey, who took me to lunch. 'You have a dog,' she said, 'and you seem to love animals. Would you like to present some shows about them for us?'

Apart from being an offer I couldn't refuse, it was also proof that Inca had helped me get a job. I have often wondered if I would have even been noticed on *Castaway* had I not had Inca. I certainly doubt my career would have taken the twists and turns that it has.

I was asked to present a series called *Countryfile*. It was hidden in the schedules on Sunday mornings, but hosted by the legendary John Craven. The first thing I made for them was a short series about islands around the UK and on each programme Inca accompanied me like a co-presenter. I loved having her with me and it further cemented us as a team. Wherever I went, people asked about her. She began receiving fan mail and she was even invited to be part of a fashion shoot for *Vogue* magazine.

Inca helped me in all sorts of ways and I'd like to think

I've been good to her, but just occasionally things didn't go according to plan.

Together we helped out with a number of animal charities, including the Dogs Trust and Hearing Dogs for Deaf People, which my father founded in the UK with Lady Beatrice Wright. Hearing Dogs had been a passion for my dad and he was instrumental in not only getting the Princess Royal as patron, but also in turning it into one of the premier canine charities in the UK. Several years ago he received an MBE from the Queen for his services. We all went along to Buckingham Palace to watch him be invested by the Queen herself. I was so proud of my father that day – but not as proud as his father, who flew over from Canada for the occasion and organized for a Scots piper to serenade us at dinner in the Garrick afterwards.

I have tried to follow my father's lead by working for and helping as many charities as possible. One of the earliest was the PDSA. My late maternal grandmother, Jean, volunteered in one of their shops in Brighton for nearly twenty years and it was hugely important to her and Russett, her little Norfolk terrier, so I felt I wanted to do something to make her proud. The PDSA were looking for some well-known people to appear with their dogs in a calendar to be photographed by the late Patrick Lichfield, so I agreed to take part. Inca and I turned up at his studio on Oxford Gardens in West London, where her feet were covered in talcum powder to ensure she didn't mark the floor, and we had a most enjoyable day of biscuits and Bonios.

Before the calendar went on sale, copies were sent to all the national newspapers and glossy magazines. I was in

Canada at the time, paddling in Muskoka with my friend Jake, and I turned on my phone one day to pick up my messages.

Beep. Beep beep. Beep beep . . . on and on it went. My phone was filled with messages and texts. My heart sank. As a rule anything more than four messages usually means something bad. My heart started racing as I called the answerphone number.

'You have seventy-seven new messages.'

Whoa! Either I had suddenly become Mr Popular or something seriously bad had happened.

'Hi, Ben. Saw your number in *Heat* magazine and thought I'd call,' said the first message.

'Hi, Ben. Radio One told us where to find your number, so we thought we'd give you a ring.'

What on earth was going on? A little detective work and a call from Orange to tell me they had disconnected my answering service after a flood of more than three thousand messages, and I worked out what had happened.

Heat had published a full-page photograph from the calendar of me hugging Inca. The problem was that her ID tag was clearly visible with my number on it.

I got an apology from Mark Frith, the editor at the time, but still I find it hard to believe they didn't notice the error before it went to print. I suppose it helped bolster the charity and that's the most important thing. Inca got a whole lot more fan mail after that.

Inca was still learning the complexities of life away from the island and it wasn't long before she almost got me in trouble again.

I had been invited to a private polo ground to watch a match in which Prince Harry and his team were pitted against Prince William. It was a small, intimate affair to which I rather foolishly decided to take Inca. We stood close to the field as the horses got into position and the game began.

The horses thundered down the field, sending clumps of turf into the air. Inca got caught up in the drama of the moment and decided it would be good to join the horses out on the field. She squealed, barked and pulled at her lead and collar. Before I knew it, the collar, which was too large for her, had slipped from her head and she had bolted straight towards the horses and the young princes.

What followed could have put John Fenton to shame. With some lightning-quick reflexes I was able to rugby-tackle her to the ground just as she crossed the line on to the field. I still shudder to think what chaos might have ensued had she got past me. I might have been locked in the Tower for all eternity.

One thing is for certain: dogs keep you on your toes. There was never a dull moment with Inca. Shortly after writing my first book, *The Teatime Islands*, I was sent part of my advance from the publisher in the post. It was the largest cheque I had ever received and contained much-needed funds. The problem was that Inca got to the post before me – and ate it. I still haven't forgiven her, although the publishers were kind enough to reissue the cheque.

Countryfile took Inca and me to some weird and wonderful places. We travelled to Bardsey Island off the coast of Wales and to the Isles of Scilly. We visited Islay and sailed around Cornwall on the *Deu Kerens*, a traditional Cornish lugger.

It was about this time that I was asked to make a short strand of films for another Sunday-morning show called *Heaven and Earth*, a programme about spiritual and religious beliefs. I was given a short series called 'Living Legends', in which Inca and I travelled around the country exploring just that – living legends such as the Loch Ness Monster, mermaids, Dracula and the Black Dog.

For the Dracula film, Inca and I travelled to Whitby, where Dracula is described as having come ashore in the guise of a growling, angry black dog. Most people assume it was a Dobermann or Rottweiler, but we didn't have much of a budget so Inca was moonlighting as the 'angry dog'. We had to film a sequence in a church, where, so the story goes, a wild, salivating dog ran down the aisle. It took us the best part of the morning as Inca bounded down the middle of the church with what my rather exasperated director described as 'the happiest, friendliest smile' she had ever seen. All well and good if you're shooting an Andrex ad, but not when you're making a film about Dracula. The final edit is very funny. Inca bounds up with an evil snarling and growling overlaid. She wouldn't have won an Oscar for her performance, but she loved doing it.

It was while filming the legend of the Black Dog in Norfolk that Inca had her first real health scare. We were filming a sequence of her playing against the local football team, called the Black Dog. It was a very hot summer's day and Inca was going berserk with the ball, when suddenly she keeled over.

I don't think I have ever run so fast in my life. She was foaming at the mouth and breathing deep, rasping breaths. I fumbled in my pocket for my mobile and called my father.

'Inca's collapsed!' I screamed, struggling to keep my composure. He asked about her symptoms and what she had been doing.

'Heat exhaustion,' he replied. 'You need to get some cold water on to her, particularly her bare belly.'

It was strange watching camera crews and football players running for buckets of cold water. We doused her and it wasn't long before she was back on her feet. It was only a scare – but sadly it was also a prelude of what was to come, which would turn both our worlds upside down.

Over the years I have made literally hundreds, perhaps thousands, of hours of television and I'd be lying if I said I was proud of it all, but if there is one programme that stands out as the lowlight it would have to be *Death By Pets*. I've erased it from my CV (and even got someone to remove it from Wikipedia), so I probably shouldn't be telling you any of this. It really was a dreadful show, but we all have to make a living and this was mine.

The title was supposed to be a play on words: *Death By Pets* rather than *Death By Chocolate*. It was a prime-time BBC1 show that was supposed to show the lighter side of people and their pets. We covered the story of the taxi driver who got electrocuted when his terrier cocked its leg on a live lamp post in Newcastle; the story of the woman with the largest rabbit in the world; and the family with the most pets. All well and dandy, until they then threw in the brain-damaged woman who had been thrown from her horse, sustaining life-changing injuries. It was simply too much of a gear change for the show and it made for uneasy viewing.

I was asked for my own animal-encounter story as an opener for the show. I have had more than a few debacles with animals both great and small over the years, but in keeping with the original light-hearted proposal for the show I decided to tell the story of my first encounter with a gerbil, which the BBC proceeded to recreate in its full dramatic, gory detail, complete with scary shadows and ominous music. The story went like this.

When I was ten, my friend Barnaby had a pet that rather scared and fascinated me in equal proportion. He kept it in a cage in his bedroom. I was always rather wary of this creature, but as time went by I became more and more confident, until one day I finally decided to 'make contact'.

I held out my hand and carefully moved it towards the cage, with my index finger horizontal like ET calling home. I neared the cage and stared without blinking at the object of my fears. As my finger reached the cage, the animal came up to the bars to investigate. My heart raced, but I held my ground. It sniffed at my finger then, like a lightning bolt, opened its mouth and clamped its teeth on to my finger. I recoiled in horror, clutching my bloody finger. The room began spinning and I could feel the blood draining from my head. The world started going dark and suddenly there was blackness. I collapsed like a felled tree, fainting outright. I soon came round to find a tiny trickle of blood on my finger and a little set of teethmarks. And there in the cage, grinning from ear to ear, was Trevor the gerbil.

Now I'm ashamed to admit that this is a true story, but it

was told and recreated for its comedic power. Unfortunately, the programme style was so confusing with its mix of light-hearted and near-death drama that it got completely misinterpreted and taken seriously. It led to one of the meanest reviews I have ever read (although in retrospect it is quite funny). Ian Hyland wrote in the *Daily Mirror*:

> The only things that have died during this series are the brain cells I have killed by repeatedly banging my head against the wall. This episode instantly reached new depths of blandness with these words '. . . presented by *Ben Fogle*'. I'm sorry, but any presenter who accepts a script boasting a line like 'We are barking mad about our animals' deserves no respect.
>
> Ben is so dull he makes Terry Nutkins's choice of Gemini the sea lion as a life-companion seem quite reasonable.
>
> Still, I was intrigued to learn that Ben once had an accident involving a *gerbil* when he was sleeping over at his pal Barnaby's house. Sadly, Ben ended up with nothing more than a tiny prick on the end of his finger. Public schoolboys, eh?

Inca and I had become an inseparable team, both in front of the camera and behind. Rarely was a photograph taken or an interview published without mention of Inca. She had become a stabilizing force in my rapidly changing world. She had seen me through my loss of anonymity and had remained my loyal companion throughout. Little did I realize she was also about to have a profound impact on my personal life.

3

The Lady and the Dog

For as long as I can remember we have walked our dogs in Hyde Park: Honey, Liberty, Lexington and now Inca. Even as I moved further away from the park, I would still drive the extra distance to the place I love so much. For me it is a little taste of the countryside in the middle of the city.

I have said it before, but I firmly believe Inca made me more accessible to the public. I think having a dog is a sign of being a caring person. Of course there are instances of appalling abuse, but ultimately dog-owners are good people. After all, agreeing to become a full-time carer for a creature that moults all over your house, chews things, sometimes poos and wees in the wrong place, has smelly breath and likes to roll in fox poo is quite a sacrifice. But we wouldn't change it for the world, because the rewards far outweigh the sacrifices. In my world a house becomes a home only when it has a dog in it.

The world of dog walkers is an interesting one. In this life of social mores, most people will think you are a complete loon if you stop them in the street and start to talk to them, but add a dog into the picture and it's like a licence to chat. Dogs break down barriers and defy social etiquette. My father once had a client who used to hold a champagne and Bonios party in Kensington Gardens each year for all the local dog walkers. I've always wanted to restart that tradition.

When Inca was a puppy, I was astonished at the reaction I'd get from girls. I'd walk into a pub with her under my arm and be literally swamped. I won't go into the details here, because it probably wouldn't be appropriate now that I am a father and it would embarrass my children, but Inca bought me a fair share of kisses over the years. However, I'd argue her greatest achievement was finding me a wife.

I already credited her with finding me a job and a career and a best friend, but she was about to step up to the plate and make a family man of me.

I love routine, and when I am in London my life is a little like Groundhog Day. I get up, have a shower, feed Inca, put her in the car, drive to a coffee shop and buy a strong caffé latte, then drive to Hyde Park where I walk for an hour. Hyde Park is my thinking time. I have never been particularly sociable in the park; I like to use it as a time to reflect and plan. It is like my open-air office.

Inca and I would have our set loop through the park and we would get used to seeing the same people . . . until one day I spotted a tall, hot blonde running with an athletic, agile brown dog. She was soon christened 'Park Girl' and I became rather infatuated.

I hope I don't sound like some dreadful stalker now, but I would look out for her in her familiar red tracksuit. I learnt to recognize the gait of her run from a great distance and Inca and I would redirect our walk accordingly. The problem was that Marina had what I call 'pretty-girl radar' and would alter her course to avoid a potential stalker like myself.

For more than a year we would watch in awe as this beautiful blonde and her dog dashed across the horizon in a blur. Occasionally our paths would cross and I would get butterflies, but I was always too shy to talk. If Inca would only 'talk' to her dog and start playing, then it would be the excuse I needed. The problem was that Inca has never really liked other dogs. I put it down to her lack of socialization during our year on Taransay.

So one day I set a trap. Inca and I lay in a bush (I promise, I wasn't a stalker) and waited until she appeared. I booted Inca from the bush into the path of her sleek brown dog. Inca growled, the brown dog ran faster and the pretty blonde carried on oblivious.

It took a chance meeting at a party to finally say hello. Out of her running kit, I barely recognized her.

'You're the man with the dog,' she smiled. That smile was so sexy.

I discovered her real name was Marina and that her dog was called Maggi. Maggi had been bought from a rescue centre in Henley and was in fact half Lab, half collie. She was a beautiful dog. Fast, agile, sleek and very, very funny.

Once again I feel the need to rationalize to non-dog-owners how a dog can be funny. Well, every dog has a unique personality. It is true that it takes time to develop, and I've no doubt that it is through observing a dog's habits that we learn to understand its individuality.

Inca has a massive personality. I can laugh just looking at her. She also has many, many names: Inca, Ink, Inca Pink, the Pink, the Stink, the Big Stink, Inca Pinka Stinka, Stinky (our Russian cleaner used to call her Inca Bazinka in her heavy Russian accent), Incalot, Incalopincola . . . the list goes on. She has always been a funny dog, but above all she has been incredibly loyal to me, putting up with my long absences and always forgiving me.

I would feel immense joy as I turned the key in the door of my parents' home after a long trip away and saw Inca bounding through the house towards me. It's true I have missed a large amount of her life. Travel has taken me to some of the remotest corners of the globe, but it has also deprived me of my dog (and, more recently, my family). I even missed the birth of her first, and only, litter of puppies.

Inca was such a wonderful dog that I always knew I wanted her to have puppies. My father found a handsome suitor and they were put together to do their thing. Nine weeks later, I found myself diving in the Gulf of Mexico while my father oversaw the birth of six beautiful little pups. I gave them all away to friends and family. One went to castaways Patrick and Gwyneth Murphy, who had loved Inca as much as me; one went to my friend and director Alexis Giradet (who would go on to produce the films of my row across the Atlantic and my trek across Antarctica); two went to clients of my father's; one went to my aunt; and one went to my sister Tamara. Tamara called her Lola and she is the spitting image of Inca. The puppies were even born on the same day as Inca so share her birthday.

I digress from Park Girl, or I should say Marina, and Maggi. We had finally met, but it took another six months before I finally built up the courage to invite her out to dinner. I like to think it was love at first sight, but it could never be true love until we knew the dogs liked one another.

Love me, love my dog.

I was terrified that Inca would try to attack Maggi when we first got together, so we organized a neutral ground, the Ladbroke Arms Pub in Notting Hill Gate. Apart from a little grumble, they loved each other straight away.

With the exception of my parents, I had never really entrusted Inca to anyone else, but suddenly Marina presented a new challenge. One day after meeting in the park, she suggested that she carry on her run *with* Inca and then keep her for the day while I went off to film.

I was torn. I really liked Marina, but would I trust her with Inca?

'Sure,' I agreed.

'Come on, Inca,' she beckoned.

Inca ran to Marina and Maggi and never looked back. So much for loyalty – but I was smitten, and this gave me the chance to reciprocate and impress Marina.

I had been off filming *Wild in Africa* in Namibia. That Christmas Marina was going to Mozambique with her family. Her sister Chiara was doing her medical elective out there and the whole family was joining her for a couple of weeks.

'We'll look after Maggi for you,' I suggested. If Inca could have choked, she would have. For five years she had been an only dog and now I was inviting another canine into our world.

So Maggi came to stay and I soon got to know her better than I knew her mysterious and bewitching owner. I like to think you can tell a lot about an owner through their dog, and my infatuation only grew as I got to know Maggi.

I invited Marina to spend New Year with me down in West Sussex at my parents' house. They were away and I wanted to show her where I had spent much of my childhood. One of my favourite beaches is Climping Beach and I took Marina and the dogs there for an afternoon walk. It was low tide, leaving a vast expanse of sandy beach on which to walk. A midwinter sun cast its weak glow on to the sand while a gentle wind blew Marina's blonde hair. She looked so beautiful. I still had to pinch myself that she was with me. We had been dating, but I still wasn't sure about her feelings for me.

Maggi and Inca were splashing around in the surf, chasing a tennis ball. I picked the wet ball up and threw it as hard as I could. We were nearing the end of the beach where an estuarine river, the River Arun, separates Climping from nearby Littlehampton. A long wooden groin divides the beach from the estuary. The ball landed on the pebbly beach just next to the groin. Maggi raced towards the ball, grabbed it in her teeth ... and for some unknown reason kept on running. She leapt off the groin like a base-jumper off a mountain, only she had no parachute and it was a long, long way down. Twenty feet to be exact. I'm not sure why she did it or even how she survived, but Marina, Inca and I rushed to the groin and peered over, fearing the worst. There below us, circling in the muddy waters, was Maggi, proudly clutching the tennis ball in her mouth. She had survived. Now we had to work out how we were going to get her out.

The River Arun surges at more than 5 knots when the tide is ebbing and flowing, and there was no way for her to swim across to Littlehampton without being swept out to sea. A small patch of sand had been uncovered by the low tide close to the wall of the groin and we were able to coax her on to this little island, where she was marooned like a shipwrecked sailor. By now a small crowd had appeared, attracted by our furious cries of direction to Maggi.

'How are they going to get her out?' I heard a woman ask her husband. How indeed?

As the crowd looked on I became increasingly panicked. Marina was beside herself with worry. I had to do something and do it fast, before the tide became too strong, submerging her small sandy refuge and sweeping her out into the English Channel.

'I'll have to call the RNLI,' I thought. I needed someone with a boat. I was just searching through my mobile when a young boy pointed to a hidden ladder built into the wall of the groin. A series of rusting handholds had been recessed into the wall. Some of them were either missing or broken, and the rest were covered in thick slippery algae and weed, but it was our only chance.

Slowly I clambered over the barrier and began to descend. I looked up at the small crowd of people, who were shaking their heads. If I slipped, I would join Maggi in the drink and we'd both be swept away to sea.

Carefully, I climbed down until I splashed into a shallow pool of water. I trudged through it to reach Maggi, then I swept her up in my arms and returned to the wall.

Now climbing a partly broken vertical ladder with 25kg of soaking wet dog is not an easy task. I held her as tightly as I could under my arm while I used my other arm to hoik myself up the ladder. I had to time each movement very carefully, because whenever I let go of a rung we were contactless and free to plummet back down into the sea below.

I looked up at Marina's face above. It was torn with worry as we slowly made our way back up the ladder. 'If this doesn't impress her nothing will,' I thought to myself as I fought against gravity.

We reached the top to a round of applause from the gathered crowd. Maggi was still clutching her ball and our fate was sealed ... Marina and I got married less than eighteen months later.

We tied the knot in Portugal. It was too far to take our matchmakers, so the dogs were immortalized as figurines on top of our wedding cake (we still have them somewhere) and also in a letter I read out to Marina and our guests purporting to be from the dogs.

To make up for them missing the wedding, we devised our whole honeymoon around the dogs. I had organized for us to spend a week on Taransay. It was important for me to show Marina the island that had changed my life, but subconsciously I wanted to take Inca back and allow her to share it with Maggi. The two dogs had become thick as thieves and were inseparable. There had been no jealousy; they had simply adapted to family life together.

The excitement in Inca's behaviour when we leapt from the RIB on to the shore was unforgettable. She was home. She raced around the island to all her favourite spots. She knew where the fence was high enough to crawl underneath and where the gates were. Pretty incredible, after more than five years. I found it quite moving and began to doubt myself as a good owner. How could I have dragged her from this paradise and taken her to London?

The fact of the matter is that she has had a pretty charmed life. She has been in more helicopters, trains, planes, buses and hotels than most people in their lifetime.

Life was pretty good. In fact, you could probably have said it couldn't have got any better. But they always say disaster strikes when you least expect it, and for me it happened when I was in Svalbard in the Arctic Circle.

When we were growing up, my father used to take my sisters and me to various veterinary conferences, but our big treat was to go to Crufts at Earls Court in London.

I loved going to Crufts.

'The BBC would like you to present Crufts,' said my agent excitedly down the phone. It was quite an honour. The BBC coverage of Crufts was a broadcasting institution watched by many millions and it was a stellar event to host. I can remember watching the evening coverage as a child, hoping I might catch a glimpse of myself at the show. I never did. But now, suddenly I was being asked to host it. Honours don't come much greater.

'Who will I be co-presenting with?' I asked.

'On your own,' came the cheery reply.

This was quite a big ask. I had been working in television for six years and had done little pieces of live broadcasting, but never on the scale of this and certainly never on my own.

I would have my own studio above the show, from which I would broadcast an hour live each evening for a week and for two hours on the Sunday. Quite frankly, it was a terrifying prospect – but a little like a moth to a lamp, I have always been attracted to challenges. Without risk there is no gain. I agreed to do it.

I always knew I would be a controversial choice of host. Previously it had been presented by Clare Balding, but she had a prior commitment hosting the Commonwealth Games, which clashed with Crufts in 2006.

The dog-showing world is a strange one. If, like me, you've seen the film *Best In Show*, then you'll have an idea of what I mean. I want to be careful what I say here, but the people who show dogs are a breed unto themselves. I think you can broadly divide dog-owners into two categories. The first is those who love dogs unconditionally as a member of the family. They don't mind if a dog gets wet and muddy. It doesn't matter if he or she is scruffy and badly behaved. They will love them even more for it. And then there are those who 'show' their dogs. These are dogs that are pampered and primped and crimped almost beyond recognition. Talcum powder, hairdryers and curlers are all part of the daily routine. A dog is for show and must be impeccably well behaved at all times.

Now of course these are sweeping generalizations, but I don't think they are too far from the truth. I fall firmly into the former category and I think my appointment ruffled some feathers in the latter camp. The Kennel Club have always ruled the show with an iron fist and I'm sure they were nervous about my new role. Clare Balding had brought some thoroughbred gravitas to the broadcasts with her close association with the horse-racing world, but I think some thought I lacked the professionalism necessary for such a formal event.

'Nothing against you,' said a stuffy-sounding woman as I walked into the Birmingham NEC for my first day, 'but why isn't Clare presenting it this year?'

That set a precedent for the week. It never ceased to amaze me how rude people could be.

I've never really understood the dog-showing mentality. I'm not saying it's wrong, I just don't get it. For me a dog is about a wild creature that we have domesticated to share our lives. Man has a long history with dogs and there is a reason we call them man's best friend. But there is a formality to dog shows that I find a little oppressive. It can also be inherently cruel. In the United States, for example, to qualify for Westminster (their equivalent of Crufts) a dog needs to take part in a great number of shows in a year. That means a dog must live in a cage, rather like a shirt lives in a suitcase, as it travels on commercial planes from state to state. To my mind that is no life for a dog.

When I was presenting I was always brutally honest about what I thought. I always planned to present for doggy people like myself: families and their dogs curled up on the sofa together. And whatever people's reservations, I had my secret weapon – Inca. If I was presenting Crufts, then Inca would be my co-host.

It has been proved by science that stroking a dog can reduce your heart rate and indeed I have always found it incredibly therapeutic. Marina likes to sniff Inca's giant paws and I like to curl her ears. It relaxes me and calms me. Having Inca on the sofa with me was a sure-fire way of making me less nervous.

It takes a very large team to make a live broadcast. Around 150, to be exact. Our cameras and crews dominate the event.

'Have you ever used autocue before?' asked my producer.

'Yes,' I lied.

How hard could it be, I wondered? Well, as hard as you make it, especially when you are blind.

I have always had a problem with my eyes. When I was fifteen I was given a glasses prescription but I never wore them, partly through vanity and partly through the mis-conception that if I wore them I would train my eyes to rely on them, thereby worsening my vision. The result was that I was blind as a bat when it came to distances. I would squint my way through films and often couldn't spot Marina in a busy pub. I really was shortsighted, but the problem was that I never did anything about it; I just squinted my way through life. It is one of the reasons I have so many lines around my eyes.

The morning of the first live show we had a run-through in the studio. The words were simply a blur.

'Can you make it bigger?' I asked.

'Bigger?'

'A little bit bigger.'

This went on until there was barely space for a word on the screen. I had brought an old pair of prescription glasses that were four years out of date; they made things marginally better. It was going to be a long week.

'Good evening and welcome to Crufts from the NEC in Birmingham.' We were live on air to 6 million viewers. The next hour could only be described as chaotic, confused, but full of energy and fun. I loved it. The breeders weren't so sure.

I may not have been slick and seamless, but we certainly had fun and viewing figures began to rise.

I thought it would be nice to get as many dogs in the studio as possible to give us a chance to get to know the animals themselves. After all, that was what it was all about. At one stage we had twenty-three golden retrievers in the studio at once. Inca and I were forced to perch on the edge of the sofa. The camera started on a close-up of me and slowly pulled away to reveal Inca, then a golden retriever, then another . . . and so on, until all you could see was a sea of blond hair. The problem was that the two retrievers closest to the camera had taken a liking to one another and started humping. As the camera pulled back to reveal the whole room, in the foreground, right in front of the camera, were the two dogs locked in passion. It was very, very funny, and to this day I'm sure it's what the majority of the viewers wanted to see.

On the second day I thought it would be fun to have my father on the show. As a vet and animal behaviourist, I thought it was a perfect opportunity to enthuse and debate breeds.

It was strange interviewing my father. In truth, it was more of a chat as we talked about all sorts of things, but then we got on to the topic of breeds. My father has always been apathetic towards the Kennel Club but he warned me before I took the job of some specific rules and requirements which he argued were to the detriment of a dog's health and well-being.

Now Dad began to wax lyrical about new varieties of dog which combined the best traits of different breeds while at the same time diversifying and enlarging the gene pool. One of the inherent problems with pedigree dogs is the small pool of breeding, which has long-term physical effects on the breed themselves. He enthused about the rise of the labradoodle (a cross between a Labrador and a poodle), which at the time was one of the most popular breeds in the UK. He talked about puggles (pug and beagle), cockerpoos (cocker spaniel and poodle) and, my personal favourite, the bullshit (bulldog and shih tsu).

The audience loved it, but the Kennel Club were furious that we were extolling the virtues of cross-breeds that they didn't recognize. 'This is a show about "pedigree",' they fumed. It set my father and me on a collision course with the club.

The filming had its ups and downs, but somehow I blagged my way through. Not without my fair share of mistakes, I might add, but then that's what live telly is all about. I still regret introducing Peter Purves as Peter Perves.

The audience viewing figures had risen from 5 million to 6 million and I was invited back the following year . . . with Clare Balding as co-presenter. I loved working with Clare. She too grew up surrounded by dogs and animals and was great fun in the studio. Me, Clare and Inca. Happy days.

In 2008 the BBC aired an exposé called *Pedigree Dogs Exposed*, which highlighted what my father had always worried about. The public were appalled and the BBC were forced to pull their coverage of the event. They still haven't resolved the issue with the Kennel Club and haven't broadcast *Crufts* since.

Throughout all of this, Inca had been my rock.

Before Crufts began, I had started filming a new series for the BBC called *Extreme Dreams*, in which I took people on life-changing journeys around the world. I had already been to Peru and Guyana and now we had just finished filming a particularly difficult shoot in the Arctic Circle. We had arrived back in the capital of Svalbard, Longyearbyen, when Marina called.

'Inca has had some kind of fit,' she said.

She had suffered a form of seizure in the night and was with my father while he did tests to find out what had caused it.

I was beside myself with worry. An over-active imagination has always played havoc with my emotions, but I never anticipated that this time things would be as bad as they were.

I went straight from the airport to my parents' home, as I had done for many years. I put the key in the door. Their golden retriever, Macy, bounded up, but there was no sign of Inca. I walked through to the lounge to see her sitting by the fire. She could hardly move. She looked up at me with her big sad eyes and struggled to her feet. She wobbled towards me but before she could reach me she collapsed on the floor.

One leg started kicking out, she threw her head back and started to salivate and then foam at the mouth. Her eyes rolled back so I could see the whites. It seemed to go on for an eternity. It was awful.

'Make sure she hasn't swallowed her tongue,' warned my father as I held her head, 'and be very careful when she comes around. She will be very disorientated and aggression is common. She may bite you.'

I couldn't believe what was happening. She was suffering an epileptic seizure. I had seen one before in a human, but I never even knew dogs could suffer from the affliction.

The seizure must have lasted a minute. During that time she didn't breathe. As it finished she made a sharp intake of breath and sat bolt upright. She was there, but she wasn't there.

'Inca,' I said. Nothing. There was no reaction. She was staring off into the middle distance. My father explained that it was quite common for dogs to remain in a trance-like state until they could be snapped out of it. Given Inca's lifelong love affair with food, I rushed to the kitchen to get some ham from the fridge and I held it in front of her mouth. Still nothing.

She continued to foam from her mouth and salivate, and she began panting heavily, but Dad reassured me that this was perfectly normal.

My beloved Inca. What was happening to her? I felt helpless.

It took about twenty minutes for her to come round from her trance. She was sluggish and had difficulty walking; her back leg was twitching and kicking uncontrollably.

My father put her on phenobarb and did test after test to try to establish what was causing the seizures. She was sent to a neurologist for an MRI brain scan and had all the fur shaved off the back of her head for a spinal tap. The tests found nothing and in the meantime she had more seizures and, although she would come out of the fits themselves, she remained in a trance-like state, unable to control her leg kicking and twitching. He added potassium bromide. The fits continued.

It drove my dad to despair. He couldn't bear the fact that the cause was eluding him and that the recognised treatments for epilepsy weren't working.

As the weeks went by, the doses of anti-convulsants were increased but Inca's condition deteriorated and she lost the use of her back legs. It was heartbreaking.

My father took me aside one day.

'You're going to have to think about what is best for Inca,' he said.

What did he mean? What was he saying?

'You're going to have to think about her rather than you,' he continued.

No, no, no, this wasn't happening. Please, no. Not Inca. My best friend.

Euthanasia is a terrible thing. It gives us the chance to play god, but it also allows us to end suffering. Is there a difference between euthanizing a dog and a human? Controversial. All I know is that if ever I were under unbearable suffering and pain, I would like my exit to be swift.

That doesn't make the decision any easier for those around you. For the first time I realized the emotional burden of being a vet. Many people aspire to work in veterinary medicine, to alleviate illness in animals and make them better. I wonder how many realize the emotional toll the decision-making takes on vets? My father has rarely, if ever, spoken about the hardship of putting dogs down, the distraught owners weeping uncontrollably. There is something about seeing the raw emotion of grief that is contagious. If I see a grown man weep, then I weep.

For my father to make that suggestion, and sometimes even the decision, and put a beloved friend to sleep must be an unbelievable emotional burden to bear. But he has done it for more than forty years. He has never complained or dwelt on it. He always returned from work with a smile on his face. But here's the thing. I'm his son. We are similar in so many ways that I find it inconceivable that he wouldn't be emotionally affected by such decision-making. I have always worn my heart on my sleeve; perhaps Dad is just better at hiding it. I have often wondered about it and never asked.

I think I know the answer. My father can bear it because he has always had the animal's welfare and happiness as a priority. It is all too easy for us, the owners, the carers, to think about ourselves over our animals. We think that feeding them lots of food is kind, but it's not; an obese dog's life is a terrible life. In the same manner, we think keeping a dog alive through illness and suffering is a kind thing to do. It is not. It is selfish. You have to ask yourself, are you keeping a dog alive for itself or yourself?

Believe it or not, it is possible – and rather common – for people to love their animals too much.

The prospect of losing Inca was too much to bear, but my

father was right: there was the prospect that she may lose the use of her back legs and the control of her bladder. She would have a life consigned to a two-wheeled chariot and would be incontinent. That is no existence for a dog. Not in my world anyway. No matter how much I loved her and wanted her, I wasn't prepared to put her through that.

The weeks wore on and we got no nearer to a successful treatment for her idiopathic epilepsy, her 'seizures of unknown origin'. Dad told me it was probably in her family, something that some Labs unfortunately inherit. As a last resort he tried a new, eye-wateringly expensive human drug. The gamble paid off! Her seizures stopped completely, although the honeymoon period lasted for only six months before they returned, but now every two weeks. We learned that excitement triggered them so we removed the front doorbell and checked for the presence of squirrels before letting her into the park.

I now take her fits for granted. They are part of who she is. To this day my father has paid for her medication. I have offered, but he has always refused. I think subconsciously it is his way of saying how important Inca is to him too. My paying would have muddied the waters between his work and his love. After all, Inca has spent as much time with my parents over the years as she has with me. My parents love my dog and she loves them. I hope my father knows how grateful I am for his generous gesture. He does now. Ultimately, though, it doesn't matter if it cost a million pounds, because we all know man's best friend is priceless. You can't put a value on that and my father hasn't.

Sometimes Inca's fits can do very strange things indeed.

Each summer, for the last five years, we have packed up the car with dogs, and latterly babies, and driven from England to Salzburg in Austria, where my parents-in-law rent a house on the lake. It is dog heaven. They get to spend a month swimming in the lakes and wandering in the mountains.

One morning I came down to breakfast to see my father-in-law, Jonathan, sipping coffee with Inca. He looked up at me, rather puzzled.

'I think there's something wrong with Inca,' he said.

I looked at her. She was sitting up, staring at me. She seemed fully conscious and was even wagging her tail. She cocked her head from side to side and to the eye looked fine.

'What's wrong with her?' I asked, a little perplexed.

'Call her,' he said.

'Inca,' I called, '*Inca!*'

She stood up and started to walk – backwards. She stopped and I called her again.

'Inca!'

Again she walked backwards away from me. I picked up a slice of bread and offered it to her. Inca would never turn down food, but she simply walked backwards further away from me.

She had temporarily lost the ability to walk forwards. It sounds quite funny now, but for the rest of the day she could only walk away from us each time we called her. We still refer to the day Inca could only walk backwards.

As the years have rolled by, Inca and Maggi have both grown older and greyer, but they have both remained graceful in old age. In Inca's case, with each epileptic seizure the cumulative damage to her brain has started to take its toll, but the arrival of our two children had an unexpected effect on her.

Although Marina and I were both delirious with excitement about bringing some little Fogles into this world, we were also slightly apprehensive about the effect they might have on the dogs. After all, for more than a decade the dogs had effectively been our surrogate children. They had been loved and doted on, but suddenly they would lose their place – not in our hearts, but in the pecking order.

What I hadn't anticipated was what the children would do for two dogs who have spent their lives thinking about and living for their tummies. Inca's lifelong passion for eating suddenly got a boost in the form of two little children dropping food from their highchairs like rain. For Inca, the arrival of Ludo and Iona was like a delivery from food heaven and I swear it has added a few years to her life. She may have grown a little rotund, but hey, she's in her twilight years.

I always hoped that Inca would live long enough to meet my children and she has now met both Ludo and Iona. Ludo has carried on the family tradition and fallen head over heels in love with her. It probably has something to do with the fact that she can't get out of the way in time. He squeals with delight as he envelops her in a hug. He places his face close to hers and stares into her eyes. He doesn't even mind her smelly breath. He rugby-tackles her and climbs all over her. He straddles her and repeats her name over and over again as he nuzzles his head into her thick fur. So Inca now has a little boy to live for. She loves that little boy and he loves her.

He and Iona have brought a sense of purpose (and food) into her life, and nothing gives me greater pleasure than to see the children and the dogs together.

It's been quite a trip, Inca and me. That little dog with the swollen eye has helped mould my life from something into everything.

Is life directed by fate? Do we all follow a predestined path? Was it just a coincidence that the shy little boy who dreamed of working with animals has fulfilled his dream? Was it luck that I met my future wife walking in the park? Or did a little black dog help me all along?

I like to think that destiny brought Inca to me. I know it may sound saccharine, but I think she and I were always meant to be together. I have shared the most important years of my life with her. Whatever the future holds and whatever course my life takes, I will always be thankful for Inca, the best friend I ever had.

Part Two

The Moo

4

Killing Chickens

The day I had to kill a chicken was one of the worst days of my life. Now that might seem a strong sentiment and rather over the top, given some of the things I have done over the years, but at that particular time, place and moment it really was.

I was in a forest on the border with Wales. It was late June and I was cold, tired and hungry. I had been living in a makeshift shelter for more than twenty-four hours and, quite frankly, I was ready to go home.

'Dinner,' said Lofty with a smile, handing me a live chicken.

Sweet little chicken with its feathered crown. It stared me straight in the eyes as if to say, 'What are you doing?'

A small crowd of bedraggled campers gathered round.

'Ben is going to show you how to kill a chicken,' Lofty said.

Was I now? This was certainly news to me.

'I'll show you first,' he said gruffly, pulling another chicken from his coat. 'First you hold its legs firmly between two fingers and then you place the forefinger and index finger of your other hand on its neck. Then you hold the chicken upside down and, in one swift move, pull and twist.'

There was a quiet cracking followed by a furious fluttering of wings, then deathly silence.

Life can be cruel, but then as a carnivorous *homo sapiens* I am part of that cruel cycle. I have frequently fought with my meat-eating conscience and have often contemplated vegetarianism, but the problem is that I enjoy hamburgers and bacon baps too much.

I have always firmly believed that if you are a meat-eater you must be prepared to face what that really means. It is so easy to hide behind the façade of the Waitrose meat counter or Marks & Spencer's pre-packaged 'finest cuts'. What that counter and packaging don't show you is the bloody reality of how we get that produce – and the truth ain't pleasant.

Could I kill an animal myself? I had never done it before. The idea repelled me. What is the difference between a chicken and a dog? Or an elephant for that matter? A chicken also has a brain and a heart. It is a living, breathing thing just like us. But if I was to become the farmer I aspired to be at that time, then I had to face up to this challenge. Especially as it was issued by Lofty Wiseman.

Lofty is an institution.

John 'Lofty' Wiseman was born in 1941 and at the age of seventeen joined the British Army's Parachute Regiment. A year later he became the youngest man ever to join the

Special Air Service (the SAS) – and, since today it is impossible to join the service at such a young age, this is a record that cannot be beaten. Wiseman served in the SAS for twenty-six years and in that time was involved in military campaigns around the globe. Meanwhile he was responsible for running the SAS selection course and training new recruits. The recruitment tests for the SAS are the hardest in the world, with only 5 per cent of applicants being judged fit to join the service. He was also responsible for training the first recruits of the American 'Tier One' counter-terrorism unit, Delta Force. As an officer, Wiseman helped to set up the SAS counter-terrorism team, which first came to fame after storming the Iranian Embassy in London during the siege of 1980. The operation was covered live by the world's media.

Yet it was only after retiring from the SAS in the mid-1980s that 'Lofty' Wiseman became a household name. In 1985 he wrote the *SAS Survival Handbook*, which was published the following year and has been in print ever since, going through three editions and selling over 2 million copies. The book contains instructions on how to survive in the many terrains of the world, including advice on how to track and kill animals, setting up camp, first aid and signalling for rescue. Since retiring from the service, Wiseman has been a trainer at Trueways Survival School and has worked as a 'survival consultant'.

Every boy my age had grown up with the *SAS Survival Handbook*; you only really became a man when you got your own copy. And here I was under the tutelage of the master himself, and to tell you the truth I was completely in awe and rather star-struck.

'Now Ben will show us,' he said.

I clutched the chicken close to my body, feeling its heart beating next to mine. I held its feet in my left hand and turned the poor bird upside down. It must have sensed my nerves or apprehension because it began beating its wings furiously, which acted like a cantilever and made the chicken swing like a pendulum. I had to pull my face to the side to avoid being swiped by its flapping wings.

'You need to do it quickly,' urged Lofty.

I felt sick. I wasn't sure I could do it.

Fumbling in the air for its jolting head, I tried to hold the chicken still, but it had begun to panic and was struggling against my grip.

Once again it was like standing on the edge of that little cliff. I knew I had to do it but the longer I waited the harder it became. I was losing my willpower.

'Come on, Ben,' I thought to myself. I took a deep breath, held the chicken's head a little tighter and began to pull. It was still struggling and I tightened my grip. Still the chicken beat its wings.

'Pull harder!' said Lofty.

The small crowd looked on in silence. Some covered their eyes with their hands. The early-morning sun had broken through the canopy of trees, creating shafts of light as the smoke drifted from our little fire.

Harder and harder I pulled. I could feel the neck stretching but the chicken was still struggling.

'Twist!' shouted Lofty.

With a sharp jerk of the wrist I rotated the neck ... silence. The bird's wings collapsed by its side. A couple of

Above: My sister Emily with my mother Julia Foster, her beloved dog Honey and me, aged three, in central London in 1976.

Right: The 'mobile animal clinic' parked next to Honey outside Dad's veterinary surgery. It was the first of its kind in the UK and doubled as the family car.

Below: Mum and Dad with Humphrey (aka Humphretta) and Liberty at home above the clinic in 1985.

Left: The farmer's haystack near our cottage in Horsham where I would spend hours playing before I was chased away.

Below: My grandfather Morris built this treehouse overlooking Lake Chemong in Canada, where my grandparents lived.

Bottom: Dad, my grandmother Aileen, my sister Tamara and me off on a newt and tadpole fishing excursion in West Sussex.

Left: Aged four with a friendly sea lion at London Zoo in 1977. My father began his career at London Zoo and I spent a lot of time there as a child.

Below: Grandpa Morris and me in Canada. I spent eight weeks there each summer with my grandparents and they were more like parents during that time. Grandpa always had a great love of the outdoors and nature.

Bottom: Grandma Aileen, Grandpa Morris, Tamara and me, aged nine, in West Sussex. I spent a great deal of my childhood surrounded by farm animals like this lamb.

Left: Aged eight with Liberty. I loved Liberty. She was the first dog I ever really had and was a firm part of my childhood.

Right: With Milly the Maine Coon cat. My puffed cheeks say it all, really. She came as a kitten and grew to the size of a lion.

Below: Liberty and Lexington in West Sussex. Those dogs loved mud and water, and I could spend hours watching them at play.

Above: With Bill the macaw – the first parrot we ever had – at my father's veterinary clinic. I may look a little wary, but I did love him.

Right: I spy. Humphrey peering through one of the holes in his blanket.

Above: With Inca and Maggi at Putsborough in North Devon, where we used to go for holidays together until the children came along and stole the limelight.

Right: With my father at Buckingham Palace after he received his MBE for setting up Hearing Dogs for Deaf People, a charity for which he has worked tirelessly over the last twenty years.

Above: Ludo, aged two, with Ricky the rockhopper penguin at London Zoo.

Right: Ludo and Inca at Easter. She followed him like a shadow on his Easter-egg hunt.

Below: The Fogle family: Marina, Iona, Ludo and me with Maggi and Inca in West London, 2011.

Farmer Fogle. On Taransay with one of the lambs in 2000 (*right*) and with Angel the cow and Inca (*below*), December 2001. I'd returned to the island to make a film about my time there for the BBC: we came for a day and ended up staying a week.

tiny downy feathers floated in the smoky sunlight, dislodged in the bitter struggle.

A small tear formed in my eye and zigzagged down my cheek. I swiped it away before anyone could see, but the devastation on my face gave it away. I was horrified. I had just taken the life of a breathing, living thing. It seemed to highlight how fragile life is. How can it be ended so easily? It seemed so unfair that I had the power to change the course of a living thing's existence. It sounds daft, but I worried about those it had left behind. The family and friends wondering what had happened to their sibling or their child.

'It's only a chicken,' lamented Lofty – but was it? Is it *only* a chicken? Twelve years on and I still don't know. Even as I write this I'm not sure what I think or feel.

Who gave us the right to end anyone or anything's life?

'Well done,' smiled Lofty, patting me on the back. 'Now you can pluck it, clean it and cook it,' he added, handing me a sharp knife and a small camping pot.

I don't think you can overestimate the impact that day had on me. Not only did it raise more questions than it answered about eating animals, but that damp weekend would change the course of my life, as it was an important stage of the selection process by which volunteers were chosen to be marooned on Taransay for a year as part of the BBC's *Castaway*. The idea of the social experiment was that our community would become entirely self-sufficient within a year. I would get to be a real-life Robinson Crusoe on a windswept, treeless island, but more crucially I would finally have the chance to become a farmer.

* * *

I spent every weekend as a child in a tiny farmhouse cottage near Horsham in Sussex. My parents rented the house from the local farmer and we were in the thick of the action.

Next door to the little house was the farmyard, which was filled with empty stables, several haystacks and barns full of rusting machinery. Our garden looked on to a muddy field of cattle.

I used to spend hours in the haystacks, moving the heavy bales to build little houses or dens. My favourite trick was to stack them up to create a form of diving board. I would then loosen one of the bales and spread the hay or straw in a large springy pile below to act as a sort of soft-landing crash mat. I would then take a striding leap into the straw-filled abyss. Sometimes I would miss and one leg would slip into the gap between two bales – there was more than one occasion when my sister Emily had to rescue me after I got stuck waist deep – and sometimes the teetering bales would collapse on top of me. The farmer hated us playing in the bales. We would have lookouts for the familiar clackety-clack of his big red tractor and if we heard him approaching we would race to hide, either in the haystack, covering ourselves with loose hay, or in one of the empty barns where Emily liked to catch rats.

She would set an empty biscuit tin upside down in one of the feed barns, propping one end up with a stick attached to a long piece of string. She would set the trap with a large piece of cheese and stretch the string along the barn and out of the door, then pull the door closed, leaving just enough of a gap to spy on the biscuit tin. She would then lie in wait for any unfortunate rat or mouse that fell for her ploy.

When we weren't playing in the haystack, we were playing

on the farmer's agricultural machinery, sitting in the seats and pretending to harvest the field or plough the land. The farmer really hated us and I have many memories of running from him.

'Ger off me hay!' – although as he came from Sussex I'm sure I've made the West Country accent up, but you get the picture.

I used to squelch through the muddy field to an old broken-down tractor that lay derelict and rusting in the corner of the field. These days I'd probably consider it an eyesore, but I loved that yellow tractor with its broken windows and rusty gear stick. I would spend hours on it as the cattle grazed in the field beyond.

When I was eleven years old I saw a giant gorilla in the field and it reduced me to hysterical tears. It's not every day you see King Kong wandering through a field in Sussex.

As usual I had been playing in the yellow tractor, pulling its wheel from left to right and virtually 'ploughing' the field, when something caught my eye in the distance. I was used to the familiar silhouettes of the Friesian cattle, but this was different.

I stood up to get a better view. Its head seemed to be much higher than its back; so too did its front legs. As it got a little closer I could make out its form. It was brown and hairy and seemed to have very short back legs. Then I made out its tall neck and long arms. Suddenly I realized that it was a gorilla. I knew it by its distinct shape and the way it moved its head. There was an enormous gorilla in the field!

I burst into tears and ran into the house, leaving one of

my wellies in the thick, swamp-like mud. I hopped into the kitchen in my muddy sock.

'There's a huge gorilla in the garden!' I cried to my father.

We raced to the bottom of the garden, where I pointed to the giant beast.

My father looked at King Kong and then back at me.

'It's two cows mating,' he said with a smile. And on that day I learnt the facts of life. That incident feels as if it was yesterday and I still believe that from a distance mating cows can look like a gorilla.

I loved that little farm and always had aspirations to become a farmer myself, and Taransay gave me the opportunity.

I came down for my first day on the island farm looking like something from central casting. I had gone to town on the gentleman farmer look: I had a tweed jacket and Viyella shirt with green wellies and matching tweed cap. All I needed was a piece of straw in my mouth and the Wurzels' 'I've got a brand-new combine harvester' CD and I was set.

I had volunteered to help with livestock. We had two cows, a dozen chickens, a horse, a hundred sheep and one enormous pig. Our first job was to get the pig from the land-ing craft and on to the beach, through the little village and into her new pen, which we had spent the week building. We had made a sort of 'herding' device out of some sheets of corrugated iron and some long wooden timbers. It took half a dozen of us to shepherd – or 'pig herd' – her to her new home.

I was tasked with looking after the cattle. We had two

cows, Misty and Angel, which had to be milked twice a day, morning and evening. We set up a small milking team who would be responsible for looking after and milking the cows for the duration of our stay.

I loved milking the cows. Even on the windiest and wettest days in the bleak midwinter, when it didn't get light until after 9 a.m., I loved getting up at six o'clock and trudging through the howling gale with Inca at my side.

At first we tried hand-milking; later we moved on to a hybrid device that still had to be worked by hand, though it had an artificial sucking mechanism. I would tether one of the cows to the side of the stable and set my little milking stool close to her udder. Inca was never sure of the cows, nor they her. There was a stand-off, but they put up with one another; besides, Inca loved their milk. I would hold the long teats in my hand and pull down hard on them. A great, powerful jet of milk would crash against the side of the pail. I could only manage two teats at a time and would occasionally squirt one straight into Inca's mouth. She loved that. I would rest my head against the cow's belly and slowly but methodically pump her udder, making sure I worked both sides equally.

It was always important to keep the cow calm and still. We learnt the hard way how easy it was for her to move and kick the bucket over, spilling the hard-earned milk all over the stable floor. The other hazard was peeing and pooing, both of which the cows did far too often for my liking. If you weren't careful you would get covered in the splashback of both; or, worse, it would end up in the bucket of milk. Philiy Page used to sing to the cows to soothe them, and Padraig

Nallen played his tin whistle. I used to talk to them. Inca, me, the cattle. We were a team and we became very close to those cows.

In order to produce milk, a cow must be pregnant or suckling a calf, so we always knew that Misty and Angel were pregnant, but it didn't make things easy when they both gave birth to male calves and we were meant to eat them.

Before that we had to castrate them; with such a small herd and relatively confined conditions we couldn't risk either inbreeding or testosterone-fuelled adolescent bulls running amok in our little community. We had been taught how to castrate the sheep using tiny little rubber bands that would be stretched using a special tool and placed over their testicles. The band, about the size of a 5-pence coin, would squeeze and restrict blood flow and several days later the testicles would fall off. I can still remember my shock at seeing the field littered with tiny balls.

The cattle were a slightly different matter. We may have been castaways, but we still had to adhere to guidelines and the local vet, Hector, was choppered in to help with the castration.

How do you castrate a bull? It makes me want to cross my legs just thinking about it. Hector put down a pail of feed and cupped the testicles in his hand before drawing his knife. He sliced along the sack and with one deft movement removed the balls.

As if that wasn't bad enough, what happened next still makes me feel a little uneasy.

Hector held the severed balls over the stable gate where I was watching with Inca and threw them into Inca's mouth.

She caught each one and without as much as a chew or a bite swallowed them whole.

'At least they didn't go to waste,' smiled Hector, stitching up Taran's scrotum.

Inca and Taran had an uneasy relationship from that day. I'm sure he resented her for eating his balls, but then who can blame him?

It was the farming that created one of the most difficult decisions of our castaway year.

I came into the stable one day to find Angel lying on her side, unable to get up. I rushed to the rest of the 'cow team' but none of us could shift her. We tried bribing her and then physically pushing her up, but she was simply too heavy. None of us knew what was wrong and it took a satellite call to the local farmer to find out.

She was suffering from milk fever, a calcium deficiency. We needed to get her on to her feet before her sheer weight crushed her lungs, but without a pulley, crane or tractor we simply didn't have the means.

'Well, there's one way we farmers sometimes do it,' explained the farmer. 'Have you got a car battery?'

We had.

'You need to rig up the battery to two large metal kitchen spoons,' he explained carefully. 'Then you give her an almighty shock on the behind. It works every time.'

This presented us with a quandary. We had to get her on to her feet but none of us wanted to electrocute her, especially not on national television, where we were sure to further infuriate the Animal Liberation Front, who were already bombarding us with hate mail. Eventually one of the castaways volunteered to do it on the understanding that it wasn't filmed.

The camera was lowered and the spoons charged. I looked on with worry as he brought them towards her behind.

'Snap!' The spoons made contact and, like the phoenix rising, Angel was up from the stable floor. It was another reminder that sometimes you have to be cruel to be kind.

We loved all those animals, but they weren't there as pets. They were there for our sustenance. We had only a limited amount of food on the island and we had thirty-six mouths to feed three times a day. So when the piglets were born it wasn't long before their time was up. I will never forget the first time we killed one of our pigs in our little home-made abattoir. Even though we were a small, self-contained community, EU policy at the time stipulated that animals had to be killed in an EU-certified slaughterhouse by a registered butcher. We spent weeks carefully building a little abattoir to fulfil the criteria and Colin Corrigan became our registered butcher and executioner.

We led the pig into the small building and put a rope around its neck. Whatever people tell you, pigs are incredibly intelligent animals and that pig knew what was happening. It squealed and snorted as Colin readied the equipment. He put a small bucket of slop on the floor. The pig's last meal. A little like Inca, pigs think through their stomachs and I like to think that this one went doing what it liked most. It's a bit like the male fantasy of dying during sex – not that that is my fantasy, I should explain, but you get the analogy. I'm rambling . . .

Colin held the humane killer to the pig's head. A 'humane

killer' is an oxymoron if ever there was one. Killing is killing. It looks like a gun, but rather than releasing a separate bullet it simply fires a large bolt which then returns to the barrel of the gun – a little like a bullet on a yoyo. It is vital to pick the correct point at which to fire so that the bolt penetrates the brain and kills the animal instantly.

I watched with morbid fascination as Colin fired the weapon. It was instant. The pig collapsed to the floor, at which point it began to jerk and flip around like a floundering fish. I had heard about death throes, but nothing prepares you for the horror – or the power, for that matter.

The pig was dead, but the muscle spasms sent it flying around the room. It struck Colin across the face, breaking his nose and giving him a black eye. Not that it stopped his professionalism. In one deft movement he had put a rope around the pig's back legs and shouted at us to pull on the other end of the rope. We heaved, hoisting the hindquarters up into the air and, as the pig flew up, Colin took a knife and sliced it clean across the neck, allowing the blood to pour to the ground below.

All of this had taken less than twenty seconds. Colin was bleeding from his nose and the air was thick with death. It was a visceral, primal thing. I was horrified, mesmerized, fascinated, appalled and moved all at the same time. I had been part of this. I had helped condemn an animal and take its life, and now we would eat it. Once again I found myself confused about life and our relationship with animals.

While killing farm animals may have been a necessity, what happened next divided not just the community but the whole country and even sparked a question in the House of Commons.

We sometimes forgot that we were living in a goldfish bowl into which 9 million people were peering, living their lives vicariously through our every action and decision.

It was 3 November. I remember the date because it also happened to be my birthday. We had been on the island for nearly eleven months and we had created a pretty perfect life. We were fully self-sufficient. We were growing more than twenty different kinds of vegetable and fruit in our polytunnels and we had a huge assortment in the vegetable patches that we had cut into the sandy soil.

We had used Ailie, the horse, to turn the soil with a heavy old plough. She had panted and sweated her way up and down the plot for several days until the job was done, which made it all the more embarrassing when less than a week later she gave birth to a foal. I can still remember my surprise at finding two horses in the stable when I came down one morning.

We planted potatoes and kohlrabi and cabbage and beetroot. Everything we could want was sown into that soil. We then harvested kelp from the beach and left it to soak in one of the freshwater rivers – or burns, as we referred to them – to wash off the excess salt that could burn the crops.

It didn't take long for a bumper harvest of fresh organic produce, but suddenly we found ourselves at war with the resident herd of red deer. The island was home to more than a hundred of them. They had remained elusive until now, when they suddenly found a free supermarket in their back yard.

So we decided to put up a deer fence to keep our hungry neighbours at bay. We proceeded to erect more than 3 miles of 6-foot-high fencing. It was back-breaking work hammering the huge stakes into the ground. Then we unfurled the heavy fencing and pinned it to the stakes. The result was a Fort Knox-style fence that could have kept Attila the Hun out. Nothing could breach our fence and the crops remained ours.

North Atlantic storms often battered our island, however, and by late October a series of winds had damaged a section of the fencing, allowing the deer to find a way in. For several days we failed to stop them raiding our outside larder, until one November afternoon when they were spotted in the enclosure.

We were furious, but this also provided us with an opportunity. The owner of the island had given us the rights to half a dozen deer. We could do with them what we wanted, including eating them.

At the beginning of the project the community had decided by unanimous vote that we would be unarmed. We had been offered the use of a gun for such an eventuality, but, given that we were all strangers with no CRB checks, it seemed only prudent not to accept one.

Some of the castaways now suggested we try to catch one of the deer; after all, for the first time in eleven months they were corralled into a small area with just one exit point. If we could corner one animal then it was ours.

Colin armed himself with the humane killer and a dozen of us marched off into the gathering dusk with candles and torches. We had eaten nothing but mutton and pork for eleven months and we were after something else.

To be fair I don't think any of us ever expected to catch a deer, let alone kill one. We were swept up in the excitement of the moment. Besides, our priority was protecting our valuable crops.

We marched along the line of the fence and could just make out the silhouette of a dozen deer against the red sky. We picked up one of the old fishing nets that we had found on the beach and used to protect the crops from thieving birds, and with it we herded the deer uphill towards the north-west corner of the enclosure. Spreading out in a long line, stretching the net between us, we created a sort of human barrier. Slowly, quietly, we crept up to the deer. They knew something was up and a group of them bolted, bounding past us as they escaped, but, for better or worse, one deer remained. Frozen with fear, it was unable to move.

We marched forward, closing the gap. There were just a few metres between us and the deer. Behind was the 6-foot fence. We held the net aloft and, without warning, the deer bounded forward, straight into our net.

The animal was surprisingly powerful as we threw ourselves on top. Without taking a breath, Colin ran forward, held the gun to its head and – *POW!* It was dead.

We were stunned. None of us had thought we were really going to catch a deer; indeed, there were even vegetarians among our party. Once again I felt physically sick at the speed with which we can end a life.

I had been part of dozens of slaughters over the previous eleven months, but this brought back those sentiments I had felt about the chicken. Did we really have to kill the deer? Did we need its meat? Were we starving?

None of those things rang true. Sure, we were self-sufficient and therefore reliant on the flora and fauna around us, both farmed and wild, but I don't think any of us could have argued that we really *needed* that meat.

Logic told us that these deer would have to be culled anyway. If we didn't kill them, then some wealthy banker would be choppered in to do it for sport. Better us than that? After all, we would use every part of the beast.

Whatever our sentiments, we had done it. We had taken the life of a deer and nothing could reverse that. What we hadn't anticipated was the wave of revulsion back in mainland Britain after the scene was shown on television. Newspaper headlines described us as going 'native' and said that we had moved beyond the scope of a TV project. The RSPCA was consulted and we became the subject of national debate.

The deer incident dominated headlines back on the mainland but only began to filter through to us by post in the form of hate mail and threatening letters – awful, hideous, terrible letters in which the writers threatened to come and kill our children. They described how they would decapitate them and mutilate them. It makes me sick to think of those letters. We handed them to the police and for a while we were all a little uneasy. Where the island had once been a safe outpost, suddenly it took on a more ominous feel. We became much more wary of strangers and visitors to the island.

By now you will have seen how badly affected I am at the idea of killing an animal and how close I have come to vegetarianism. I find it hard to be selective about the different importance of each creature, hard to accept the different values we put on different species.

Eating animals is a subject that is fraught with sentimental dangers, whether you are a carnivore, a vegetarian or a vegan. Our eating habits highlight our tumultuous, often confusing relationship with animals and they can also emphasize cultural differences.

We Brits have a nostalgic and rather squeamish approach to animals and we look on anyone who deviates away from our rigid conformity with disdain and disgust. For most Brits, chicken, beef, pork and lamb are all acceptable to eat. Anything away from this is getting into dangerous waters. Most of us will accept eating game, like pheasant, grouse or partridge, and of course the odd duck or goose is fine, though this tends to be a class thing.

Our Gallic cousins across the water have always been a little more creative with their eating habits. In England we have special 'frog crossings' under roads to allow the creatures safe passage, while in France they'll think nothing of polishing off a dozen frogs' legs as a starter. Whereas we in the UK love our horses, the French see no problem in eating them. Sparrows and songbirds are a delicacy in some parts of Europe. The Haitians, meanwhile, like to eat cat and the Koreans enjoy dog, while the Thai love nothing more than crispy locust and fried tarantulas. On the other hand, while we are happy to eat cows, in India and Nepal they are sacred. We have always had a horrified fascination with other people's diets.

Of course hunting some animals for food can be such an

emotive matter that people are willing to risk their lives in a bid to prevent it – for instance, aboard the anti-whaling ships in the Southern Ocean. Commercial whaling has been around since the 1700s. While I can accept that for some peoples – such as the Inuit, who have hunted whales from time immemorial – there is a degree of tradition crucial to their very heritage, it is debatable whether the Japanese can really justify their annual 'hunts' in the Southern Ocean in the name of science. Personally I have never approved of killing whales and as far as I know I have only once eaten whale meat, and that was high in the Arctic Circle in Spitzbergen which I have visited several times over the years.

It's actually quite difficult to eat an animal by accident, unless you are in some dodgy restaurant, as with the whale. However, over the years I have eaten species I probably shouldn't have. Was it an accident? Not really. I have tried them partly to avoid giving cultural offence, but also to understand more about a particular society and its relationship with animals.

There is one animal I really wish I had never eaten.

I was in Papua New Guinea for my BBC series *Extreme Dreams*, leading my five teammates on a ten-day journey down the Black Cat Trail, a notorious route through the rainforest used by the Australians and Japanese during the Second World War. We had been trekking through the leech-infested jungle for days.

I hate leeches.

If you will forgive the digression, I thought I would get that off my chest. All animals are equal blah, blah, blah . . . but leeches?

I can still remember my first encounter with a leech, when I was in Canada as a child. I was on a camping holiday in Algonquin Park with my father and my friend Toby. It was with a mixture of horror and fascination that I found my first bloodsucker on my foot. Who can ever forget the scene in *Stand By Me* when the young boy emerges from the swamp covered in leeches? It is one of those powerful images in cinema. The leech on my foot was my own small equivalent and I have never been able to reconnect with them since.

The problem with leeches is that they are cleverer than you. No matter how long you spend taping sleeves and ankles, they will always find a way on to your body, usually your crotch. They have an incredible ability to feel the vibrations of a footfall from an approaching animal. Contrary to what many expect, they lie in wait, hanging from leaves and branches. As the footsteps approach they make a death leap, hoping to land on whatever is below for their dinner. Once on the body, they have a sort of heat-seeking infrared tracking facility that directs them towards the warmest part of the body – invariably the groin. I remember the first time I ever found a leech attached to my testicles. How could you forget such a thing? My scream could be heard back in England.

Leeches have this ability to wear you down slowly with their relentless march. No sooner have you finished picking the little suckers from your body than you find another battalion working their way up your leg. The most I ever found was twelve on one leg.

Once you're resigned to being sucked to death, it can be quite fun to watch the reaction of others, particularly if they are leech virgins. I remember an expedition across the

Nepalese Himalayas in which we had to trek through the rainforest before reaching the higher peaks. My team had no idea that leeches lived at such heights until one day I advised them all to check their feet and torsos. There was a long period of silence as boots and socks were carefully removed. I could sense the fear and trepidation in the air.

'Aaaaaaaaaaaaaaaargh!'

One of the little parasites had been discovered. It can actually be quite funny. I can still picture one of my team-mates physically falling over backwards holding his foot.

Back to my story. We had been trekking in PNG for many days, living off tins of tuna and damp crackers, when we reached a small settlement. It was hidden deep in the rain-forest and consisted of a number of longhouses. The village children were particularly excited to see us and arrived clutching one of the cutest animals I have ever seen – a tree kangaroo.

Tree kangaroos are native to the rainforests of Papua New Guinea, some of the nearby islands and the far north-east of Queensland; they are effectively kangaroos that have evolved to live in the trees. The major threats facing them are hunting and habitat loss. Tree kangaroos have been hunted for food by indigenous communities across their range and for a number of species this factor alone has contributed to a sharp decline in population numbers. Habitat loss and degradation as a result of logging and timber production, or through the conversion of land to coffee, rice or wheat production, mean that many species now inhabit a restricted range. This loss of habitat can also expose tree kangaroos to predation by domestic dogs.

The tree kangaroo and the cassowary are the two creatures we had been hoping to see during our short expedition, and here, now, we were confronted with our first tree kangaroo.

Before long a large crowd had gathered around to share our wonder at this beautiful creature. It was being held on a branch, clutching on with its long claws, then one of the village elders took the animal and placed it on the ground like a teddy bear. We took turns crouching down, taking photographs of this lovely little thing.

It was at this point that a great yawning void of miscommunication and cultural difference came into play. The village elder lifted a large machete and swung it at the tree kangaroo's neck, taking its head clean off.

My mouth dropped open in surprise. It was completely shocking. How could the scene have changed so dramatically? I looked at the rest of the team; they too were standing with their mouths ajar.

Before anyone could say anything a woman got to work on the headless corpse, pulling out its insides and stripping it of its fur, while the children laid an enormous fire. Within ten minutes of playing with this highly endangered species we were handed its cooked legs to chew on. It seemed astonishing that the villagers had so misinterpreted our attitude towards this little creature that they had killed it and cooked it for us.

For days I felt profound guilt that I hadn't intervened. Why had we not said anything? It all happened too fast and was over before we knew it, but there was also an element of not wanting to insult cultural sensitivities. Where do you

114

draw the line in intervening in cultural identity? For the Papua New Guineans this had been an extraordinarily kind display of friendship and sharing, a truly generous offering on their part.

I have been in plenty of situations over the years where I have been confronted with foods that I have eaten only for fear of offending my host. I have seen goats and pigs killed in honour of visiting groups, but the tree kangaroo was different and affected me more than I expected. Here was an endangered species killed for us.

Cultural killings by indigenous communities are one thing, but I have never been able to understand wanton killing for the sake of it. I have never understood hunting or shooting something for sport – though I have plenty of friends who do both and I would never judge them on it; indeed they are all decent, kind-hearted people. But big-game hunting and pig-sticking are totally unfathomable. There is something deeply gladiatorial and bloodthirsty about chasing pigs with sharpened sticks. And as for big-game hunting – how can anyone glean pleasure from taking the life of such magnificent, often endangered creatures? I would be quite happy to sit down with the king of Spain or Donald Trump Jr (both of whom hunt big game) for a discussion. I would genuinely like to hear their reasons. Why does anyone want to kill, murder, an animal like this? Why? I have spent the best part of thirty-eight years trying to understand the mentality.

I bumped into the provocative writer and bon viveur A. A. Gill recently. 'I hear you want to kill me,' he smirked.

I had once worked as Mr AA's PA and have always enjoyed

his writing, but in this case he had written a particularly provocative piece for the *Sunday Times* about the time he killed a baboon for fun. He had described shooting the animal while travelling in Africa and said that there was no reason for shooting it, but that he 'wanted to get a sense of what it might be like to kill someone, a stranger'. The article caused a massive uproar in the British press and Gill was targeted by animal rights groups. It was a provocative, deeply offensive piece and, as a passionate conservationist and supporter of animal welfare, I felt sickened. But I didn't want to kill him – I would never use, or condone the use of, violence.

Now vegans and vegetarians will point out at this stage that there is nothing different between killing a monkey and eating a bacon bap; both, they will argue, involve the bloody and untimely demise of one of this planet's creatures. What, they may say, is the difference between a pig and a baboon? They are both highly intelligent creatures.

Which brings us full circle back to where we started and the question of why we find it acceptable to kill some animals and not others. It is an issue that will for ever be complicated and beset by different attitudes, cultures and religions. I suppose, like everything in life, it is down to personal choice. As humans, at the top of the food chain (or intelligence chain, at least), I would argue that it is our responsibility to be as sensitive and humane as possible. The reality of the matter is that there is no simple answer. The question, like life, is circular and unending.

Even more complex are the culls that take place across the world. Seals, elephants, deer – the list goes on. Culling of animals is a highly emotive issue but one the world has to confront. Here in the UK, the government's plan to cull badgers in order to control the spread of TB in the country-side is a difficult debate that has divided opinion across the country, pitting small furry animals against the harsh economics of farming. The Badger Trust argues that badgers are not to blame for the rise in TB in cattle, while farmers, many of whom have lost stock, argue otherwise. The reality is that TB in cattle is on the increase.

The badger debate is a fascinating one. Any cull would be useless unless every badger were culled – it cannot be a localized eradication; it must be a complete one. But can we justify wiping a species from the countryside? On the other hand we have farmers faced with putting down TB-infected cattle. They claim that badgers threaten their very liveli-hoods. Whom do we favour, man or animal?

My father is not only a vet but also chair of Humane Society International and he, like me, is torn on the ethics of favouring one species over another. He has warned that it would be impossible to catch badgers humanely and then test them, and there is always the fear of positive/negative inaccuracies.

So in the red corner we have the badger – fluffy, emotive badger with his little black eye-mask, an iconic figure of the countryside and part of many people's childhoods alongside Ratty and Toad. In the blue corner we have the farmer, hard-working stalwart of the countryside, sweating and toiling to scratch a meagre living from the land to give us the food we need. Cattle, of course, provide us with many essential food-stuffs, but can that really justify the outright cull of another species? The massive increase in the number of dead badgers littering our roads in recent years is often attributed to farmers taking the law into their own hands, but now the government has accepted their call for a cull. The Badger Trust, however, is taking the government to court over the proposed destruction of an entire species.

The truth is that there is no simple answer – no clear right or wrong. The debate will divide society in the same way that foxhunting has and is yet another example of the highly complex and fragile balance between man and nature.

5

All Creatures Great and Small

I left Taransay with a much greater understanding of farming life and the trials and tribulations of working the land and the sea. But my ideas of becoming a farmer were postponed when, shortly after leaving the island, I was offered a job as a presenter alongside John Craven on the BBC's rural affairs programme, *Countryfile*. A couple of people laughed and sneered at the idea, but I loved my eight years on *Countryfile*. During that time I travelled the length and the breadth of the land reporting on just about everything rural. The experience gave me a fascinating insight into man's working relationship with animals.

The first film I ever made for *Countryfile* was about dog-sledding in Aviemore, in the Highlands of Scotland. I was so nervous as I boarded a train from London ready for my first presenting assignment. I actually practised in the mirror of the train loo on the journey north.

'Hello, I'm Ben Fogle,' I said, sounding ridiculous. I had absolutely no idea how to present (Ian Hyland would be quick to add that I still haven't).

Aviemore is a pretty little resort and once a year it plays host to the Sled Dog Rally, Britain's largest husky race, organized by the Arden Grange and Siberian Husky Club of Great Britain. Over two hundred teams of between two and eight canine competitors, along with their human companions, run a 4-mile course around Loch Morlich. Rallies have been held since 1984, when only twelve out of twenty teams managed to complete the course in that original race. However, one veteran competitor, Rob Hyden, has taken part in every single Sled Dog Rally.

In the absence of snowy conditions, I used a three-wheeled sled. There was something magical about hurtling along forest tracks under 'dog power'. Until now, dogs had only ever been pets to me, but here, in the Scottish mountains, I was experiencing working dogs for the first time and it was magical. There is something about the energy and excitement of the dogs that is electric. They exude a keenness and enthusiasm that we humans tend to temper and restrain. In some ways it is an organic, natural form of greyhound racing. Gone is the stadium and the stuffed rabbit, replaced with the vast outdoors and a natural theatre. Beautiful, and deeply moving to watch.

I soon found myself back in England, this time reporting on the Hound Trailing Championships. This is a traditional Cumbrian sport that has been practised since the eighteenth century, but only formally organized under the auspices of the Hound Trailing Association since 1906. Observers bet on which hound will be the first to complete the course, as the dogs follow a trail of paraffin and aniseed across the Cumbrian landscape. The trail is marked out by two people carrying woollen rags, who walk together to the halfway point, then split and continue to either end, thereby laying the scent for the whole course. It's a demanding sport: puppies start training from six months old. Puppies have from fifteen to twenty minutes to complete a trail, while the senior dog races have to be completed in less than forty-five minutes. Special trails are laid for veteran racers, and for maiden trail hounds. Prizes are also awarded to dogs with the best appearance. To make sure sly competitors don't swap dogs mid-race, all hounds have a coloured mark placed on their head; and to avoid overheating, the dogs are shaved bald.

I watched as several dozen of them waited on the start line before being given the scent and released into the mountains. It was strange seeing a pack of dogs heading off on their own. It's a little like watching remote-control dogs. Once they are on the trail there is very little the owner can do to encourage them.

The most bizarre sight is when the dogs first appear on the horizon, having completed the course. The owner of each animal holds out a bowl containing the dog's favourite food, which they shake frantically while hollering their dog's name.

Despite the colour-coding, the hounds all look identical until closer inspection. With all the yelling and hollering of names, many owners end up temporarily grabbing the wrong animal, which leads to a rather comical 'dog swap' at the end of the race.

I teamed up with a dog called Lucky Billionaire. He came last. I've never been very lucky when it comes to racing.

During the April–October hound-trailing seasons, trails are run up to twelve times a week, but not long after I was there it was affected by the outbreak of foot-and-mouth disease, and in recent years the sport has been threatened by the lack of younger owners. It seems a shame that the art of hound trailing may be on its way out. As with so many aspects of rural life, things have moved on, but I hope there will be a movement to keep up this extraordinary teamwork between man and dog.

If my time on Taransay had fuelled my fascination for farm life, then working on *Countryfile* had deepened my understanding of rural affairs. Indeed it wasn't uncommon for people to mistake me for a farmer. They were always surprised to hear that I lived in central London, but my work with *Countryfile*, and later on *Animal Park*, kept me in the countryside and I became a regular at agricultural shows. In some ways I was living out my farming aspirations, only with Inca as my sole livestock.

It seemed only natural, then, that the BBC should ask if I'd like to be involved in *One Man and His Dog*. I leapt at the opportunity.

The first sheepdog trials were held in 1867 in Wanaka, New Zealand, and within five years similar events had been held in Australia, Wales, England, Scotland and the United States. In a trial the dog must perform a number of specific tasks which would frequently be carried out on a working farm, such as fetching sheep from a distance, guiding them through gates, splitting a group of sheep in two and driving the flock into a pen. The handler controls the dog with a known set of whistled or spoken commands. The trial must be performed within a set amount of time and each of the various tasks is marked by judges. The International Sheep Dog Society was founded in 1906 and today it holds a worldwide dog trial once every three years. Sheepdog trials can be a big-money sport too: in an auction in February 2011, £6,300 was paid for a dog called Dewi Fan, who had been the International Supreme Dog Trial winner in 2009.

One Man and His Dog ran for twenty-four years, between 1976 and 2000, on the BBC. Its original presenter, Phil Drabble, worked on the show for eighteen years and the original commentator, Eric Halsall, for fourteen. They were subsequently replaced by Ray Ollerenshaw, Robin Page and Gus Dermody. The series reached the height of its popularity in the mid-1980s, gaining an audience of up to 8 million viewers. It ran regularly before the weekend news, but during the late 1990s it was moved to an earlier slot, much to the distress of many farmers, who could no longer watch it due to the demands of their work – although the programme also had a large urban audience. The series was axed in 2000, but beginning that year the BBC has always produced a Christmas special, which remains popular to this day.

Clarissa Dickson Wright, probably best known as co-presenter of the eccentric but very successful cookery programme *Two Fat Ladies*, had replaced the rather cantankerous Robin Page as presenter of the first Christmas special. Despite her sex, they retained the title and the show was incredibly popular. Clarissa is quite a character and a force to be reckoned with. She is one of the most astonishing people I have ever met, with one of the most colourful pasts of anyone I know. I loved working with her. I felt rather awestruck in her company. I had been a big fan of *Two Fat Ladies* and Clarissa exuded a charisma and confidence that I envied and admired.

I was invited on to the programme in 2003 as one of the team captains to 'jolly' the farmers along. With no disrespect to the farming community, farmers can be a little shy and retiring, which doesn't always translate on to the screen very well. The presence of some bouncy, chirpy presenters was intended to speed proceedings along.

My team triumphed in the championships that year, and not only did I win one of the sought-after *One Man and His Dog* crooks, but also the coveted role of presenter.

So the next year I returned as host, replacing Clarissa. We were broadcasting from Chatsworth and I was working with Gus Dermody. It was great fun making *OMAHD*, as we used to call it. Inca would sit in the hay bales with me while the farmers coaxed their dogs around the course. During the intervals we would be entertained by children who had taught their dogs to round up ducks and geese. It was very, very funny to watch the geese waddling round the course.

In 2006 the recording coincided with the thirtieth anniversary of the programme and the Duchess of Cornwall had agreed to come along with her daughter Laura for the final. I sat there with the Duchess on one side and Inca on the other, thinking how strange life had become as I tried to explain the intricacies of sheepdog trials to Her Royal Highness.

'We loved you on Crufts,' she told me with a smile. 'And we were all gripped by *Through Hell and High Water*,' the programmes about my rowing across the Atlantic with James Cracknell. I have remained a most loyal fan of the Duchess ever since.

When I was a child my late grandfather, Dick, loved *One Man and His Dog*. He watched it religiously every Sunday night and my one regret was that he didn't live long enough to see me host it. I'm sure he would have been proud.

Over the next few years I built up something of a reputation for all things rural. I had become president of the Campaign for National Parks and had started writing a weekly column for the *Sunday Telegraph*, so it seemed right for me to present a programme called *Escape in Time*.

In 2009 the BBC had been surprised by the success of a series called *Victorian Farm*, which followed a team of experts – historian Ruth Goodman and archaeologists Alex Langlands and Peter Ginn – as they attempted to live in Victorian conditions as farmers and labourers at a farm in Shropshire on the Acton Scott Estate. The series chronicled the trials and tribulations of life as a Victorian farmer and seemed to tap into the right zeitgeist for viewers. The follow-up, broadcast the next year, was *Escape in Time*, which I was asked to host.

The idea was simple. I would live on the farm at Acton Scott with some families who would spend their week attempting various aspects of a Victorian farmer's life. They would do everything from ploughing the land to threshing corn and feeding the pigs. It would be an authentic experience of life as it would have been. It would also give the families a chance to bond together through a shared experience, while at the same time learning new skills and understanding the history of our ancestors.

Acton Scott is a pretty extraordinary place. The 1,500-acre estate has been managed by the Acton family for nearly nine centuries. They can date their genealogy and possession of the land back to the days of William the Conqueror in 1066, when the land was held by Eadric the Wild, an Anglo-Saxon noble who played an instrumental, if ultimately unsuccessful, role in the rebellion against the Norman Conquest through an onslaught against the castle and town of Shrewsbury. The estate itself was the site of brief conflict in the Civil War, during which time Prince Rupert, nephew of King Charles I, stayed here.

Acton Scott is now most famous for being home to the UK's first historic working farm, a fully functioning recreation of nineteenth-century farming conditions. It was the brainchild of estate-owner Tom Acton and gives visitors the opportunity to learn traditional crafts and skills, such as woodworking and hand-milking. As well as celebrating the techniques of the past, the estate also looks to the future, developing ways to lower Acton Scott's carbon footprint, such as through the use of solar panels and woodchip burners for heating.

I lived in a small cottage just next to the estate for a month and once again Inca was there with me.

It was great fun teaching the children how to milk the cattle and how to grind corn. We threshed the hay and learnt how to shear the sheep with old-fashioned clippers. But my favourites were the working horses. They are such magnificent creatures. I had had very little experience with Shire horses before this, but suddenly I had the opportunity of learning to carriage ride and getting them to pull heavy ploughs.

Draught horses have been bred to be large and muscular in order to be able to carry out heavy labour. Horses have been used in this way for thousands of years – there is evidence of their use in Roman times. They usually stand at 16–19 hands high (1.6–2 metres) and weigh 550–900kg. They are descended from forest horses, but during their domestication were bred for ploughing fields; it's believed that some of today's breeds, such as the Percheron, are the descendants of medieval war horses. Many of our modern breeds were developed in the nineteenth century, when industrialization meant that heavier, more powerful breeds were needed in factories for haulage and also to drag the heavy new agricultural machinery. Jethro Tull, for instance, believed that it was better to use horses to drag his newly invented seed drill, rather than the oxen that were more commonly used at the time. In England the most popular breed of heavy horse, and also the largest, is the Shire. The biggest draught horse on record was a Shire called Sampson, who weighed over 1.5 tons, and stood 21.6 hands (2.2 metres) high.

For the entire month of September the sun shone on Acton Scott and the beautiful Shropshire landscape around it. There was something very simple and pure about the project. There was no mean-spirited TV contrivance to instigate arguments or rivalry. It was good, old-fashioned family values, and I was very envious of the families and the opportunities they had together as a unit.

One of the most memorable experiences of my time at the Victorian Farm was when we went out ferreting for rabbits. This ancient art has been practised for hundreds of years. It never ceases to amaze me how we have been able to work with the most unlikely of species, and ferrets must be up there with the strangest. I have never been their biggest fan. They have a musky, slightly unpleasant odour, not to mention a very sharp set of teeth, and I have had more than my fair share of ferrets rooting around the inside of my shirt, having disappeared down my sleeve. I've always been puzzled by the tradition of stuffing ferrets down your trousers, but here I would see first hand the remarkable partnership between man and beast.

Killing rabbits, however you do it, is unsurprisingly controversial. Across the Channel they are a staple part of the French diet and arguably a national dish, but here in the UK rabbits fit into the 'cute, cuddly and furry' category alongside guinea pigs and badgers. British sentimentality combined with rabbits in popular culture have led to an emotive attachment that overshadows the damage that marauding rabbits can do. They really can be astonishingly destructive to crops and land alike, and for many who live and work in the countryside they are a real pest. There are different ways of dealing with them: poison, shooting or ferrets.

Long ago farmers learned that, unless they could chase

rabbits from deep inside their holes, it could be a very long wait to catch them. They soon discovered that if you sent a ferret into the hole, it would chase the rabbit out and then by placing a net over the hole, you could catch the rabbits. Sounds simple; all they had to do was train the ferrets.

As a natural predator, ferrets made an ideal partner. The problem was ensuring they didn't catch and kill the rabbit themselves underground, as experience had taught the farmers that the ferret would then fall into a deep sleep that could last for days. Suddenly, from waiting for the rabbit, the farmer was left waiting for the ferret.

I joined a team of ferreters who work the land as their ancestors have for centuries. We reached a large pockmarked field, dotted with the holes of rabbits. A small net was placed over every hole before the ferret was sent into one.

I don't like hunting and can't stand the thought of killing animals, but here, now, in the Shropshire hills, I had a small feeling of excitement. I hated myself for it, but this was two animals pitted against one another in an underground arena. It wasn't a bloodthirsty excitement but a fascination and wonder at the natural order and man's ability to harness the land and the wildlife around him.

There was silence and then a very quiet, distant thudding. It was the sound of rabbits warning others about a danger. Suddenly, all around us, rabbits leapt from their holes like jack-in-the-boxes, then into the nets. One, two, three, four . . . nine rabbits I counted within thirty seconds. It really was extraordinary. The rabbits were swiftly killed and sent off to the butchers.

My time at Acton Scott was not only a reminder of the

hard life of a farmer, both Victorian and present-day, but it had demonstrated once again the strange and complex relationship between man and animal.

I had a whole new respect for ferrets after that, although I still think they stink.

My involvement with horses on *Escape in Time* took me back to my childhood, as I have always loved horses. My wife jokes that I know nothing about equine things as she has never seen me on a horse, but the reality is that when I was growing up I spent much of my time on horseback.

Having two sisters meant I ended up with a slightly feminine-based childhood: Barbie dolls, ballet and horses. We used to go riding every weekend at a little stable nearby and during the holidays we would even go to Pony Club camps. Sometimes we would just trot around the outdoor school and other times we would go out for a hack across country. I really enjoyed hacking. I felt free and loved being on a horse. I still preferred my dogs, though. Horses always seemed like too much hard work – all that mucking out and grooming didn't appeal to me. But over the years since then I have ridden horses all over the world: in Namibia, Kenya, the Falklands, Peru and New Zealand to name just a few places. Each time I have regressed to those childhood days.

I should clarify, though, that I am a confident rider rather than a good one. I never sit upright and sometimes find it hard to trot or canter in time with the horse. But as with so many things in my life, I have never let poor technique get in the way of opportunity.

In the run-up to the wedding of Prince William and Kate

Middleton in 2011 I was invited by the US network NBC to make a film about the Household Cavalry. I was given the opportunity to go out with the soldiers and horses who would escort the royal carriage – on the understanding that I could ride.

The Household Cavalry consists of the two senior regiments of the British Army: the Blues and Royals, and the Life Guards. As well as normal army duties, some of the soldiers from these two regiments make up the Household Cavalry Mounted Regiment, which since the 1660s has performed in a number of state and royal ceremonies each year – most notably the Queen's Birthday Parade every June and the famous Musical Ride in the Windsor Castle Royal Tattoo. A number of notable people have served in the Household Cavalry, including both Prince William and Prince Harry.

Before I could ride out with this iconic regiment, they insisted I had a 'test', so on the morning before filming began I was taken to their famous indoor school, where one of the commanding officers in charge of training put me through my paces.

'Right, I want you to follow the school clockwise,' he instructed me.

Things didn't go well when I started going anticlockwise, but he must have given me the benefit of the doubt because the test continued. I practised a series of trots and canters and he got me to change direction and come to a halt.

I passed, but only just. I was allowed out into Hyde Park, carefully flanked by two uniformed officers who never let me stray far from the horse track. It felt pretty special to be riding with the Household Cavalry. I wondered what my bossy little riding teacher would say now.

A few months later I found myself out in Canada with NBC once again. This time I was given a chance to ride with the Royal Canadian Mounted Police.

'Well, I've been out with the Household Cavalry,' I explained when they asked if I was up to it, and before I knew it I was riding through the streets in my red jacket with one of the most famous mounted regiments in the world.

I felt I should keep this up and blag my way into the famous Spanish Riding School in Vienna.

The great appeal of riding with the Household Cavalry or the Canadian Mounted Police is the ceremony. I have always loved our rich tradition of pageantry in the UK, from the Changing of the Guard to the State Opening of Parliament, but one of the most unusual historic events in which I have had the privilege of participating takes place each year at Marlow on the River Thames.

Between 18 and 22 July visitors to the Thames can witness a historic royal ritual: Swan Upping, the annual swan census. The ceremony dates back to the twelfth century, when the king declared all unmarked mute swans his property. At the time, swans were an exquisite delicacy at feasts and banquets, so Swan Upping acted as a practical means of catching and dividing the birds for this purpose. Nobles would lay claim to their fowl by carving signature designs into their beaks, while unmarked swans in open water were rightfully the Crown's.

The ceremony has undergone some significant changes in its 800-year history. Emphasis has shifted from catching to simply counting. By the nineteenth century swan was no longer such popular banquet fodder and today, other than the royal household, only fellows of St John's College Cambridge have retained their right to dine on swan. While the seventeenth-century Upping took place on a single day, today's events span a full five. In the early twentieth century Queen Alexandra demanded the carving of less elaborate markings, as she was concerned by the damage inflicted on the beaks of the swans. Carving has since been entirely superseded by the use of rings on the birds' legs and there are now only two organizations who continue to mark their swans: the Worshipful Company of Vintners and the Worshipful Company of Dyers. Royal swans continue to be unmarked.

July is the optimum time for swan counting, as the cygnets have not yet learned to fly and the adults are also largely earthbound as they are in moult. Swan Upping involves a count of both young and adult swans and a survey of any signs of illness. 'Uppers' dressed in scarlet travel in six traditional boats (two each for the worshipful companies and two for the Queen) and cry 'All-up' before herding together and lifting a family of swans out of the river.

In 2005, shortly before I set off to row the Atlantic, I was lucky enough to be given a place by the Queen's Swan Marker and joined the royal party on their boat to make a film for *Countryfile*. The Swan Marker was in a rich red jacket with starched white trousers and on his head was the captain's hat that has been worn for decades. The Vintners and the Dyers all wore the smartest red T-shirts I have ever seen, with 'ER' emblazoned on their fronts. They looked a little like Italian gondoliers with their white boat shoes and slightly short trousers.

We rowed up the river as crowds of people looked on from the shore. I had never realized quite how heavy and powerful a swan can be until we caught our first one.

The swans are weighed and checked for any debris, like fishing lines or any other rubbish that may have got caught on their bodies, before they are released back on to the river.

Just as we reached Henley, a gust of wind caught the Queen's Swan Marker's hat and tipped it into the river, where it promptly sank into the murky depths. I like to think that many years from now some mudlark will discover the missing cap and consign it to a museum.

As a child I had always been wary of swans. I had heard tales from my father of dogs and even people attacked by these moody birds. Indeed, I was once chased from the banks of the Serpentine in London's Hyde Park by hissing swans. My experience with the Uppers, however, gave me not only a different perspective but a whole new attitude to these majestic birds. As with so many creatures, we sometimes fail to marvel at their beauty. For many, including myself, they have simply become a part of the furniture. Stop, stare and explore, and you begin to scratch beneath the familiar surface and rediscover nature's true beauty.

It has never ceased to surprise me how animals have cropped up in my life at the least expected moments. I once came across a flock of sheep on London's Savile Row and I once ended up on a flight in Bolivia with a pig on my lap; but perhaps one of the least expected encounters came during the 2009 Hay-on-Wye literary festival, where I was launching my book *Race to the Pole*.

Hay-on-Wye is always fun, with its heady mix of writers, authors and poets. You always meet interesting people there, but this particular year I bumped into my old colleague Giles Coren. Giles is the son of the late great Alan Coren, with whom I had appeared on *Call My Bluff* several times, and brother of the writer and presenter Victoria Coren. I knew him from the time I worked for *Tatler* magazine in London. He was one of the only other males in the office and our restaurant reviewer. Most days he was paid to lunch out, so he always kept us entertained with his late-afternoon rants. Our lives separated when I went off to Taransay for the year and Giles left to work for Rupert Murdoch on *The Times*. Now nearly ten years later our paths crossed again here in Hay-on-Wye, where Giles was co-presenting the *Arts Show* for Sky with Mariella Frostrup.

Giles thought it would be fun for me to teach him how to shear a sheep – for a book show. I know, I thought it sounded pretty odd too, but I loved the idea of seeing Giles covered in sheep shit.

We drove several miles from town to where a farmer had agreed to 'lend' us some sheep.

'My car's all muddy,' huffed Giles, stepping into the farm-yard. You can take the man out of the city, but you can't take the city out of the man.

We went to a small shearing shed where the farmer wanted to show Giles how to do it before filming began. He carefully manoeuvred the clippers back and forth, removing large swathes of wool with each movement. Soon he had removed all the wool from the head and it was time to move to the trickier rear end. Carefully he worked his way around the end, cutting the matted hair from the sheep's behind, but as he reached the delicate genitals, he clipped the skin and a great flood of blood streamed out of the sheep.

Giles made a retching noise. 'Have you just shaved off its cock or its fanny?' he asked.

It was very, very funny. It was only a tiny cut, but Giles was beside himself with worry that he would do the same.

'I came to shear a sheep, not to castrate one or perform a hysterectomy,' he lamented.

Eventually he agreed to have a go. It was very surreal. The two *Tatler* boys shearing a sheep together in a Welsh field. The sheep didn't get the best haircut, but at least he kept his balls.

It wasn't the first time sheep and *Tatler* had come into the same sentence. When I first arrived on Taransay I decided to name all the sheep after the girls back in the *Tatler* offices in Hanover Square. Hermione, Lucy, Vassi and Harriet were all immortalized in woolly animals. The only thing was, I hadn't understood that these sheep were all castrated males destined for the cooking pot. So not only had the girls suffered the ignominy of having eunuch sheep named after them, but they all ended up as lamb chops too.

Agriculture and the rural way of life have frequently crept into my life as over the years I have been given small opportunities to sample different aspects not just of farming but of man's working relationship with animals.

We are a farming nation, but all too often we forget about

our heritage or even where our meat and veg come from. A farmer's life is a tough one and I have experienced my own trials and tribulations over the years as I have come to terms with our relationship with animals and all the complexities it involves. From our rich cultural heritage to the simple need to eat, this relationship has always been strained and often contradictory.

As a child my father had told me so many tales about tails, but of all his animal stories it was the ones from his time working as a vet at London Zoo that captivated me the most. I always wondered what it must be like to work with those magnificent creatures, and I was about to find out.

6

Lion Country

In a way I have two wives. There is my real wife Marina, who nags me, teases me and kisses me, and then there is my TV wife, Kate Humble, who nags me, teases me but never kisses me. Well, not on the lips anyway. I'll get in trouble from both of them for saying this, but that's how it has always been and how it will always be.

Kate once described me in an interview as 'the bravest person I know, because he's actually scared of everything . . . including guinea pigs'. I think that statement sums Kate up perfectly. She has an effortless way of giving me a compliment while ensuring I remain firmly grounded.

I dread her opinion but I also value and respect it. I often find myself thinking, 'What will Kate say?' I suppose that makes her more of a mother figure, but our friendship is far more complex than that.

If I had to describe Kate, she is my 'humbler'. She is

extremely easy to annoy and difficult to impress. It makes me wonder what Ludo, her husband, did all those years ago. But that's what I love about her. Kate has always called a spade a spade and in the world of sycophancy in which we both work I have found it a stabilizing force. It is one of the reasons we have become such good friends and it's also why she has become such good friends with Marina, because they are really quite similar.

Kate is one of the most loyal, caring, thoughtful and generous people I know. Sure she is opinionated and sometimes a little short-tempered, but aren't we all? Over the years she has become part of the furniture of my life. Not in a comfy-sofa sort of way, but in a wood-burning-stove kind of way, sometimes giving a nice warm glow, sometimes a little fiery, needing to be refuelled but always comforting.

For many years people used to think we were together both on and off screen, but Kate has been happily married for nearly twenty years. She and I just have a chemistry that works. It is partly founded on mutual respect, but it is mainly based on the fact that we actually like each other.

I have heard tales of some 'camera partners' who despise one another. They are professional enough to smile through gritted teeth while the camera is rolling, then they walk away without a word once the filming is over. There are stories of hatred and envy. There is one famous presenting duo who watch back the final edit of their show with a stopwatch in hand, calculating the screen time each has had in order to make sure it wasn't biased.

I have always found it far more enjoyable co-presenting than doing it alone, and without doubt my favourite and most constant co-host has been Kate. A brief calculation on the back of a napkin suggests we have made about three hundred hours of television together. We have lived together and travelled the world together.

The first time I met her was in 2000. I had been asked by the BBC if I'd like to present a new TV series called *Animal Park* which followed life behind the scenes at Longleat Safari Park down in Wiltshire. It had already been going for a season with Paul Heiney and Kate Humble as presenters and the BBC wanted to know if I would take over from Paul and co-present with Kate. I had never met her or, to be honest, seen her on television. Little did I know what an important person she would become in my life.

I had just touched down from a trip with the World Wildlife Fund to Nepal, where I had been relocating Asian rhino, when I picked up my voicemail messages.

'Hello, it's Kate Humble here and I'm afraid you're stuck with my company for the next few months whether you like it or not. So I thought we should meet. How about Sunday lunch at mine?'

It was Saturday afternoon and, as I have learnt with Kate, she didn't really give me a chance to say no. So next day I packed Inca into the Land Rover and we made our way to Chiswick to meet Kate and her husband Ludo.

I was a little nervous. What if she didn't like me? What if she felt annoyed that she had been landed with a 'reality show' participant as a co-host? For many years I had an enormous complex about my provenance and I was unsure about what Kate would make of me.

With Inca at my side, I knocked on the door. It was

opened by a mop of blonde hair, but before I had time to introduce myself Inca had rocketed through the hall, through the lounge, through the kitchen, out into the garden and straight into their fish pond. It would have been rather impressive if it hadn't been quite so embarrassing. I had never seen Inca move so fast – well, except for at that polo match with the royal princes anyway. She literally leapt into the air and belly-flopped into the pond. She had lilypads on her head and I half expected to see displaced goldfish flapping around on the patio.

My face glowed red with embarrassment.

As if things could only get worse, Inca was stuck in the pond, floundering around in the murky water unable to get out. I knelt down and hauled at the scruff of her neck, growling under my breath as I tried to hide my scarlet face.

'I don't suppose you have a towel I could borrow, do you?'

I dried her off as best I could and she skulked around the kitchen smelling of pond water – and then she spotted the rats.

I like to think of Inca as a worldly dog, but I don't think she'd ever met a rat before and these rats had certainly never met a young Labrador. She must have looked terrifying. Whenever Inca gets excited she begins to sing. She can even make different notes. The movement of her tail shook her whole body as she sang excitedly to the unimpressed and frankly terrified rats.

At this stage Kate pointed out that they may well have heart attacks if Inca continued breathing her stinky breath and singing uncontrollably, so the rats were relocated to the top of the house.

Kate loves rats. In fact, Kate loves just about any creature that everyone else hates. But that is the joy of Kate – her infectious enthusiasm for life and for nature in particular.

The first day of filming at Longleat was with the elephants and their keeper Andy Hayton. We turned up at the large elephant house and while the film crew set up for the shot Kate handed me a spade. 'Get shovelling!' she urged as she began sweeping the floor with a broom.

I was puzzled. We weren't filming, so why were we sweeping and shovelling? It was one of the best lessons I ever learnt: that we were no more important than the keepers themselves. By showing a willing hand, helping out and joining in, Kate was demonstrating our respect for those around us. All too often, people in television can be swept up and engulfed in a cloud of self-importance, but the reality is that those around us are often far more talented or knowledge-able than we are ourselves.

It was the first lesson Kate taught me in the importance of being Humble. Humble by name, Humble by nature.

I sometimes wonder whether I would still be working in television after all these years had it not been for Kate and her professionalism. She taught me a great deal about presenting. I still aspire to be as good as her. She makes it look effortless. She has always been able to share information and explain things in a brilliantly simple way.

Kate used to joke that I couldn't tell my lions from my tigers or my elephants from my meerkats, but the fact was that I found myself focusing so much on the presenting itself that I sometimes forgot about the content.

I can't really remember time Before Kate (BK). She had

known a number of my girlfriends over the years and she was the only person I confided in when I first saw Marina. I asked her advice on what to cook Marina for our first date; she suggested salmon and potatoes. It paid off and before long she was giving a reading at our wedding. Kate was one of the first people I called after the birth of my son. She was in John Lewis at the time and she burst into tears when I told her we'd named him Ludo after her husband.

Kate is Ludo's godmother and she has taken on an almost rock-star status in my little boy's obsession with tractors and diggers and cows and pigs.

Several years ago Kate and Big Ludo (he loves that name) made the move out of London to Wales, where they bought a farmhouse. In just a few years they went from urban-dwelling Londonites to farmers. These days Kate occasionally comes down to London in her muddy boots to stay with us, bringing photos of tractors. Better still, we go for weekends in Wales.

Kate has become a vital fixture in my life. Without her I doubt I would have been able to pursue my passion for wildlife and nature, and I'm not sure I'd ever have had any longevity in television.

When I first told her about this book and suggested it might be called *The Accidental Naturalist*, her immediate response was, 'But you're not one.' She has a point, but I hope that when she reads this (and she will), she will understand, even if she still disapproves of the title.

She is an extraordinary presenter and a great friend, but for me she will always be my great Humbler.

* * *

If Kate is my second wife, then Longleat is my second home. Don't worry, I'm not about to reveal that I am the illegitimate son of Lord Bath (or at least I don't think I am, unless there is something my mother never told me), but over the last decade I have become entwined within the fabric of the Wiltshire estate. Inadvertently, I have become a small part of Longleat's long, rich history.

Longleat is one of the finest Elizabethan houses in the United Kingdom. It was built by Sir John Thynne, member of parliament and steward to Edward Seymour, 1st Duke of Somerset; his descendants became the marquesses of Bath and Longleat is still the Thynn family seat today. The house was designed by Robert Smythson and took twelve years to build; it was largely completed by 1580. The 900 acres of parkland that surround it were designed by Capability Brown and there are a further 100,000 acres of woods and farmland. In 1949 it became the first stately home to open to the public, and it also boasts the first safari park outside Africa.

Longleat Safari Park opened on 1 April 1966 as the result of a gentleman's agreement between the then Lord Bath (the 6th Marquess) and Jimmy Chipperfield of the famous Chipperfield's Circus family. The dynasty goes back more than three hundred years, making the Chipperfields one of the oldest circus families in Europe, and for many years they toured Europe and the Far East with their big top.

The idea of a safari park within the grounds of the stately home was embraced by Lord Bath's father as another way to supplement the increasing costs of running and maintaining the house. When Chipperfield put the idea to the 6th Marquess, he was slow to grasp his vision.

'Won't the cages have to be awfully big if cars are to drive into them?'

'No, it's the people who are going to be in the cages – their cars – and the lions who are going to be free,' Chipperfield replied.

At the outset, fifty lions, extras from the film *Born Free*, were brought in to roam the 100-acre reserve. Three thousand cars visited the park in the first weekend and within five months the capital cost of the venture had been repaid.

To begin with the park was home just to lions, then giraffes moved in along with the hippos a few years later.

The BBC had been granted access to the estate to make a series that looked behind the scenes at a safari park. It replaced an earlier series based at Longleat, *Lion Country*, and was to be called *Animal Park*. And they were offering me the job of co-presenter.

Correction. They would give me a job depending on how I fared in a screen test. Given that I had never presented before – I had yet to be offered the job on *Countryfile* – that was fair enough.

It was a cold January morning when I made my way to Chessington World of Adventures. I drove down the A3 in my noisy Land Rover Defender with Inca in the back. I was nervous as hell. I had no idea how to present. What if I was no good?

My life had become directionless since my year on Taransay. I had found myself drifting around London doing the odd interview or chat show, but I had no idea where it was heading.

My confidence had taken a dent and I had dipped into a minor depression, unsure of what I wanted to do with my life. The opportunity to work on *Animal Park* seemed to offer a structure and a course. I hadn't even got the job but I was already relying on it. I had never thought of being a TV presenter; my childhood aspirations had centred on either becoming an actor or working as a vet. Neither had happened, but suddenly here was a golden opportunity to dabble in both. I didn't have a degree in zoology and knew little about animal behaviour, but the series was looking for someone with a passion and interest who could act as the foil to the show itself.

I had been on television dozens of times before in *Castaway*, but this would be the first time I had 'performed' for the camera as a presenter. The night before the screen test I spent several hours in the bathroom staring at myself with a hairbrush as an impromptu microphone.

'Hello and welcome to the show . . .' I'd practised. It looked as stupid as it now sounds, but I really wanted that job.

It was a freezing cold morning when I met the crew – Chris Powell the producer, Mark Chan the cameraman and Stu the soundman. I struggled to hide my nerves.

'We thought we'd start with a snake,' said Chris, smiling.

'Great,' I replied through gritted teeth. Oh why oh why had he chosen a snake? Of all the creatures he could have picked, it had to be a snake. I hated snakes. Correction. I was terrified of snakes. It was a fear that had increased over the years and is, of course, a common phobia, known as ophidiophobia.

'We thought we'd get you to hold the snake and introduce it to the audience,' explained Chris.

We found a bench in a small paddock and Mark set up his camera while Stu attached a mike. I was shaking, but these were no longer nerves about the screen test; they were about holding the snake.

But if I was going to make it as a wildlife presenter, I had to overcome my fear.

My heart pounded as one of the keepers brought out a box containing the snake. 'How do you hold it properly?' I wondered to myself. 'What if it escapes – or, worse, bites me?'

My brain was muddled and distracted with fear.

'Here you go!' said the keeper. 'Sophie, meet Ben. Ben, meet Sophie.' And with that he handed me the snake.

I had been expecting a large snake, but suddenly I found myself with a tiny corn snake and that was far, far worse. It may sound strange, but the smaller the snake, the more fearful I am. They seem to have much more unpredictable movements. They are fast and agile.

I took a deep breath as I held her in both hands. A snake is unexpectedly cold to the touch and has a strange, almost leathery texture.

'Action!' shouted Chris before I had gathered my thoughts.

Sophie started winding herself around my wrist, her little tongue flicking out of her mouth. I juggled her between my hands, trying to control her. I needed to keep her in my sight, but I knew I had to talk to the camera, which would involve taking my eyes off her.

'Hello, I'm Ben Fogle and this is Sophie the corn snake,' I

said, smiling to the camera before looking back down at Sophie. In horror, I realized she had disappeared halfway up my jumper sleeve. If I pulled her back I was worried she might bite me or pull harder and disappear all the way up my arm.

'Ah – Sophie appears to have disappeared up my sleeve,' I beamed to the camera, gently tugging at her. I fumbled with my sleeve, trying to coax her out.

'Here, Sophie,' I said with a short whistle, as if I were calling Inca. I was hopelessly out of my depth.

She wriggled and squirmed and before I knew it she had gone. Lost in my Guernsey jumper.

I stared wide-eyed down the lens of the camera, frozen in fear as Sophie wriggled towards my armpit. I caught Mark suppressing a laugh and Chris was grinning from ear to ear.

I was petrified with terror, but I had to get Sophie out. I pulled at the neck of my jumper and peered down. There was no sign of her. I was terrified about sticking my hand in in case she bit me.

Slowly I lifted my jumper and began to feel around. 'You're supposed to be presenting to the camera,' I reminded myself.

'As you can see, Sophie loves my jumper. In fact, she is looking for a warm place and I can assure you my armpit is very warm just now.' I said all of this with fleeting glances to the camera as I fished around for the snake.

Then I felt a movement and, as I pulled at my clothes, her head appeared from the neck of my jumper. I froze like a rabbit caught in headlights as she slithered under my chin. I didn't need to say anything; my fear was clear to see. Slowly I gathered her back into my hands.

'Cut!' shouted Chris.

I had messed up. I had wanted to look smooth and professional, and instead I had lost my interviewee in my jumper and fluffed the whole screen test.

Chris had a large grin on his face.

'I think we can safely say you have the job,' he said with a big smile, shaking my hand.

It had been an inauspicious start, but it had given me the confidence to be myself and to play along with whatever happened.

Life was good. I had got the job and I'd be spending several months living down in Wiltshire on the Longleat estate. Suddenly my life seemed to have a little direction. I felt excited about the future once again. I bought myself half a dozen books on wild animals and began to learn about some of those I would be working with.

And then disaster struck.

Foot-and-mouth disease had been discovered among a herd of cattle in Northumberland. Before long it had swept across Britain, closing down the countryside with it.

Foot-and-mouth is a contagious disease of livestock, mainly affecting animals with cloven hooves, such as cattle, sheep, goats, pigs and deer. It causes blistering of the animal's hooves and gums, a high fever, and can lead eventually to death. It is endemic in much of the world, but there had not been an outbreak in Britain since 1967. The 2001 outbreak started in mid-February with a report from a farm in Heddon-on-the-Wall in Northumberland and within days further announcements of animals suffering from the illness were made across the country. The government responded by putting in place two regimes of control: first, all livestock within a small distance of any proven case of foot-and-mouth were to be culled; and second, a ban was instituted on moving livestock across large areas of the country. Using these strategies the government was able to announce by April that the epidemic was under control. In the end over 7 million animals were culled between February 2001 and January 2002. Although farmers were able to claim compensation for culled animals under the Animal Health Act of 1981, the disease had a devastating effect: many farmers lost their entire livestock and the tourism industry across the British countryside suffered tremendously. In total, the epidemic cost the British economy over £8 billion.

Dad had taken time off from his London surgery and had volunteered to help out in Shropshire. The countryside was littered with dips for boots, and vehicles had to be sprayed before entering or leaving farms. It was a frightening time for all and a heartbreaking one for farmers. I saw toughened men in tears as they watched bodies burn on long flaming pyres.

It was not only farms that were affected. Longleat was on total lockdown, shut off from the outside world. Foot-and-mouth affects all cloven-hoofed animals – even the elephants were at risk, as they too are susceptible to foot-and-mouth – and they couldn't afford to take any risks with their priceless collection. Filming was a logistical nightmare. The Land Rovers had to be fumigated before and after entering each paddock or enclosure, and we had to wash our clothes and boots after any interaction. The safari park was deserted.

Although no animals had to be culled at Longleat, there were cases of foot-and-mouth in the vicinity. Consequently, the park was opened two weeks late for the 2001 season and suffered a large dip in visitor numbers (only 360,000 people visited the park in 2001, compared to the expected 400,000). As a result, Lord Bath decided to auction paintings, furniture and historical artefacts from Longleat House to raise the £15 million needed to cover the shortfall caused by the lack of tourism.

The epidemic had made filming almost impossible. We weren't allowed access to many of the animals and the shortened series turned into a rather bleak look at life on the park during foot-and-mouth. The cold, wet weather and early darkness only accentuated the grimness. I was down on so many levels and I still feel guilty about my own self-pity during that period. At the time I felt my career prospects were being jeopardized, but the real issue was that this awful disease had decimated the country and ruined lives and livelihoods. It was not me but other people who were experiencing real suffering and hardship.

With time, of course, some of the wounds have healed, but the scarring remains very real across the countryside. Longleat was lucky; there was loss of income from being closed, but the animals were spared, unlike many hundreds of thousands of cattle throughout the country. It was a dark period for all those involved in the countryside and one we must never forget.

In a little field near to Pets Corner at Longleat was an old barn from which an ill-fated balloon tour of the park operation had briefly been run. I suppose it had seemed like a good idea at the time, until they realized that the balloon terrified the animals and it was shut down.

The balloon office, as it was known, became our home for six months each year. In it, half a dozen desks and computers were neatly lined up side by side. Set within a fenced field, the office also provided a perfect place for Inca to spend each day while I went off to work with the tigers and the camels. She would spend her time wandering in the field, listening to the distant howl of the wolves and roar of the lions. I always used to wonder what she made of all the smells on my trousers at the end of each day. However, I think the Notting Hill Gate foxes must have had an even greater surprise when they came across lion poo carefully spread over my garden in my bid to keep them away. The foxes, that is, not the lions.

The animals for which Longleat is most famous are its lions. You can hear their roar from as far away as Warminster and it still makes my hair stand on end. The park was home to three prides: Charlie's, M'fui's and Kabir's. They had to be kept apart at all times for fear of a territorial battle.

Brian Kent and Bob Trollope were in charge of all the big cats in the park – lions and tigers – and also the wolves. Each Friday the park fire alarms would be tested at 10 a.m. and the sound of the alarm would trigger the wolves to start howling.

The three elderly tigers used to roam Tiger Territory like three pensioners. They would slowly patrol their enclosure, occasionally getting agitated by a rogue pheasant, which would be promptly dispatched with the swipe of a paw. Old and arthritic, they were slightly grumpy and would spend hours sunbathing next to their little pond. Kaddu, or 'Dudus' as Bob called her, was definitely his favourite, although he would rarely admit it. He would hand her small pieces of dripping red meat on a skewer through the bars. They had such a close relationship, and Bob was in tears when Kaddu died in April 2008.

Amongst the most important aspects of keeping animals in safari parks is to ensure they are as enriched, both physically and emotionally, as possible and to try to maintain as many of the natural traits they would display in the wild as possible. For all the big cats and the wolves, this always meant an exciting feeding routine with the park's famous feed truck. It worked a little like a reverse cage, with me caged rather than the animals. A small hatch at the back allowed large chunks of bloody meat to be dropped at intervals while the animals chased alongside.

We would set out from the yard with blood dripping from the back of the truck and carefully enter each enclosure, making sure our fingers never curled on to the outside of the bars. Lions would chase us at quite a lick and it was always the alpha males who got the first pick of the cuts. The tigers, due to age and lethargy, would move at a slightly slower pace, ambling rather than cantering like the lions.

I never liked to look too closely at the cuts of meat piled up around our feet. It came from local farms and abattoirs. Look too closely and you could sometimes make out a snout or a head.

Feeding the wolves was a little more gruesome, as we would often leave whole carcasses in their enclosure. These might be horses or ponies that had died of old age or been put down. It was staggering to see how fast the wolf pack could tear a carcass apart and strip it to the bone. It sounds tough, but I think it's better that the animal should be used rather than buried or burned. I have always been a firm believer in using all by-product and feeding deceased animals to Longleat's carnivores was as good a way as any.

When I first visited Longleat it was home to five magnificent elephants called Marge, Limbo, N'dala, M'bili and M'kali. They lived up in a far corner of the park under the care of keeper Andy Hayton, and Ryan Hockley worked in the elephant house with Bev Evans and Kevin Knibbs. They all loved those elephants, but they were particularly special to Andy. The elephants were like his children. He fed them, washed them and took them out for walks in the woods. When I think of Andy, I still see him spraying them down with his powerhose and then scrubbing them with a brush. One of the greatest privileges I ever had at Longleat was helping him give them their early-morning shower and taking them for a walk. The five elephants would walk in single file, holding each other's tails with their trunks. It was like a real life Disney film.

N'dala, M'bili and M'kali were only three years old when Andy first got them and they were fourteen when they left in 2003. He effectively saw them through their childhood and was extremely close to them all. But all good things have to come to an end, and an EU dictat saw the end of the elephants of Longleat. The estate simply couldn't meet the conditions of the new law on keeping elephants and they had to leave.

Whatever your thoughts on elephants kept in captivity, it was a traumatic time for all. The day we had to say goodbye to N'dala, M'bili and M'Kali, Andy was heartbroken. For more than a decade he had cared for those three elephants and now they were being taken from him, like children taken into care. It was a devastating time for the keepers, as they had built up such strong relationships with all their elephants, and it took Andy a great deal of time to get over it. For a while you couldn't really mention the elephants.

While I had only known the elephants for a few years, they certainly left a glaring hole at Longleat. I always found it sad to drive past their old house. In fact I've always had mixed feelings about elephants in captivity. A little like my dilemma over our relationship with farm animals or species native to this country, I can remember feeling a glimmer of sorrow for the elephants at London Zoo. True, here at Longleat they had wide valleys and fields to wander, but of all the animals they always seemed the most out of place. A psychologist would come up with some academic reasons for the emotion elicited by elephants. Maybe it is their ability to remember, or their little pleading eyes. Whatever it is, they can tug at human emotions that other animals can't reach. We were all sad to see them go, but I was sadder for Andy than anything else.

They left Andy and Ryan for ZooParc de Beauval in St-Aignan in France. The two keepers accompanied the elephants to France and stayed with them for the first couple of weeks to ease them in to their new surroundings and help their new keepers bond. They had to teach them all their commands in French. I still can't fathom how Andy was able to do that. It would be like me handing over Inca – inconceivable.

The next few years were tough for Andy, but he turned his attention to Longleat's 'hoofstock' section, looking after the endangered Rothschild's giraffe, zebra, camels, llamas and tapirs, to mention just a few. He has bred many Rothchilds over the years, making Longleat's one of the most successful breeding groups in the country. But he never really got over losing his elephants, so it was particularly sweet when he helped save an elderly African elephant called Anne and he and Ryan were finally reunited with their first love.

Anne the elephant arrived at Longleat on 3 April 2011. An ex-circus animal, she had travelled all over the world with the Bobby Roberts Circus. She arrived amidst a media furore after it was reported that she had been abused by one of her handlers; however, this has not been proved and she is certainly in safe hands now. At nearly seventy, she is the oldest elephant in captivity, and it shows. She suffers terribly with arthritis, so Andy and Ryan needed to execute a strict routine of scrubbing, massage and manicures to maintain her health.

I love that things have come full circle for Andy and his elephants. He and Anne were destined to meet. When I first saw the pictures of her in the papers I had a suspicion that Andy would come to the rescue and there is something deeply satisfying in knowing that he is once again lovingly showering and walking an elephant, becoming once again Andy the elephant man. Longleat hope to extend their 'elephant sanctuary', so Andy and Ryan could soon be looking after a lot more.

After the lions, perhaps Longleat's most famous residents were the gorillas, in particular two Western Lowland gorillas named Nico and Samba. Mark Tye looked after them and all the animals in the lake area.

Nico arrived at Longleat shortly after it opened in 1966 and Samba got to the park on 13 October 1986. They lived together for twenty years. Although they accepted one another, they didn't have a particularly loving relationship – in fact, it was really quite tempestuous. Sam would get very frustrated with her grumpy, messy flatmate. Mark only ever saw them having sex once; he just thinks they weren't that into each other! They were more like a brother and sister than a couple, and they would often squabble and fight. It was not uncommon to see them sulking in separate corners after a tiff, unable even to look at one another.

Gorillas are extraordinary creatures. For me, it's all about the eyes, which are mesmerizing mainly because they look so much like our own. Those eyes sometimes give the impression of a man in a gorilla costume.

After elephants, gorillas must surely take second place amongst animals that create strong emotions in us. Like many, I dream of visiting them in the wild. I loved *Gorillas in the Mist* as a child. They have an air of haughtiness about them, a superiority that demands respect. Forget about the power of a gorilla; I sometimes believe it could outwit and out-think me. It would be just as likely to beat me at a game of chess as in a boxing bout. I could spend hours gazing at Nico and Samba, but unsurprisingly they didn't like being stared at and would often turn their backs on me. Never underestimate a gorilla.

Mark had an incredible relationship with both the gorillas, hand-feeding and medicating them through the bars on a daily basis. Nico's favourite drink was Ribena mixed with yoghurt. He loved it and used to guzzle it down from a baby bottle held between the bars. Although he and Samba had the whole island to explore during the daytime, they were always brought into the Gorilla House at night. To alleviate any boredom, Mark installed a TV and a Sky box. He used to leave it on Animal Planet and latterly they were allowed to watch *Animal Park* and see themselves on the BBC. They really did love watching television. I heard rumours that they had once been allowed to watch porn to try to get them frisky and in the mood to procreate, but I'm not sure if that's really true.

We saw so many animals come and go at Longleat, but there was a huge sense of devastation and loss when Samba passed away due to old age on 3 March 2007. Mark was torn. Bereaved, he went into a form of mourning. Surprisingly, Nico didn't seem to be affected as much as everyone else. And he is still going strong at the age of fifty! That really is a ripe old age and although he has a large covering of grey fur, you wouldn't know he is so old. Nico has suffered from colds and even pneumonia, and we all breathed a sigh of relief each time he made it through another winter.

A little like Andy and Anne, exciting times lie ahead for Mark: at the time of writing he awaits the arrival of two new gorillas. It's a long time since he has worked with any primates other than Nico and Samba so it will be a challenging time for him, but what I have seen over the years is that the keepers thrive on challenges.

The gorillas' island is surrounded by Half Mile Lake and the California sea lions that live in it would occasionally tease the gorillas, but in reality they were terrified of them – a gorilla could tear a sea lion to pieces in seconds.

Who ever knew that sea lions could live in a freshwater lake in Wiltshire? I still think it is one of the most fantastic quirks of the safari park. They would be fed salt tablets hidden in their mackerel to compensate for the lack of salt in the water. They were by far the noisiest residents of the lake and, a little like rabbits, they seemed to be a continually growing population, all due to the virility of the big male, Buster. He had quite a harem. I always used to think that if there was one animal like Lord Bath in character it would be Buster the sea lion.

Also living in Half Mile Lake were Spot and Sonia, the park's two very grumpy hippos. In my eight years down at Longleat I never did see them out of the water and only ever caught the occasional glimpse of them in the murky water from the safari park boat. It always seemed amazing that arguably two of the largest creatures at Longleat were the most camouflaged and hidden. They had a large field, called Hippo Field, which was churned up with mud. In the summer the soft earth would dry into the most extraordinary shapes, left behind by their mud-wallowing baths. I always wondered when they did this and how I always managed to miss it. We used to hide infra-red cameras to try to capture footage of them bathing at night. Without the scale given by their surroundings, however, they just looked like cows grazing in a field.

* * *

While the larger animals used to dominate our time, as it was trickier to set up filming with them, it was often the smaller animals that gave us the most entertainment and they usually came from Pets Corner, which is now known as Animal Kingdom.

Pets Corner was home to an eclectic mix of the weird and wonderful, from the football-loving Vietnamese pot-bellied pigs to Sophie the python and Rosie the Chilean rose tarantula. Meerkats, otters, rabbits, guinea pigs and iguanas all competed for everyone's affections under their curator Darren Beasley. Pets Corner always gave us the best opportunity to be hands-on, and I still bear the scars from cuts and scratches inflicted by beaks, claws and sometimes teeth.

My father's hands are also scarred from years of working with animals and the bites and scratches inflicted on him by irate or confused animals. I have always thought his hands bear the mark of his dedication to his profession. He has never complained about them, or even talked about them.

Kate would use any excuse to get hands-on with arguably my least favourite creatures in the park: the rats and the meerkats. She used to love allowing them to scurry up her sleeve or down her leg, but I was never sure about them – particularly after I got a few little nips.

They weren't actually my least favourite, however. That position was still reserved for Rosie and Sophie. Spider and snake. To be fair, I did start to overcome my fear a bit, but I still trembled every time I had to hold either of them.

* * *

160

While we were making *Animal Park* Kate and I would relocate down to the West Country and for several months each year would share a little cottage on the Longleat estate.

I loved the drive down to Wiltshire. If I had to nominate a favourite road in England it would probably be the A303. There is nothing quite like leaving London early in the morning and seeing Stonehenge at sunrise. The road would then take me across the Bovington range, where I would often see little plumes of dust as tanks rumbled across the fields; sometimes I would be held up by a convoy of a dozen tanks as they clattered across the road.

My old Land Rover would finally rumble up the tree-lined drive into the estate and, as I summited the hill, the rolling landscape designed by Capability Brown would open up before me. There was something rather settling and comforting about reaching Longleat. It's strange, because it always meant work, but it brought with it a different pace of life. It never ceased to give me a thrill to see giraffes and rhinos roaming the Wiltshire countryside.

I like to think that over the years Kate and I were awarded honorary keeper status. That's not to say we were at all comparable to the real keepers, but I think we built up a trust with them. After all, the keepers, the animals and the location were the real stars of the series, but, as is so often the case, the presenters got to bask in other people's glory.

One of the hardest things was keeping track of the chronology of events. There was often a long lead time between filming and broadcast on TV, so, combined with the high turnover of animals that were born and those that had passed away, it was sometimes difficult to know which animals were which. I'd often get stopped in the street by a very concerned fan who would ask how Becky the giraffe was recovering, or how Denzil the tapir was getting on. The reality was that we saw so many animals come and go that it was often impossible to give them an accurate answer.

The park was divided up between a number of key keepers whom I got to know like old friends. At the top of the hierarchy was Keith Harris, who looked after the whole park. Deputy head warden Ian Turner was another of the important keepers with whom we used to spend time. He would oversee the entire collection of animals and he would often be there to help me give a mud pack to a rhino or to help the local vet when he had to take ultrasounds or treat an injured animal. In addition to the keepers we have already met in this chapter, there was also Tim, who was in charge of the deer and the Rees macaque monkeys.

I learnt so much about the wildlife at the safari park, and the real lessons came from these magnificent keepers. They are some of the most generous, selfless people I have had the pleasure to meet. They don't do the job for financial gain, but for the love of their charges. Animals don't take weekends, bank holidays or summer breaks. They need care 24/7 and here at Longleat they receive it without question through all the highs and lows that come with looking after such a wide, varied and complex collection. The fact that so many exotic animals thrive at safari parks like Longleat is testament to the expertise, care and patience of their keepers.

I have struggled to come to terms with my own feelings and opinions on keeping wild animals in captivity. Is there a difference between keeping a dog in your home and a lion in a field? There is no simple answer, and as with anything that involves nature it is bound to be an emotive subject.

While there are some who believe that zoos and safari parks should be consigned to the history books, I beg to differ. It is the only chance many people ever get to see some of this planet's great creatures. The best way to ensure people care for our environment is to show them what they stand to lose. Many safari parks have become pioneers in the art of conservation, and indeed the Zoological Society of London is responsible for vital conservation initiatives around the world. Without them, the outlook for animals in the wild would be considerably poorer.

While Longleat might be famous for its lions, it is arguably overshadowed by its loins, in the eccentric guise of Alexander George Thynn, the 7th Marquess of Bath. Lord Bath is as much a part of Longleat as the house and the lions. Tall and broad, he has tremendous presence. Slightly dishevelled with his huge white beard and long curly hair, he looks like a cross between a pirate, Henry VIII and Father Christmas. He has a unique and quirky dress sense, which usually involves a combination of floral waistcoat, velvet trousers, a beret and colourful jacket. His style has been described as 'Kabul chic', although it often looks more like Captain Sparrow.

I have always loved his style and his individuality and would argue that he embodies the true English eccentric, but he is far more complex than that. Lord Bath is full of contrasts. He is ranked 359th in the *Sunday Times* Rich List, with an estimated wealth of £157 million, yet he likes to drink wine from wine boxes and sent his children to state school. He is married but he doesn't believe in monogamy. He is aristocracy but he doesn't like conformity. He stood for election in 1974 in an attempt to devolve Wessex and sat in the House of Lords as a Liberal Democrat.

Married to Hungarian actress Anna Gyarmathy since 1969, he has two children. The rest of his private life is open to speculation, often fuelled by the irascible lord himself. While Lady Bath may be the chatelaine of the main house, dotted around the estate are some of Lord Bath's famous 'wifelets', or mistresses.

A prolific painter, he has covered much of the historic house in his own creations. Using a porridge-like combination of oil and sawdust, he has created murals of every shape, size and colour imaginable. They stare out from walls and ceilings like naive 3D art. He is particularly fond of the Kama Sutra room, stuffed with pornographic art. The murals are his proudest achievement; his efforts now cover a third of the walls of Longleat – and he is still going strong. Not everyone is happy with the murals, though. Not because of the style or even their proliferation, but because they are highly flammable and are therefore an added fire hazard. The local fire brigade in nearby Warminster has had to change its whole drill in case of a fire at Longleat.

In addition to the murals, there are about 150 portraits of the marquess's royal ancestors, as well as sixty-eight paintings of the wifelets adorning the staircase known as Bluebeard's Gallery.

'Some people have notches on their bedpost,' Lord Bath explained the first time he showed me the collection. 'I prefer to paint them. Far more flattering, I think you'll agree.'

The house is open to the public – all, that is, except for Lord Bath's private apartments. In these the rooms are interconnected and include a modern kitchen, its shelves stacked with tins of processed peas and jars of Chicken Tonight, and a futuristic dining room, a little like the Starship Enterprise from *Star Trek*.

Hidden in the top of the house are the collections of his late father, Henry Thynn, the 6th Marquess of Bath, founder of the safari park, who with his authoritarian tendencies was an avid collector of Hitler's paintings. At prep school, Alexander tried to please him by being as fascist as possible. As a school prefect, he punished some boys by putting them under the floorboards with a table on top. He then wrote to his father, boasting of what he had done. Henry responded by reporting him to the headmaster for bullying.

Lord Bath's most loyal friend and companion is Boudicca his yellow Labrador. I didn't think anyone loved their dogs as much as I love Inca until I saw the relationship between Lord Bath and Boudicca. They are literally inseparable. Invariably his arrival was heralded by a deep holler, 'Boody-boo! Boody, Boody-boo!' He is never without his loyal friend. The house staff used to joke that they would have to follow his lordship everywhere he went to prevent the trail of destruction caused by the ever-excitable Boudicca as her tail knocked against priceless vases and paintings. Their descriptions always reminded me of the scene in *Mary Poppins* where they have to hold on to their possessions each time the retired captain fires his cannon.

Lord Bath was very much a part of my years at Longleat. He would invite us for dinner in his private apartment and occasionally hold parties for the staff and us in the Great Hall. And Inca and Boudicca used to spend hours and hours playing in the grounds by the house.

I used to love being shown around the house by Lord Bath; it made me feel enormously privileged. He may not have a conventional lifestyle and some may disapprove, but I have always admired his honesty and the fact that he dares to stand out. So often in society we are bowed by conformity. I would love to be eccentric and different, but the truth of the matter is that I lack the confidence and I'm not sure how Marina would feel about my taking twenty-six wifelets!

I have had such a wide and varied career that it is sometimes difficult to define myself through my work and challenges, but without doubt the television series that has had one of the greatest effects on my career is *Animal Park*. More often than not, if I am stopped on the street it is as 'that man from the wildlife show'.

'Animal Park!' people holler. 'Longleat man!'

I was once sent thirty-six pieces of work from a school in Belfast who had used me and the series as the basis for a whole-school project. I was so touched and flattered that I paid them a surprise visit. You should have seen the looks on their faces. I loved that visit. It's moments like that that make everything I do worthwhile.

Shortly before I left Longleat when the programme finished in 2009, I went to visit Lord Bath. I was devastated to be leaving and I had something important to ask him.

'You know how much I love it down here,' I said, trying to find the words. 'I'm really going to miss it.'

He stared at me.

'I was thinking . . .' I continued, blushing, '. . . was wondering whether there might be a spare cottage on the estate that I could rent?'

I hate asking for things, but I'd done it.

Lord Bath looked at me with a mixture of surprise and confusion.

'Well,' he replied, 'you don't really qualify for one of the cottages because you're not a wifelet. And while you're very handsome, you're not really my sort. But I'll see what I can do,' he said, smiling and offering me a drink from one of his wine boxes.

Lord Bath and his loyal army of keepers, Spot and Sonia the hippos, Nico and Samba the gorillas, M'fui the lion, Buster the sea lion and Denzil the tapir had all given me an insight into their unique world and a much greater understanding of the animal kingdom. Unknowingly, they had helped nurture and educate me in natural history. They had all unwittingly been part of my transition from aspiring naturalist to budding naturalist. I now needed to take my lessons from the classroom out into the field.

Part Three

The Roar

7

Everything Was Illuminating

I had been in Central America for nearly eight months. I was on a soulless, meandering and sometimes meaningless journey from nowhere to nowhere. And now I found myself on a wild beach on a remote peninsula of a forgotten land in the middle of a tropical thunderstorm.

Sheet lightning created snapshots in my head like Polaroid stills. Inky blackness was shattered by dazzling white flashes that sent my mind reeling.

I was lost. It was the middle of the night. My torch had broken and all I had was a bucket of warm turtle eggs. I was miles from the nearest settlement and somehow I needed to get off the beach and out of the storm.

'This way,' said Bonnie, pointing to a dark shadow set against the white sand.

The rain was so torrential it felt as if we were in a shower. The raindrops were so large that they seemed to merge with one another into a single continuous flow. Water cascaded off my face, which created its own unique weather system as the rain streamed down my forehead and off my nose. My eyes stung from the salt and even in the tropical heat I began to shiver.

Slowly we approached a large upturned canoe that had been hollowed out from a tree. Next to it I could just make out the shape of a figure. It was a person. At least I was sure it was a person. I could see the distinct outline of a head and a torso and what looked like an arm held aloft, as if waving or gesticulating.

'Hello!' I cried, but my words were drowned out by the din of the rain.

'*Hello!*' I repeated, but once again my words were washed away by the flood of rainwater.

We had been out for hours. We were tired, hungry and scared. We needed to find the path back to the village.

With an electric snap, the sky lit up like day. There in front of us, just a few feet away, was a man, his face contorted and confused, his hand held aloft clutching an enormous machete.

'Run!' cried Bonnie, grabbing my hand. '*Run!*'

It's funny how we find ourselves in places we never expected to visit and never knew existed.

Latin America had become my passion. It all began with pink dolphins on the Amazon. As an eighteen-year-old fresh out of boarding school I was determined to travel the world. In January 1993 I bought myself a one-way ticket to Brazil and within a few days of landing I found myself aboard a cargo ship travelling 3,000 miles up the Amazon.

The first time I saw one of the famous pink river dolphins was at dusk and I was sitting cross-legged on the roof of the boat, alone; I often used to escape up there from the chaos below. I was staring into the murky water around the boat when I noticed a long nose break the surface. My eyes opened in wonder as I realized it was a dolphin.

Pink river dolphins have long been a source of wonder and superstition in their Amazonian habitat. Known in Portuguese as *botos*, these creatures are thought to be the most intelligent of the freshwater dolphins. Indeed their brain capacity exceeds that of humans by 40 per cent. These dolphins are also famous for their pinkish colouring and their ability to turn their heads round a full 180 degrees. *Botos* are largely solitary animals, but sometimes cluster together in small family groups. In the early nineteenth century French naturalist Geoffrey St-Hilaire reportedly presented a specimen of the creature to Napoleon, a fact commemorated in the species name *Inia geoffrensis*. While once a common feature of the Amazon and Orinoco rivers, the pink river dolphin is now an endangered species.

But here, in this busy stretch of the Amazonas, were not one but two dolphins. I stared in wonder as the magnificent creatures played around our boat. I had seen dolphins at sea, but here were dolphins hundreds of miles inland – and they were pink. What quirk of evolution had turned them this colour, I wondered.

Local mythology has bestowed a number of sinister powers upon these human-sized dolphins. One of the most famous folktales of the region is that the souls of men who drown in the Amazon enter the bodies of the river dolphins, enabling the possessed creatures to transform back into men at night in order to seduce and impregnate human women. Babies born with spina bifida were sometimes thought to be the offspring of dolphins, as unfused areas of the spinal cord were explained as dolphins' blowholes. Killing a river dolphin is thought to bring bad luck, while looking a *boto* straight in the eye can lead to nightmares. Tales also exist of more benevolent *boto* behaviour, with reports of dolphins helping capsized individuals to the shore and fetching objects from the river.

From the Amazon I headed further south to the vast wetlands area known as the Pantanal, where I went on a safari deep into the swamps in search of the famous anaconda. This huge region of Brazil is home to a wealth of biodiversity, including both the green and yellow anaconda. The name *anaconda* is thought to be derived from a Tamil word meaning 'elephant killer', reflecting the snake's infamous reputation for crushing and swallowing giant prey whole. Anacondas are not known for their sense of maternal care. Rather than laying eggs, female anacondas give birth to live young in shallow protected pools, producing up to forty offspring at once. The infant snakes are expected to swim away and fend for themselves as independent hunters from birth. The yellow anaconda, the less formidable of the two species, can grow up to 4 metres long and uses backwards-facing teeth to maintain a grip on its unfortunate prey, while crushing it with the rest of its body.

At up to 9 metres long, the green anaconda is the largest snake in the world and can open its jaws wide enough to swallow jaguar. Anacondas can consume so much in one sitting that it can be months before they need their next meal. They are swift swimmers, spending the majority of their time in water, and are able to hold their breath for up to ten minutes at a time. There have been many supposed sightings of giant anacondas and the American Wildlife Conservation Society has offered a US$50,000 reward for a live anaconda longer than 30 feet (10 metres). No one has yet claimed the prize, but I was shown a photograph by a local farmer of an enormous anaconda coiled in the back of a pick-up truck with a very large bulge in it which the farmer claimed was his brother. The scale of the photograph was convincing, but I wanted to find an anaconda for myself.

We went out on horseback through the watery swamp. The water varied in depth from just a few inches to a couple of feet and occasionally the horse would be up to its belly as we went past the little jacare or caiman, a local species of crocodile that inhabits these waters.

To find the elusive anaconda we left the horses and took to the water. Walking in bare feet, we shuffled along looking for one. Occasionally my guide would dip his hand into the water and feel around. It was extremely disconcerting: I couldn't believe I was wandering through a crocodile- and snake-infested swamp barefoot.

My guide dipped both his arms into the water once again and started rooting around. I could tell that he was struggling with something, as his weight shifted and his whole body disappeared under the surface.

I have rarely felt as vulnerable as I did standing in that remote swamp while my guide disappeared under water. But soon he reappeared, clutching the impressive head of an anaconda. It wasn't a 30-footer by any means – it was more likely 5 feet – but it was impressive none the less. I was open-mouthed that he had been able to find and catch this snake with his bare hands.

He held its head tightly and passed me the body, which was surprisingly heavy with its thick walls of muscle. It was the largest wild snake I had ever seen. I had never been fond of snakes – little did I know that this encounter would be just the beginning of a long working relationship with them. Holding a snake taps right into a vein of primal fear in the psyches of most people, and being in such close contact with a fearsome creature was at once exhilarating and terrifying. More scary than holding it was watching my guide return it to the swamp. As quick as lightning, it bolted back into the murky depths beneath our feet. It still makes me shiver to think of that enormous snake lurking in the very water in which we were walking . . . and it was only a baby.

The Pantanal and the Amazon were both richly rewarding experiences, introducing me to some fascinating wildlife, but it was another country altogether that would strengthen my understanding of the natural world and the plight of this planet's flora and fauna. As a child I had been obsessed with the Paul Theroux novel *The Mosquito Coast*, which sub-sequently became a film with the late River Phoenix. As with so many twists in my life, I followed my fascination to the ends of the earth and, a year after my Amazon trip, found myself out in Honduras on the Mosquito Coast – or La Moskitia, as it is known to the people who live there.

One Man and His Dog, 2005. Robin Page (*below*) has always been very vocal about his dislike of the BBC's rural affairs output, but I've always respected him as a farmer, even if he is a little grumpy.

With the Duchess of Cornwall on the thirtieth anniversary of *One Man and His Dog* in 2006. She was surprisingly interested in the sport.

Above: At Acton Scott Historic Working Farm in Shropshire, filming *Escape in Time* for the BBC in 2009.

Right: Swan Upping – the annual swan count on behalf of Her Majesty the Queen – on the Thames at Marlow with the Worshipful Company of Vintners for *Countryfile*.

Below: On horseback with a Canadian Mountie in Ottawa during the royal visit of the Duke and Duchess of Cambridge in 2011.

Above: If you look carefully enough you can see my grimace. I'm terrified of snakes, but if Kate was going to do it then so was I.

Below: With one of Longleat's cockatoos. It reminded me of my childhood to be surrounded by so many birds, although I also got my worst injury from one of these feathery 'friends' when it bit my finger to the bone.

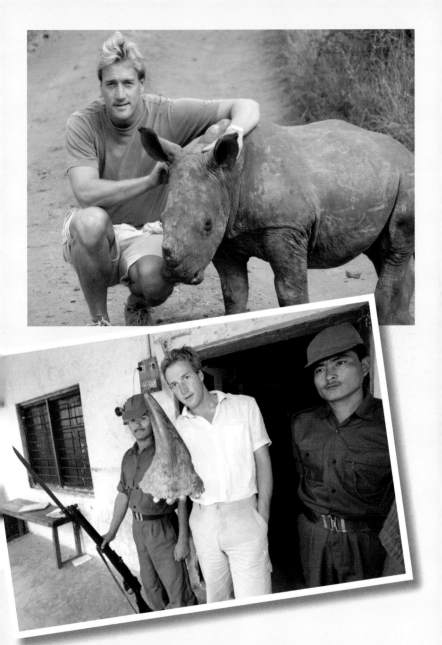

Top: Max the orphaned rhino at Lewa Downs in Kenya, where he had been brought up by the Craig family alongside their Labradors. He would later be slaughtered for his horn.

Above: Poaching is a concern that has reached pandemic proportions. Here some Nepalese park wardens show me a horn confiscated from poachers.

Above: In Chitwan National Park, Nepal, on an Asian elephant from the orphanage. I got to help give her a bath in the river.

Right and opposite: Helping relocate an Asian rhino from Chitwan to Bardia National Park, Nepal.

Above: In the Falkland Islands photographing a baby albatross. The islands are a haven for wildlife.

Right: At AfriCat in Namibia carrying Pixie, a tranquillized caracal, to the operating theatre. I came up covered in hives from an allergic reaction to its fur. I'm still allergic to the fur of cats both big and small.

Below: At AfriCat this elderly wild warthog would walk in on its elbows each evening to lie by the fire before disappearing back into the bush at dawn.

Rudderless and without focus, I had rocked up in the region's tiny capital, Puerto Lempira. It's strange how you can follow your heart without a clue where it is taking you.

It was here that I met Bonnie, a forty-something American from California who worked for the US Peace Corps.

The Peace Corps is an organization run by the American government with a mission to promote world peace and international friendship. It was first established in 1961 by President John F. Kennedy and at the time was highly controversial, as Richard Nixon, who had recently lost his presidential campaign, believed that volunteer work for the organization would allow young people to avoid conscription to the army during the ongoing Vietnam War. Since its establishment, however, over 200,000 people have volunteered for the Peace Corps and they have worked in 139 countries. Today the corps is still active in sixty-eight countries around the world. Volunteers on the scheme are typically college graduates, but range in age, and will usually work for two years after a three-month period of training. Soon after the attacks on 11 September 2001, George W. Bush announced that he was increasing funding to the Peace Corps in order to double the size of the organization in five years as part of America's war on terror.

Peace Corps volunteers have worked across the whole of Latin America, but today the programme exists only in Belize, Costa Rica, El Salvador, Guatemala, Honduras, Mexico, Nicaragua, Panama, Colombia, Ecuador, Guyana, Paraguay, Peru and Suriname. Between fifty and three hundred volunteers currently serve in each of these countries. Many of the volunteers in Latin America work on agriculture, education, community development and environmental projects.

In 1994 the Mosquito Coast was still considered too remote and too dangerous for Peace Corps volunteers, but Bonnie had been sent to recce the region looking for ways in which the organization could help. Unbeknownst to me, our paths were about to collide and I was about to take my first steps into wildlife conservation.

I had spent the previous year in Ecuador – after my Amazon trip – where I had helped in an orphanage. Its proximity to the Galapagos Islands was too much for my father, who flew halfway across the world to join me six months into my gap year for a two-week tour of the islands. It was an unforgettable experience and a rich bonding experience for father and son. We flew to the main island where we boarded our little boat, which we shared with my friends Guy, Tamsin and Jo. We had an excellent guide and for twelve days we plied the chilly waters of the Galapagos, marvelling at the blue-footed boobies and the marine iguanas. I can remember being serenaded to sleep by the sound of barking seals, and exploring the mangrove swamps full of colourful polka dot rays. We went snorkelling in the Devil's Crown and frolicked in the sea with seals. It was a magical experience, and now, a year later, I found myself with an opportunity to work with wildlife. Serendipity had played another part in the meandering course of my life and through luck and determination I had found myself on the Mosquito Coast in search of fulfilment. I didn't know what that would be or what it would entail, but a chance encounter with an American anthropologist sent me in search of Bonnie.

Bonnie had learnt that there was a problem with turtle populations along the Mosquito Coast. Traditionally locals have always collected their eggs for food and their numbers were diminishing at an alarming rate. A number of conservation groups had flagged up their fears and Bonnie thought it might form the foundations for a new Peace Corps project.

I had found a small wooden stilted room to rent overlooking a swamp. It was a hot, humid, sticky place, which, as the name of the region suggests, was full of mosquitoes and sand flies. It was so damp and humid, in fact, that I developed a fungal growth all over my skin that would take more than a year to disappear.

It wasn't long before Bonnie had come up with a plan. The Mosquito Coast Turtle Conservation Program was an education-based project aimed at teaching the local communities about the plight of the turtle and trying to encourage them to ration the number of eggs they took. The idea was that, by creating their own quota, they would manage their turtle egg stocks themselves, thereby ensuring supplies in years to come. It is a simple model, much repeated the world over, but it is very difficult to tell those who have nothing that they must give up the one thing they do have. It would be rich enough coming from a peer, let alone from two white interlopers.

Bonnie had drawn up a simple education programme which the two of us could deliver in schools and at village meetings. It was straightforward, clear and unpatronizing (or as unpatronizing as it could be coming from us). But after the first talk I think we both realized we were on a collision course with the locals. While they agreed with our principles, they refused to change the habit of a lifetime. 'Why should we give up the eggs when they are all we have?' they asked, quite rightly. I had no answer and it seemed we were fighting a losing battle.

'What if,' suggested Bonnie, 'we collect the eggs ourselves and keep them for conservation?'

There was much debate as the locals chatted with one another. They had a strict meritocratic rule about turtle-egg hunting: first come, first served. The first person to spot the turtle laying could lay claim to those eggs. They metaphorically stuck their flag in the ground to mark their ownership.

Bonnie had reasoned that two could play at that game. If we too could mark 'our' turtles, then we were free to do what we wanted with those eggs.

There was much heated debate before they returned a verdict. 'Why not?' shrugged the village elder. In retrospect, I think they were so sure of their own ability to find the turtles before us that they rather arrogantly thought we wouldn't be a hindrance.

It didn't take us long to work out where and when the turtles came ashore and soon we were collecting hundreds of eggs each night. Our plan was simple. We would stalk the beach from early dusk, flashlights in hand, waiting for the turtles to come ashore. We would stake our claim to the laying mother with a small white cloth attached to a piece of driftwood, then we would lie in wait, hidden in the dunes, until the turtle had buried the eggs and returned to the sea.

At this point we would remove the eggs from their nest and take them to a safer place immediately, before anyone else had a chance to find them. We could then rebury them so that they could hatch out of harm's way.

One of the great arguments against Darwin's theory of successful evolution is the survival of turtles. They must be the worst creatures in the word at hiding their eggs, and how they have survived for this long is a matter of wonder. They might as well have had a 20-foot neon sign and an enormous arrow pointing to the ground saying 'Yummy Eggs Here – Come and Get Them'. Their great weight – they can be up to a ton – means that they leave vast drag marks all the way up the beach, which they haul themselves across using their front legs. They then proceed to make a construction site by digging a hole with their back legs, throwing the sand into huge piles before burying the eggs. The result looks as though a tractor has been working on the beach, but crucially it means the nest and its booty of eggs is highly visible even to the untrained eye.

Despite spending their lives at sea, turtles need to come inland to lay their eggs, which they do once every two or three years after they have reached maturity. Several weeks after mating, the female will lay between fifty and two hundred eggs. The eggs are soft-shelled and covered with mucus. The mother turtle then covers the eggs with sand and returns to the sea. Turtles will often migrate many thousands of miles in order to lay their eggs. Most will lay on the same beach each time they go through the reproductive cycle, and some species will return to the beach on which they themselves were born. Some species of turtle, such as the Kemp's Ridley turtle and the Olive Ridley turtle, arrive at egg-laying sites in a large group referred to as an *arribada*, which is Spanish for 'arrival'.

New research in 2011 showed something extraordinary about turtle eggs: by releasing chemicals during incubation, they are able to communicate with each other about the state of development of the young inside, allowing a whole clutch of eggs in a single nest to hatch at once.

Ancient Chinese texts from the seventh century BC are the earliest records of human consumption of turtles: they suggest that the meat from the giant soft-shell was a prized ingredient in soups. Since those times many cultures around the world have continued to eat turtle meat. During the seventeenth and eighteenth centuries ships on trade routes through the Caribbean would often stop at the Cayman Islands to pick up green sea turtles, which could then be used as a source of food. But by the early nineteenth century the natural stock of turtles had been massively depleted, meaning that the large-scale production of turtle meat in the Caribbean moved to the coastal waters of Nicaragua, while turtles in the Caymans were hunted more sustainably during the nineteenth century.

Meanwhile, in Mexican and Costa Rican folklore, turtle eggs are regarded as an aphrodisiac, although the governments of these countries now forbid their consumption. Collecting the eggs is illegal these days in much of the world. None the less, there remains a black market for eggs and they are occasionally still eaten. This may in fact be relatively dangerous, as a single turtle egg can contain as much fat and cholesterol as twenty chicken eggs.

Throughout the nineteenth century turtle soup was considered a delicacy in Britain and the United States; it was President William Taft's favourite food. Indeed, in some areas of the United States where particular species of turtle are not considered to be threatened or endangered, it is still eaten. Meanwhile, in Britain 'mock turtle soup' – a stew made from calf offal – was developed as a cheap home-grown alternative to soup made of exotic green turtles.

Today turtle continues to be eaten around the world, but due to over-hunting both for shells and for meat, many species are now protected either internationally or under the jurisdiction of particular countries or territories. Since the second half of the twentieth century, as technologies for conservation and sustainability were developed, the hunting and breeding of turtles for meat has developed too in order that turtle may still be eaten without threatening species with extinction. In 1968 a green sea turtle farm was set up on Grand Cayman both to provide a sustainable source of turtle meat and to breed turtles which were to be released in order to bolster the natural population around the islands. Nevertheless, 75 per cent of Asian turtle and tortoise species are threatened today, mainly as a result of their use for meat; consequently the United States currently carries on a strong trade in turtles and turtle meat to China. In areas in which turtles are protected, they are still often poached or hunted illegally. For example, poachers in Cape Verde catch female loggerhead turtles as they come ashore to lay eggs, turning them on to their backs so that they can later be killed for their meat.

Eating turtles is not without its dangers. In late 2010 six

people, including four children, died in Micronesia after having eaten the meat of the endangered hawksbill turtle during a feast. The deaths were said to have been caused by a poison – chelonotoxin – which is found in the flesh and skin of hawksbill and leatherback turtles.

Each evening, Bonnie and I would set out shortly before dusk armed with a bucket, spade and torch, and we would walk until we came across our first laying turtle. Invariably they would have been 'claimed' by a local, who had marked their prize with a little flag on a stick. It was rather galling to walk past turtle after turtle, their eggs consigned to the human gullet. Sometimes we would walk for many hours until we found an unclaimed clutch or a turtle in the act of laying. Then we would settle ourselves and wait for her to finish her business.

Watching a turtle laying is a pretty awesome experience. Highly labour intensive, there is something rather magical and even a little moving about the effort to which she is willing to go to lay her eggs. We might sometimes wait for hours until she returned to the sea to avoid distressing her or upsetting her. The locals would just wait for her to turn her back and begin her slow drag back to sea, but I could never bring myself to do it until she was out of sight in the inky Caribbean waters. I felt a little like a grave-robber as I dug up her booty of eggs. Sometimes there were up to a hundred in a single nest and we would carefully place them in our buckets, sprinkling them with sand to act as a sort of barrier, ensuring that the fragile eggs didn't break against one another.

A turtle egg is nothing like a hen's egg. It is rounder,

whiter and much softer. The shell is soft to the touch and even holding it gently could dent it. Removing them from that nest was like a surgical procedure. We would scratch away at the sand with our fingertips, like archaeologists uncovering some ancient ruin.

Armed with our loot, we would then set about looking for a new nest area. We needed to find somewhere far from civilization. The beach could be accessed by long wooded tracks leading down from the main path that linked the communities half a mile inland. Those access points were often marked with locals' boats and canoes, so to be on the safe side we would scout a location far from any boats or footprints.

We would walk in the shallow water where the sea met the beach to minimize our own footprints and leave no tracks. Once we reached a suitable nesting site, we would walk up the beach from the sea, stepping in one another's footprints to ensure just one trail. Then when we'd settled on a location we would sit on our knees and begin to dig a new nest with our little spades.

Carefully, we would place the eggs into the new nest before covering them back over with the excavated sand. Then came the real art of covering our tracks and making sure the nest was invisible. We would carefully spread the sand flat, while one of us followed our tracks back to the sea and walked up to another part of the beach to dig a fake nest. We would make this about 500 metres away, then we would return to the real nest with buckets of soft dry sand from the surface of the decoy nest which we spread over the real nest. We had found out that it was easy to spot a nest by the different textures caused by moisture in the sand; the deeper the excavation, the darker the sand. It was almost impossible to hide this colour discrepancy unless you covered it with soft dry sand.

It took us a long time to work out our system, but it became pretty effective and it wasn't long before we had saved thousands of eggs. With success, of course, came resentment. The locals had rather naively assumed we would be ineffective and they became jealous of our achievement. At times they would follow us, so Bonnie and I were forced to become more and more innovative with our technique. Sometimes we would spend hours building a fake nest and even a fake fake nest to throw them off the trail. Then while the locals dug up our pretend nest we would dig another real one.

It was hard work. Often we were out all night, but it was exciting and, above all, it was rewarding. I puffed my chest in pride the first time I watched a hatching nest of turtles emerge from the sand and begin their swaying march towards the open water. I'm not sure why, but I felt a paternal pride when I watched those turtles disappearing into the ocean. It certainly made all those sleepless nights worthwhile.

For several months we carried on with our cat-and-mouse game as we marched up and down the beach each night in our familiar routine.

Until that fateful night.

Huge storm clouds had been gathering offshore. Bolts of lightning cracked into the ocean and we could hear the distant rumble of thunder. A tropical storm was approaching, but nothing was going to put us off our work.

One of the most magical things you will ever see in the ocean is phosphorescence. I had heard about it, but until now I had never seen this natural phenomenon. It is to the ocean what the northern lights are to the night sky.

Ocean phosphorescence is a strange and spectacular phenomenon which makes the surface of the sea glow, particularly where it is disturbed by the crashing of waves or the path of a boat. The phosphorescence is caused by tiny organisms called dinoflagellates – the name means 'whirling whip' – which omit light when they are disturbed. The light, which is used as a defence mechanism against predators, is produced in the organisms by the reaction between two chemicals: luciferin and luciferase. As the light produced is blue-green, it is exactly the right colour to be transmitted best through seawater and is therefore highly visible to many sea creatures. Dinoflagellates are also responsible for 'red tides', which occur mainly around the Americas and cause the sea to turn red.

I had spent many evenings marvelling at the ocean's firework display, but this particular night I saw something that I had never seen before and have never seen since. It was something so strange and beautiful that at first I doubted my own eyes. Somehow the phosphorescence had seeped into the sand. It seemed to react to our footsteps. The result was that a circle of sand would be illuminated with each step. Imagine paving stones lighting up each time you step on one and you'll begin to get the picture. The sand glowed a sparkling white with each footprint. It took a while to fade and behind us was a long trail of glowing circles that melted into the blackness. It was breathtakingly beautiful and had I not experienced it I wouldn't have thought nature capable of such magic. A set designer couldn't have created anything more beautiful.

Bonnie and I marched down the beach while nature did extraordinary things all around. Lightning cracked into the ocean, illuminating the thick, ominous clouds. A full moon had been all but obscured by the gathering storm, but occasionally the cumulus would break and the world would be painted a bright blue.

We had unburied and reburied a clutch of eggs and started the long walk back to our community. We were usually quite good at navigating along the featureless beach, but the storm seemed to have affected our homing instinct and it wasn't long before we were lost.

At that moment the clouds overhead broke with an enormous clap and there ensued a downpour the likes of which I had rarely experienced – a relentless, tropical downpour, the water falling from the sky in great torrents. My shower produces less water.

We carried on walking in silence as the fork lightning turned to sheet. Huge claps of thunder echoed around the beach. Our torches had long gone, the batteries drowned in rainwater. We were forced to follow the tidal mark along the beach, using each flash of lightning to scan the sand for the trails and paths to the interior.

If felt as if we had been going for hours and Bonnie and I had both begun to worry. There was no sign of the storm subsiding and we had no idea where we were. It may sound strange that we could be lost on a single stretch of beach, but you must remember this was a 200-mile stretch of feature-less, remote sand far from civilization. Apart from just a few communities, there was nothing.

That's when we spotted the large upturned panga and that mystery figure.

We had known we were unlikely to be alone, but the discovery of a machete-wielding stranger was enough to send us racing for our lives. It was a surreal sight. If I hadn't seen it with my own eyes, I'm not sure I would have believed it.

I don't think I have ever run so fast. We raced towards the jungle above the beach and, through luck or fate, hit the path. I'm not sure I had even breathed before this point. We ran barefoot over roots and rocks until we reached the dark trail inland.

Compared to the beach, it was pitch black. The trail ran for several hundred miles, but we knew if we headed north-west we would reach our small community. We began to walk at a brisk pace; it was hard to run in the dark and the trail was littered with a great many roots, stumps and rocks. For an hour we marched along in silence as rain continued to fall in torrents and the path turned into a small river. We splashed ankle deep in the rainwater.

We had lost all sense of space or time and our minds began to play tricks on us. We were sure we should have reached our community by now, but we hadn't passed any sign of civilization. We were convinced we were heading in the right direction, but without a compass or even the moon or stars we couldn't be sure. We began to doubt our own navigation.

'I think we're going the wrong way,' whispered Bonnie.

We were both still on edge after our encounter on the beach, but we had to make a decision: commit to our path, or turn back.

We decided to turn back.

For another hour we walked in the opposite direction. Still there was no sign of life and it wasn't long before we began to doubt our decision again. It's easy to see how disorientated people can become in featureless landscapes. Here we were on a single jungle path and we were lost.

We decided to carry on.

I am sure humans have a sixth sense, that ability to know when someone is watching you or following you. It is nothing to do with hearing, sight, touch, smell or taste; it is something more animalistic. It involves intuitively sensing something, the way that dogs can warn epileptics when they are about to have a fit, or the way in which animals like birds and snakes have been known to predict earthquakes. Given that we are all animals of one kind or another, it seems perfectly reasonable that we should have an ability like this.

And now, here in the middle of the Honduran jungle, I knew I was being watched. I had the strong sense that someone was near. My heart began to race and I sped up slightly.

'What's wrong?' whispered Bonnie.

I shook my head and gestured for her to keep on walking.

I was sure someone was close by, but rather than thinking of it as the prospect of salvation, I was scared. The encounter on the beach had set me on edge and now all my hairs stood on end and I felt a cold chill. I heard the distant rumble of thunder and began to count down to the next lightning strike: one thousand, two thousand, three thousand, four thousand, five thousand . . .

Onwards I counted: fourteen thousand, fifteen thousand . . . *crack!* The lightning burst above the canopy. The leaves and branches of the trees were momentarily backlit to create a ghost-like silhouette. I stole the opportunity to look back.

I turned my head and there, just a few feet behind us, was the man from the beach, walking at a brisk pace – still clutching his machete.

'Run!' I screamed at Bonnie, grabbing her hand and dragging her with me.

It was as shocking and surprising as it was terrifying. No one expects to be followed through a dark jungle by a stranger wielding a machete. We ran as fast as our legs would carry us. Occasionally one of us would fall or stumble in our haste, while the other dragged us from the ground or supported us from our stumble.

We had been running for what felt like eternity before we reached a small clearing of wooden stilted houses.

'Hello!' we shouted, knocking on one of the doors. '*Hello!*' we repeated with growing panic. It was like stepping into our own horror film.

No one seemed to be around. We tried to make out where we were, but in the darkness it was difficult to work it out.

Without pausing for breath, we continued along the path. I felt sure the stranger was still behind us but I was too scared to look round.

Crack! Another lightning bolt illuminated the canopy. I peered behind and saw a figure running towards us.

On we ran. We didn't know why we were fleeing, but

instinct took over. We knew we had made enemies through our conservation programme, but we had never thought it would culminate in someone trying to kill us for the sake of some eggs.

It was to be my first experience of the passions and feelings that run so deep within the world of conservation. What I have since discovered is that someone, animal or man, will lose out when it comes to conservation. In the last few decades we have certainly created better models but, as with everything in life, none of them is perfect and, in this case, the locals felt short-changed.

I was sure it was nearly dawn, though with the deluge of rain and the heavy black clouds it was difficult to be sure. But suddenly we found ourselves in another village. We could make out stilts and then a small wooden building. Slowly our eyes began to recognize things. The water pump and the little school – we were home.

'Diego!' Bonnie called for her Honduran friend. 'Diego!'

Soon we had woken most of the village with our terrified cries. Dogs were barking and several men set off along the trail armed with lanterns and large machetes. They returned several hours later. They had followed our footprints in the soft mud and could see where we had stumbled; they had even found one of our discarded torches; but there was no sign of anyone else. No footprints, no sign whatsoever. The locals concluded that we must have been hallucinating. They speculated that we were drunk and that the electric storm had played tricks on our minds. But I knew what we had seen that night and so did Bonnie.

It wasn't the end of the project, but it took away a bit of

our mojo. We never had quite the enthusiasm or commitment to the egg-collecting that we had had during those first few months. I think subconsciously we were both a little scared. We never showed it or admitted it to one another, but it was there all right.

Too many lives have been lost over the years by those fighting for the welfare or habitat of the planet's great creatures. Humans will always seek resources and invariably we will over-exploit them. We have done so for centuries. What the whalers once did to the ocean's mighty giants, we are now doing to their smaller cousins, the cod. We humans just don't know when to stop.

It had struck me as such a simple principle: that by reducing the consumption of the turtles' eggs, the people of La Moskitia would be ensuring a plentiful supply for the future. What I would later discover is that there is a yawning gap between the developed and the developing world. Those in the less-developed world frequently live for the moment. Often hand to mouth, they exist at the mercy of nature and the weather. A drought, flood or plague of locusts can mean the difference between life and death. People in the developing world tend to live very much for the now rather than for the future.

Investment in the future is a luxury that is simply out of reach for many, and here on the Mosquito Coast of Honduras I had found myself at the sharp end of that conflict.

8

Bathing with Elephants

Ever since I was a child I have always loved elephants. Babar was one of my favourite children's books and I always dreamed of seeing an elephant in the wild. It would take me nearly twenty-two years to realize that dream, out in Nepal with the World Wide Fund for Nature.

WWF is a charity dedicated to preserving wildlife and indeed the planet. It was founded by the late, great Sir Peter Scott. He was an Olympic yachtsman. A skipper in the America's Cup. A popular television presenter. A gliding champion. A painter of repute. A naturalist. The son of a national hero. The holder of the Distinguished Service Cross for gallantry. I have always wished I could have had the opportunity to meet this remarkable man.

Like me, Peter Scott was passionate about nature and conservation, and deeply concerned about the capability of the planet to withstand human demands on its resources – an urgent issue now known as sustainable development. Another of his driving interests was preserving the Antarctic as a haven free from human exploitation; hardly surprising, perhaps, when you consider that his father was Robert Falcon Scott – Scott of the Antarctic – who died there when Peter was a mere eighteen months old. In the notes Captain Scott wrote while he was dying, found on his body, was the following request to his wife on the care of their son: 'Make the boy interested in natural history if you can, it is better than games.'

Not long after I finished *Castaway* I began working as the travel editor for *Hello!* magazine and WWF invited me out to Nepal to follow some of their work on the ground. The charity had a number of anti-poaching and relocation projects from which I would get an insight into what they did. My visit to Nepal would give me my first taste of wild wildlife. I hadn't yet started working on *Animal Park*, but the WWF had seen me on television and spotted something in my affinity with Inca and the animals around me that made them feel we would be a good pairing. I was thrilled and rather star-struck to be invited by such an august organiz-ation. As a child I had been a supporter and our old family Alpha Romeo car bore the green panda sticker with pride. It would be the beginning of a long and happy partnership with WWF, who later made me an ambassador alongside the likes of Sir David Attenborough. I am very, very proud of my ambassadorship. And it all began in Nepal.

I flew in to Kathmandu, the Nepalese capital, with a few others from WWF. It is a pretty exciting place: cars, trucks, buses, cows, bicycles and dogs all vie for space in the road, and its energy and movement are contagious. We navigated our way through the thronging streets to a tiny airfield where we would fly south to an area close to the border with India.

Only in Nepal would you find an airline called Yeti Air. Our plane was an ancient aircraft with large, yellow-tinted windows. We would be flying from the highlands to the lowlands and I had been warned that it would be bumpy, but nothing prepared me for the reality of a Himalayan flight. We jolted and jerked as the small plane groaned and swerved. The engine sounded as if it was screaming as we meandered through enormous rain clouds. Forks of lightning illuminated the dark sky around us, while vast thunderclaps drowned out the noise of the wheezing engine.

My fingers gripped into the side of the seat as we bumped our way along. It was terrifying. Over the years I have been on more than my fair share of small flights, but this really had to be one of the worst. It was sobering news when, several years later, many of the Nepalese WWF team that I was with on this expedition were killed in an air crash along the same route.

Several hours later, weak-kneed and still feeling a little sick, we stepped from the plane and into the tropical heat of the Nepalese lowlands. A safari vehicle ferried me to a small dugout canoe and on to a winding river. From chaos and fear it was suddenly peace and light. It was unbelievably beautiful as my guide slowly punted me down the river.

We were on our way to Tiger Tops, one of the most famous safari camps in the world. Tiger Tops is a company that runs four camps in Nepal, offering tourists an experience of the flora and fauna of the country. The first camp was built by two Texan millionaires, Toddy Lee Wynne and Herb Klein, in the Chitwan National Park in the early 1960s, with the first visitors arriving in 1965. By the mid-1970s the camp had expanded to include twenty-two rooms and had become a popular tourist destination for English and American visitors.

Tiger Tops has, throughout its history, always combined tourism with conservation, particularly of tigers. In collaboration with the Smithsonian Institute, it introduced long-term monitoring of tiger populations. Tiger Tops attempts to make minimal impact on the environment, while at the same time educating visitors about sustainability. It is also home to the annual World Elephant Polo Championships. When they are not playing polo, the Tiger Tops elephants take guests out on safari tours of the local reserves.

Poaching is a huge problem all over the world, including here in Nepal, where the tiger population is under threat. The first visit of my trip was to the anti-poaching unit, who worked in conjunction with the police and the army. Within their facility was a locked store full of confiscated animal parts. It was a deeply shocking sight and arguably one of the reasons I have become such a passionate supporter of the WWF and other conservation and anti-poaching organizations. Piles of animal skins filled the shelves, and there were hundreds of elephant tusks and rhino horns. Jars contained animal parts that had been on their way to the Orient for medicinal purposes.

The single greatest threat hanging over most Asian

wildlife, especially the endangered tiger, is the massive demand for traditional medicine. The annual consumption of remedies made of tiger bone, bear gall bladder, rhinoceros horn, dried geckoes and a plethora of other animal parts is of phenomenal proportions. It is believed that today at least 60 per cent of China's billion-plus inhabitants use medicines of this type. The booming economies and personal incomes of South East Asia have caused demand and prices to soar, boosting the international trade in wildlife products to an estimated US$6 billion-a-year business.

In Asia the use of endangered tiger products and medicines is seen as a symbol of high status and wealth. Some remedies list tiger parts as an ingredient, but the real animal parts are so expensive that often the medicines may have only trace elements; but even this is enough to promote the continued slaughter of the tiger. A further problem is that other communities around the globe, including non-Asian societies, are now supplementing their Western-style medicine with traditional Chinese treatments, igniting the demand for tiger parts beyond what can be supplied.

If poaching continues at its current rate, researchers have predicted that many, if not all, of the world's tiger clans will be wiped out in the near future.

The room in which I stood represented hundreds of slaughtered rhinos, elephants and tigers – and for what? All for a little ivory or a medicine reputed to make you more virile. It just made me feel sick.

The Bengal tiger is the most populous subspecies of tiger in the world; none the less, it is endangered, with fewer than 2,500 animals still surviving. It is known for its distinctive light orange colour and is the national animal of India. In Nepal there is a population of just over 150 adult tigers, all of which live in the Terai region, just to the south of the Himalayas. The population is split into four groups which exist in separate protected territories: the Chitwan National Park, the Parsa Wildlife Reserve, Bardia National Park and the Sukla Phanta Wildlife Reserve.

When I visited Nepal, it was in the grip of a civil war, which had broken out in 1996 between Maoist fighters and government forces and lasted until 2006. One consequence was that the protection of tigers from poachers, which had previously been carried out by the Nepalese Army, was significantly less effective during this period and so a large number of tigers were killed. The war also coincided with the burgeoning international demand for animal parts to use in illegal medicines, and the danger to animals was further compounded by a general increase in poverty in the region, with poaching offering a quick, but illegal, source of cash to those in need. Since the end of the conflict, the government has been more effective in protecting its wildlife populations, including the tiger population, in part through the help of organizations like WWF. The number of tigers has been steadily increasing in recent years, and compared to neighbouring India poaching rates are now very low. For endangered species overall, today Nepal has one of the most advanced and successful anti-poaching strategies in the world, the success of which was seen in 2011 when for the first time not a single rhinoceros in the country was killed by poachers. Nepal's good track record may have something to do with the low volume of wild species in the country compared to Africa, but there is no doubt that the Nepalese have found a way of balancing the human–animal conflict and beginning to deal with the poverty that often fuels it.

No one was really sure how many tigers remained in Chitwan and Bardia, so one of the early WWF in Nepal projects was to try to find out. To do that, the team had a selection of camera traps that they would hide at key locations around the parks and this was the project with which I was going to help. The cameras work on a very simple basis. They are placed near food or a key habitat and when the animal or animals approach they trip the camera, which takes a still or moving picture that can then be analysed. It's amazing the information that can be gleaned from a blurry photograph and the data can prove invaluable to scientists looking to monitor number and ages. Even the muzzle can allow future identification, meaning they can track the cats as they migrate.

We spent the day wandering through the thick forest, setting dozens of cameras near to signs of scat or footprints. It has always surprised me how elusive big cats can make themselves. They aren't even that well camouflaged against the jungle green with their bright orange smudges.

I can still remember the sense of excitement when we set off at dawn to check the camera traps, look for footprints and hope to see a big cat for ourselves. Sadly, the tigers remained elusive, but their large, distinctive pawprints led us to one of our cameras. My heart was pounding as we down-loaded the memory stick into a laptop and clicked through the various dark images. About eleven frames into the set was a fuzzy smudge close to the camera and the next picture was the unmistakable, blurry muzzle of a tiger. It was a hazy, ghost-like image, but it was my first glimpse of a wild tiger.

Nepal is also home to a small population of Indian elephants, numbering between a hundred and two hundred wild animals and a captive population of nearly two hundred. Throughout the second half of the twentieth century the country's elephant population declined massively as a result of poaching and land clearances for human resettlement. Consequently, in 1986 the Nepalese government set up an elephant-breeding centre in Khorsor in order to promote active conservation. Most of the domesticated animals also live in the country's national parks, though they are used for occasional work; for example, tourists are able to ride the elephants on excursions and at one point trained elephants helped rangers to capture wild rhinos in order for them to be translocated. More recently, elephants in Nepal have been promoted through organized elephant football matches and elephant beauty pageants, all used to change public opinion about elephants and remind people that behind the vast grey façade is a beautiful creature.

Working elephants have been used across the globe for thousands of years. Perhaps most famously, Hannibal, the Carthaginian leader in the second century BC, led an army that included war elephants across the Alps to Italy, where they were used to fight the Romans at the Battle of Zama. It has also been suggested that Marco Polo rode an elephant on his exploration of the Silk Road in the thirteenth century, although there is little historical evidence for this; the idea was popularized by the anonymous fifteenth-century painter known as the Boucicaut Master, who depicted Marco Polo with an elephant in a boat in his picture *Marco Polo with elephants and camels arriving at Hormuz on the Gulf of Persia from India*. Working elephants continue to be used today, although not in battle. Famously, throughout Kerala in India elephants are used for a range of Hindu ceremonies.

Before I left Nepal I had my own special audience with an elephant. My lifelong dream was about to become a reality. An elephant orphanage had been built not far from the boundary of the Chitwan reserve and I was off for a close encounter with one of the world's strangest-looking animals.

Elephants really are extraordinary creatures. They look all wrong, with their oversized bodies, bizarre trunks, massive ears and tiny, tiny eyes. What was God thinking when he created such a beast? I can understand the evolution and creation of most of our wild creatures, but an elephant seems all wrong. It's like a Mr Potato Head thrown together in a rush, using all the wrong pieces. Perhaps it is why they are such glorious creatures.

They are at once magnificent and ridiculous, comical and sad. Elephants have always appealed to us humans. For me they have a childlike vulnerability that taps into my emotions and makes me want to care for and protect them. I was mesmerized by this majestic animal.

My elephant was twenty years old and had been at the orphanage for nearly five years after being rescued from a destitute mahout. Many Nepalese make a meagre living by using elephants for either tourism or as work elephants. She was huge and had pink mottled skin and thick black bristles of hair all over her body; she almost looked like a child's drawing of what an elephant should be. She was calm and quiet as I approached. I'm sure she knew I was moved by her presence.

'Why don't you climb on?' asked the mahout who was my guide.

'I couldn't,' I stammered, for fear of hurting her.

'She won't even feel you,' he said with a smile, 'and besides, that is what she has always done – it is natural for her.'

Before I could refuse any more, he made a gesture to the elephant. She turned towards me and put one knee to the ground, then lowered her trunk to the ground like a slide. The mahout gestured for me to climb up her trunk and on to her back.

I slipped off my shoes and slowly walked up the trunk to her big bony head. She was huge. I could feel thick, bristly hairs on her grey skin as I straddled her neck with my legs. A huge smile broke across my face. My principles told me I shouldn't be on her – I have always felt uneasy about domesticating wild animals in this way. As at so many times in my life, I was now in a quandary, vexed by the rights and wrongs of elephant-riding. What is the difference between riding a horse and an elephant? Once again a simple situation had thrown up a great debate in my mind, further confounding my confusion about man's relationship with animals. But my heart longed for this magical experience.

The mahout made another noise and, before I knew it, she had started walking. I could feel the movement of her shoulder muscles as she strode across the grassy embankment. It felt effortless and, without a saddle, quite natural. There was something incredibly soothing and moving about being on that wonderful creature.

My bare feet caressed her thick skin as, accompanied by the mahout, we wandered further along the embankment towards woodland. Soon I was ducking under trees as she stepped over tree roots, snapping large branches like matchsticks as she went.

It has always fascinated me how we humans have harnessed animals to our benefit. Over the years I have lost track of the number of creatures I have encountered doing incredible things. I have met dogs that can sniff for mines, or even for cancer in a human; dogs that can warn their owner when they are about to have an epileptic fit and dogs who can help those with difficulties in hearing or sight. Dogs work with soldiers and the police, they rescue people from earthquakes and natural disasters, and they live with herds of farm animals until a predator comes along and they reveal their true identity. Dogs are used to pull sledges, as are reindeer, while horses, water buffalo and oxen are employed the world over for ploughing fields. I have met Shetland ponies trained to become guide horses and pigs used as therapy. Pigeons have long been used for carrying messages and birds of prey can be taught to do incredible things. Seals and dolphins have been trained by the navy to spot mines and enemy submarines in the ocean. For hundreds of years camels have been used to take men across deserts, while llamas do the same across the Andes of South America. In the Far East, meanwhile, elephants are still used for work, and it is not uncommon to see them walking down busy roads as cars, trucks and lorries rattle past.

It might not seem fair, and plenty of people don't agree with it, but I think it is pretty astonishing how we have worked with animals to make our lives better. Advocates of working animals argue that they love what they do and that we humans are simply acting as the leader of the pack. But usually we leave them with no choice. *War Horse* – based on a novel by Michael Morpurgo and followed by Spielberg's spin-off film – has become one of the most successful stage plays of all time. It focuses on the emotions of working horses, in this case in war. Should we differentiate between the rights and wrongs of riding a horse and those of getting it to pull a gun into no man's land? There is a vulnerability to any animal. They have no voice and essentially no rights.

Like so many people, my emotions are affected differently according to the species. There seem to be certain animals that elicit extreme human emotions: penguins, pandas, polar bears, to name just a few; and, as I have said earlier, I would also put elephants into this category. Perhaps it is the way their babies hold their tails as they walk or the fact that we know they mourn their loved ones (as do penguins). Despite their size and appearance they remind us of ourselves. To be honest, I find it hard to elicit the same emotions and feelings when I see a cow, a sheep or a pig. I do love pigs – some of my best friends have been pigs – but they simply can't arouse the same emotions. Is it down to our learning and education? There are countless children's books about elephants and penguins and otters, but fewer that really get into the characters of farm animals. Maybe this is the reason we are conditioned to favour one species over another. Whatever the cause, I found this first encounter with an elephant incredibly moving.

She continued her steady march through the woods until we reached a small clearing that led to a broad river. On we strode towards the water's edge. The elephant stopped at the shore, stuck her trunk into the water and sucked it up like a straw – then she swung her trunk round, held it in front of my face and squirted me with what felt like gallons of water.

Don't ever tell me that elephants don't have a sense of humour.

She then proceeded to step into the river, wading out until it was just above her knees, and knelt down. Before I knew it, the elephant began to roll on to her side. I clung on as if to a capsizing ship, but there was nothing to hold on to and I slipped into the water, my hands dragging down her side as I went. Panicked in case she collapsed on top of me, squashing me into the riverbed, I scrambled away as fast as I could. The water was up to my waist.

My elephant was lying on her side, staring at me.

The mahout had followed us into the river. 'She wants you to wash her,' he smiled, throwing me a scrubbing brush and a bar of soap.

Now this was a first, I thought, as I waded over to the enormous animal who continued to stare at me expectantly. As I approached, she dipped her trunk back into the river, sucked up another enormous scoop of water and pointed her trunk at me like a water pistol.

'No, no, no,' I warned, wagging my finger, at which point

she fired her watery bullet, catching me right between the eyes. She really was having fun.

I walked to her belly and began to scrub at her tummy.

'Harder,' encouraged the mahout. 'She likes a hard scrub.' I put some more elbow grease into it, then I clambered up her side as if it was a children's slide and continued to rub and scrub her tough skin with the brush. By now her whole face had disappeared under water; just the little pink snout of her trunk broke the surface like a snorkel. There are advantages to being an elephant.

Once I'd finished her side, she slowly rose from the water and lay on the opposite side so that I could continue with the bath scrub. I may not be an elephant behaviourist, but I could tell she was loving it – though not nearly as much as I was.

It was like a dream to be with that elephant, wallowing in a Nepalese river. There was a vulnerability and trust to this magnificent creature that I had never experienced before, and I felt a connection and an affinity that I have rarely felt since.

In many ways my experiences in Nepal raised more questions than they answered. Twenty-two thousand people had been relocated to create these national parks and make way for the wildlife the country was trying so hard to protect. It was the human–animal conflict yet again. None the less, on a personal level my time with that lone elephant will remain one of the most magical experiences of my life. I have had dozens of arguably more extraordinary encounters since, but as a place, a time and a moment in my life, it is unsurpassable.

9

Into Africa

I fell hopelessly in love with Africa the first moment I met her. It was 2002. I had been working with the animals at Longleat for a year, but I was still to meet their wild African cousins.

I would lose my African virginity to Zambia, a beautiful, exciting country in the south of the continent. I was there with my friend the photographer Ken Lennox and together we would be spending ten days with one of the early pioneers of African safaris, Robin Pope. We would visit the Luangwa Valley and stay at one of the rambling old lodges by the river while we worked on a travel feature for *Hello!*

The word 'safari' made its way into the English language in the late nineteenth century, developing from the Arabic word *safar*, meaning 'to make a journey'. But the word was describing a tradition that had its origins many decades earlier. In the early eighteenth century, as Europeans colonized much of Africa, trade expanded widely across the continent. Often large caravans would pass through unpopulated areas, carrying not only consumables and metals but also slaves. By the early 1800s these routes were being used by European naturalists, who began to survey wildlife throughout the continent, as well as hunters who prized Africa's big game. By the early twentieth century these hunting traditions had developed and were popular amongst the rich and famous, who enjoyed travelling through Africa whilst attempting to shoot the 'big five': elephant, buffalo, leopard, lion and rhino. Famous hunters included Winston Churchill and American President Teddy Roosevelt.

The hunting of big game throughout the nineteenth and early twentieth centuries had a huge impact on the population of certain species, and it was from the need to maintain stocks of animals to hunt that modern conservation began. By the second half of the twentieth century, though, hunting began to be condemned. It was understood that the only way to conserve species on the brink of extinction was to make hunting them illegal and by the late twentieth century safari animals were just to be seen, not shot – although the problem of poaching still remained.

In recent years developments in light aircraft and off-road cars have made the safari experience more immediate than ever. Guide Robin Pope has been one of the forerunners of these technological changes. Having grown up in Zambia and Zimbabwe, he joined Zambia Safaris as an employee in the mid-1970s, becoming an honorary ranger in the national parks. But it was not until the early 1990s that he began his now famous 'walking mobile safaris', in which tourists move by car and by river in a mobile camp, while going on walking safaris during the day. He has also pioneered fly-camping safaris, where tourists travel by air to more remote camps. Today the safari business is booming, with multinational investors such as Richard Branson, who owns Ulusaba Private Game Reserve in South Africa, getting in on the business.

The first thing to hit you in Africa is the smell. It is unlike anything I have ever smelt anywhere else in the world. I have always found smells evocative. They have the power to take you to another space or time. There are smells that remind me of my childhood and others of the cottage in Canada in which I spent all my summers. The smell of diesel smoke still sends me tumbling back to Latin America, but the smell of Africa is different. It is a rich, damp, musky odour that envelops your senses and feeds your mind. It is the smell of hope and despair, of laughter and suffering. It is a wild, exciting smell that stays with you.

The lodge was situated on the banks of the river, with a large wooden deck overlooking the water. I remember sitting back in my chair sipping a cocktail as a blood-red orange sun dipped into the horizon accompanied by an orchestra of honking, laughing, sneezing hippos.

We awoke at five each morning and bundled up against the early-morning chill. We would set off in our open-top Land Rover along old dusty tracks, bumping and grinding our way past vast arcadia trees and baobab trees, just like the ones in *The Little Prince*, which I loved so much as a child. There was something so romantic and exciting about the whole experience. I felt as if I had stepped into the set of *Out*

210

of Africa. Until now I had only seen lions and rhino with a Wiltshire backdrop, but here they were like caricatures from *The Lion King*. I laughed as warthogs raced past, looking like remote-controlled pigs with their vertical tails pointing skywards like antenna, and I was deeply moved to watch a cheetah curled in the branch of a tree, its long tail curling and twisting like a snake as the sun set behind her. There was the absurd moment we came around the corner of a thick body of trees to see three giraffes grazing on the branches high above, and I shall never forget hearing the deep bass roar of a lion in the distance as we tracked her in the Land Rover before settling just 100 metres from where she was chewing on a poor eland that had become lunch.

On the third day Robin took us out on a walking safari and with an armed guide we set off into the African bush. Until now we had explored by Land Rover and boat, but now we were walking towards herds of elephant and buffalo. Without a vehicle I felt exposed and vulnerable, but it also gave me a sense of freedom and excitement. To be so close to nature in its purest, simplest form was exhilarating.

To begin with, I wonder whether I had fallen in love with the romance rather than the continent itself? I remember thinking that if my career failed back in the UK, I would simply hotfoot it back to Zambia to work at a safari camp.

The camp itself was what I would describe as luxurious. My room was essentially a large tent, without walls, in the centre of which was an enormous double bed, draped with a mosquito net. That was essentially all that separated me from Africa. It was desperately romantic. I would lie in bed at night and listen as elephants and hippo wandered past my room.

Because of the presence of wild animals I had to use a small bell to summon an armed guard if I wanted to leave my room. I needed to zip up my wash bag or the monkeys would steal my toothpaste and I would read in bed by the flickering light of a candle. I fell in love with the lifestyle: the sun-downers, the early-morning safaris, the dust, the linen safari shirts, and the warm water that arrived in your tin basin each morning for washing.

But while I loved the lifestyle and the people, it was the animals that bewitched me. Here were creatures I had only ever seen in a zoo or safari park and suddenly they were in my world – or should I say, I was in theirs.

I returned to London hooked and determined to return. I became fascinated by African literature and natural history and began to read relentlessly.

It was shortly after my trip to Zambia that I was at a rather smart party in London. I don't remember what it was for or even who invited me, but it was the usual round of paparazzi photographers, champagne and impossibly beautiful girls. I have always loved the juxtapositions that crop up in my life, the drifting from one world to another. I have found it a good way to remain grounded, but above all an excellent way to appreciate the world, encountering both the haves and the have-nots.

On this particular occasion a man introduced himself to me.

'Hello, I'm John Rendall,' he said, holding out his hand.

He had a lived-in face and we engaged in some small chat

until we reached the subject of Africa. I told him about my recent visit to Zambia.

'I used to have a lion,' he said with a warm smile. 'He was called Christian. Lived with me on the King's Road.'

And with that I was captivated, and so started a friendship that introduced me to some of the most important figures in African conservation and further fanned the flames of my obsession with the natural world.

London in the Swinging Sixties, a time of free love and unusual animals. My father regularly treated people's iguanas, snakes and exotic cats. At the time, Harrods had a pet shop from which you could buy any animal in the world, from a crocodile to an elephant, and one day in 1969 two Australians, John Rendall and Anthony 'Ace' Bourke, bought a lion cub for 250 guineas from the Knightsbridge store. They called him Christian and kept him as a pet. As Christian grew larger, they moved him to live in the basement of their antiques shop, Sophistocat, on the trendy King's Road. The lion would be taken to a nearby graveyard for exercise until concern grew about his size.

Meanwhile, thousands of miles and a world away from the King's Road, wildlife conservationists George and Joy Adamson were living and working in Kenya. George was the senior game warden of the Northern Frontier District, and during his duties in 1956 he was forced to shoot a lioness. He rescued her three cubs, and he and his wife looked after them and named one of them Elsa. Together they trained Elsa to hunt, as she would have been taught by her mother, and eventually the lioness was released successfully back into the wild. Joy wrote the story of Elsa the lioness as a book called

Born Free, which was published in 1960 and later became the basis of an award-winning film. In the film actors Bill Travers and Virginia McKenna played George and Joy Adamson, working closely with the couple in the technical production of the movie.

As a result of their experience making the film, Travers and McKenna, who were married in real life, continued their conservation work and in 1984 they set up the Zoo Check campaign, which focused on rights for animals kept in captivity. The organization changed its name in 1998 to the Born Free Foundation and continues to promote animal welfare and conservation, working to prevent abuses and to encourage the release of captive animals back into their natural habitats.

One day Travers and McKenna visited Sophistocat Antiques and suggested to Rendall and Bourke that they should contact George Adamson so that Christian could be released into the wild in Kenya. Knowing that their pet was getting too big for them to look after, Rendall and Bourke agreed. So Christian was sent to Kenya and Adamson announced his release into the wild in the Kora National Park in 1971. His release was helped by another wandering soul, Tony Fitzjohn, who had ended up at Kora working for George.

Several years later, Bourke and Rendall returned to Kenya to see how Christian was getting on in the wild, and with the Adamsons they tracked him down. George Adamson was concerned that the lion wouldn't recognize his previous owners, but Christian came running up to Bourke and Rendall and hugged them as he had when he was a cub. The reunion was caught on film and became part of a documentary called *Christian, the Lion at World's End*. During the reunion Christian introduced Rendall and Bourke to the other lions in his pride, who also accepted them as friends. Many years later the film of Christian enveloping the two Ozzies became a YouTube phenomenon, catapulting the remarkable story back into the spotlight.

Over the years I have been fortunate enough to meet not only John Rendall but also Tony Fitzjohn and Virginia McKenna, and the story of Christian cemented my belief that wildlife rehabilitation really can work and made me want even more to see it for myself.

At around the time I got to know John Rendall, my girlfriend at that time, Kinvara Balfour, had just got a new roommate in her Notting Hill flat, a girl called Jecca Craig. Jecca was from Kenya, where her family ran a game reserve called Lewa. By chance, the following year I was invited out to visit Lewa and the Craigs with some of the keepers from Longleat who had agreed to do a form of job swap. Four keepers would visit Kenya, then later in the year several keepers from Lewa would visit the Wiltshire safari park as a way of learning from one another.

Once again I touched down on African soil, this time in the bustling capital Nairobi, from where I took a short flight to Lewa Downs, a 66,000-acre area in the heart of the country, in the shadow of Mount Kenya. The land was bought by the Craig family in 1922 to be used as a cattle ranch and has remained within the family ever since; in 1977 it was given to Ian Craig, grandson of the original owners, and his wife Jane, who continue to run the land.

During the 1970s Kenya's Black rhinos came under sustained attack from poachers, with the population dropping from over twenty thousand to fewer than three hundred. In 1983 the Craigs were visited by conservationist Anna Merz, one of the world's leading champions of the Black rhino, and decided to convert 5,000 acres of their ranch into the Ngare Sergio Rhino Sanctuary. Soon afterwards the Craigs worked on relocating all the wild rhino in northern Kenya to their sanctuary to protect them from poachers and so that a breeding programme could be set up. Since the establishment of the original 5,000-acre sanctuary the project has been expanding and now covers 62,000 acres. There are currently sixty-five Black rhino in Lewa Downs, over 10 per cent of the total population in Kenya, and year on year this population grows. Lewa Downs is also home to 10 per cent of the world's population of endangered Grévy's zebra.

Meanwhile, the threat from poachers remains and the Lewa estate is protected with heavy security. Like Nepal, Africa of course suffers appalling poverty and this is what underlies much of the poaching. But whereas in Nepal the wildlife is largely restricted to the national parks and poaching tends to be small-scale and opportunistic, in Africa the animals spill over vast areas that cross the continent and the simple volume of wildlife makes poaching a much more viable means of alleviating hardship.

Once again it highlights the terrible clash between desperate human need and conservation. Who has more rights, man or animal? Who are we to favour an elephant, which then goes and tramples over the meagre crop of a local family, above that family, who may well starve as a result? There is of course no simple answer. I would argue that poaching is partly a symptom of much larger man-made problems: overpopulation, demand for land, demand for food, loss of habitat. It is a vicious circle that means we are all losers.

Lewa has been at the forefront of conservation in Kenya and Ian, a one-time big-game hunter himself, was something of a pioneer in his efforts to transform what was once a vast cattle farm into a haven for wildlife. Maintaining a fenced reserve like Lewa takes an awful lot of manpower and man-agement and animal numbers must be carefully monitored and controlled.

It was during my first visit to Lewa that I met Max, a Southern White rhino who had been orphaned after his mother was killed by poachers. Ian Craig had taken him in and he had fast become one of the family. He had been hand-reared by a team of rangers, who became his surrogate mothers, lovingly feeding him every four hours with lactogen and vitamins. I have never seen more dedicated carers; it brought tears to my eyes to see the trust between animal and man. His stable was kept warm at night and a ranger would sleep next to him on the straw with a blanket stretched over the two of them. He was taken for walks during the day and his best friends were two black Labradors. One of the most joyful sights was watching him play with the dogs as they chased each other around, Max nuzzling them with his nose. Occasionally the dogs would become a little too boisterous and Max would have to remind them who was boss.

It is very strange playing with a rhinoceros the size of a large dog. It looks like a toy. Unlike other young animals, they don't look puppyish but like a miniature version of their older selves. I suppose, in a way, rhinos look old from birth, with their grey wrinkled skin and their tiny eyes. Max could have been a dwarf rhinoceros.

When he was two, Max left Lewa and moved to another conservancy, Ol Pejeta, run by Ian's son Batian. One of the sad realities of life in Africa is that the bounty on the head of a wild animal has increased; so, as is the custom with other rhinos on wildlife conservancies, Max's horn was removed in an effort to protect him from poachers.

Rhino horn can be traded illegally for up to £60,000 a kilogram in some Asian countries, where it is renowned for its supposed therapeutic benefits, and over the past few years its rising value has created a surge in poaching incidents. In 2007 in South Africa, where the rhino population is closely monitored, the number of rhinos poached was just thirteen. The following year it was eighty-three, rising to 333 in 2010.

Poaching can be highly sophisticated. As the financial stakes have become higher, so the gangs can afford to invest in more equipment, deploying helicopters as well as night-vision goggles in search of their bounty, chainsaws (to remove the horn) and shotguns. The battle between conservationists and poachers is becoming increasingly bloody, as even the prospect of excavating a few scraps from a rhino that has been dehorned makes an animal a lucrative kill.

Animals like elephants can be harder to protect because they wander over a huge range. It is easier to keep rhino alive in a sanctuary by paying for high levels of security. This can be immensely expensive, and a high proportion of Lewa's running costs go towards paying for the small army of anti-poaching police who patrol the reserve with their specially bred anti-poaching bloodhounds. But still that protection isn't infallible.

This was to be Max's bloody fate. He was six years old when, at three o'clock in the morning, Batian Craig took a phone call to say that gunshots had been heard in the conservancy. Later, Max's carcass was found lying in the warm mud. He had been shot seventeen times and poachers had sliced deep into his face in an attempt to hack out what remained of the precious stumps of his horn, leaving it a grisly mess.

The Craigs were devastated. They couldn't bear to see Max, or go near him. The death affected me greatly too, for Max's story seems to encompass everything that is glorious and everything that is wretched about man's relationship with nature. On the one hand there is the selfless act of care and love from the rangers and the Craig family, demonstrating all that is good about conservation and mankind. On the other hand there are the murderous poachers who killed him for a tiny piece of ivory, symbolizing man's selfish greed and gluttony.

As with drugs, perhaps if we could stem the demand we might also stem the flow, or reduce it at least. What frustrates me most is that this is a worldwide issue, but it is Africa that has to pay the price.

While I was visiting Lewa, they decided to translocate one of the Black rhino to the shores of Naivasha, where the wildlife painter Chris Campbell Clause had an estate. The last time I had been out to capture a rhino had been in Nepal, where we had used elephants to track our quarry. Here we were in Land Rovers, while Ian's son Batian recced from the air. Translocations are often used to dilute populations and ensure that there is little inbreeding, and that herds are divided up enough to survive disease and drought. However, they are traumatic for all involved and minimizing the time it takes is key.

I set out with Longleat keepers Andy and Darren, and Chris Campbell Clause. It was Andy and Darren's first time in Africa and they were overwhelmed by the experience. It was quite moving to watch each keeper meet their particular charges' wild counterparts. They couldn't take their eyes off them. It was a reminder of the importance of safari parks in the UK and their role in educating and also providing scientific research, the results of which can be taken back into the wild.

It wasn't long before Batian Craig had spotted a suitable female rhino to be captured. Richard, the warden who was driving us, set off at great speed and we bumped across the plateau.

We pulled to a grinding halt about 100 metres from the rhino. She continued to graze while Ian carefully filled the dart and loaded the gun, then raised the sight and fired. Although we were in a solid Land Rover, I had heard tales of elephant and rhino toppling them like tin cans – but any fear was lost in the drama and excitement of the moment. My heart raced.

The dart hit her clean on the rump. She fled in fury and

fear and we had to be careful to keep her in our sights: it was crucial she didn't lie on her side for long after she fell or she could crush herself to death. The sedative could also over-heat her. The most dangerous risk was that we might lose sight of her in the undergrowth. It may seem impossible to 'lose' a rhino, but they can run fast and some of the African bush can be surprisingly dense. Our Land Rover raced over the rough terrain as we chased after her, at the same time try-ing to keep her at a distance to reduce stressing her. It was about two minutes later that we saw her enormous body begin to sway. Soon her back legs gave way and her huge rump hit the ground. The rest of her body followed, then lastly her head came crashing down on to the rough ground. It was now a race against time. Together we ran to her sleep-ing body and twenty of us rocked her on to a large pallet and loaded her into a crate to begin her journey to her new home.

We followed close behind on the three-hour journey along a tarmac road to Chris's estate, where he had a built a *boma* (a livestock enclosure) in which she would be quarantined until her release. The rhino had come round during the journey and there was much excitement as she was released from the crate – and then a stunned silence. Her nose was bloody and disfigured. Great red clots of blood oozed from her mouth – and she had no horn.

In her anger she had butted the side of the crate so hard that she had pulled the horn from her own snout. The irony of the situation was not lost on any of us. The horn was what made her so vulnerable in the first place. It was her horn that had brought her to the edge of extinction and it was her horn that had brought her here to her new home – and now she had lost it.

I was pretty horrified. I felt sick and responsible, but it was simply the reality of working with big animals. It was nothing more than a terrible accident and, ever the optimist, Ian pointed out that at least she wouldn't be at such risk from poachers any more; besides, he said, a little like a finger nail, her horn would grow back in the fullness of time.

Over the years I was to have further involvement with Lewa Downs and the Craigs, which came about in part through my becoming an ambassador for a charity called the TUSK Trust, which operates projects in seventeen countries across Africa. It was established in 1990 in response to the mass slaughter of rhinos and elephants in the previous decades: the Black rhino population had fallen to below 2,000 animals in the world, and over 100,000 elephants were being killed each year. Since being set up, TUSK has raised over £16 million. Unlike many wildlife and conservation charities, the trust believes that in order to protect endangered species projects need to take an integrated approach, not only safe-guarding the animals but also tackling education and sustainability, often with community-led projects. Its most significant programme is the Pan-African Conservation Education Project, which has helped to educate over 150,000 children and students.

I have worked with TUSK in Kenya a number of times and even taken part in the Lewa Safaricom Marathon for them. The charity is run by an enigmatic man called Charlie Mayhew with an impressive list of trustees, and their patron is Prince William, or the Duke of Cambridge as I should now refer to him. In 2010 he announced that he and his brother Harry would be embarking on their first joint overseas tour, to Botswana and South Africa, during which William would be highlighting the role of TUSK and her projects. Together with the help of Clarence House and the full approval of Prince William, a plan was drawn up to make a film about his role with TUSK. I would follow the royal tour and talk to William along the way about Africa, TUSK and conservation.

Before the trip I had met William a number of times and, although I don't see it myself, have actually often been mistaken for him. So it wasn't a great surprise when I was greeted at Botswana's airport on my arrival with a cheery, 'Welcome, Your Royal Highness.' As usual I just blushed and smiled. I certainly never complain – after all, he is eight years younger than me and I take it as a compliment.

The two princes spent a week visiting TUSK's projects in Botswana, including the Mokolodi Nature Reserve, accompanied not only by me and the film crew, but also by an army of journalists. However, one of the highlights of the trip was a 'safari within the safari', when William and Harry took a short break from the scrutiny of pen and lens to experience a little bit of Africa on their own and I was privileged to go with them. According to the press, they had 'jetted off' to a luxury hotel, but nothing could have been further from the truth. We were in fact deep in the Okavango Delta, accommodated in a temporary camp set up by the Predator Conservation Trust whose work the princes had come to see. It was really just a research camp – we slept on camp cots in large green army tents, and camp tables had been set up under the stars. Water was heated on a fire then poured into large tin bowls next to our tents.

We arrived on a midwinter night. One of the surprising facts about the African winter is that it is very, very cold; indeed in southern Africa frosts and even snow are increasingly common. Despite the biting cold, Tico – the chief research scientist – and his family had organized dinner under the stars. A large fire had been lit, with tables around it, and to keep the chill at bay we shovelled hot coals on to the sand beneath our canvas chairs. It looked beautiful with candles placed around the camp. Later, as I lay in my cot, I could hear the deep rumble of a lion in the distance. There is something very special about the sound of a lion's roar. It makes your hair stand on end and even from a distance you can feel the reverberations within your body. I fell asleep to the call of Africa.

Next morning, with the temperature at minus 2°C, we set off in search of the lions that had serenaded me to sleep. As we drove we heard wild dogs and stopped to watch herds of elephants grazing beneath the acacia trees, and finally we found our lion. We all remained silent, but it spotted us and disappeared into the shrubs. Tico wasn't about to let it evade us that easily, however, and turned the Land Rover off the track and into the bush. We bumped and jerked our way over tree roots and termite mounds, following the lion as it swished its tail back and forth. I sensed that for William it was a magical experience.

Africa holds a special place in his heart, as does his work for TUSK. He first visited Lewa Downs in Kenya shortly after the death of his mother and has been a friend of the Craig family for many years; he spent part of his gap year with them at Lewa and it was then that he was introduced to TUSK, which appeals to him particularly because of its community-based approach.

'I love being with the animals,' he told me. 'I love making a difference to the wildlife, rather than just seeing them. It's a whole different way of life. It's peaceful. It's connecting with how we all should be, really. That's the thing about nature and the environment. It's so much bigger than us. We think we're the top dogs on the planet, but nature is.'

As the two princes' charitable duties began to grow, in 2009 they formed the Foundation of the Duke and Duchess of Cambridge and Prince Harry, which is a way of bringing together the different charities with which they are involved and maximizing William and Harry's time. The Botswana tour was one of the first examples of this. As well as the TUSK work, a group of homeless youngsters from Centrepoint had come to work in one of TUSK's projects on a nature reserve in the north of the country.

What I discovered as I accompanied Prince William was that we share many of the same values when it comes to conservation and human needs. Like me, he had also found himself attracted to remote, wild places and, like me, he had been enchanted and captivated by Africa. For both him and his brother it offered a form of escapism, a place where they could be themselves. This is where his heart was.

'When I step off the plane I'm like, "Yes, I'm back",' he smiled. 'Africa is my second home.'

Just as it is important to William, Africa has become a part of me. In less than a year I would find myself back in Botswana, just a short way from Tico's predator camp, on a pioneering project to dive with crocodiles. As I have always said, my life is far from straightforward.

It was through TUSK that I met a young man named Barty Pleydell-Bouverie, who had been working out in Kenya and was about to set off on a 5,000-mile bicycle ride across Africa, from Namibia to Kenya, to raise funds for TUSK's work with lions. He had a pretty extraordinary and tragic story to tell. Unlike me, he had been drawn to conservation not through fascination with wildlife but through a family tragedy in which his brother had lost his life to the very creature Barty was now trying to save.

In 1999 Barty's elder brother David had been working in Africa for some time when he decided to go camping. He had set his tent on an open plateau and, in order to get some air, had left the tent unzipped. A pride of lions had arrived in the night and, tragically, David was killed. It must be an awful way to go, but an even greater horror for his grieving family. It's strange how we all cope with tragedy and loss in different ways and Barty faced it head on by returning to the continent on which his brother had died, working for a cause that had meant so much to David by helping protect the wildlife that had taken his brother from him.

For me the story was another reminder of the fragility of life and of the often hopeless battle between man and nature, but also of the selfless dedication of individuals the world over who try to make things better whatever the circumstances. Barty is a true hero of conservation.

10

Wild in Africa

One of the questions I get asked most frequently is where my favourite place is. It is almost impossible to answer, but when pushed I usually plump for Namibia.

Namibia is a former German colony with a rich and varied culture as well as a stunning landscape that, in my mind, makes it one of the most beautiful places in the world. There is something insanely wild and exciting about it, and over the years I have travelled extensively through the region working with its wildlife and the people who protect its rich environment.

The first time I travelled to Namibia it was to film *Wild in Africa* with Kate Humble. I arrived with a rowing machine under my arm. It was 2005 and the lead-up to the Atlantic row with James Cracknell and I still hadn't been in a rowing boat, so it seemed to make sense that I should take an ergo machine to Africa with me instead. Inevitably, I was pulled over by a rather curious customs official in Windhoek Airport, who had never seen anything like it.

'What's in your bag, sir?' he asked.

'A rowing machine,' I replied.

'What's that?' he asked. He had me there. I wasn't really sure how to describe an ergo.

'It's like a land boat,' I tried to explain, only complicating the issue.

'A land boat?' he repeated, sounding surprised. 'Why?'

Here we go, I thought. 'Because I'm going to row across the Atlantic,' I told him with a cheery smile.

His eyes widened as he looked at me and then my bag. 'You're going to cross the Atlantic in that?' he said, pointing to the ergo.

'Sort of,' I shrugged. He waved me through without another question.

For four long weeks I lugged that rowing machine around Namibia strapped to the roof of our jeep. Each morning, long before the sun had risen, I would quietly assemble it in some new location. Wildlife filming inevitably begins at dawn, when most animals are active, and to get in enough training I would row for two hours before breakfast at 6 a.m.

It was a month to remember. The machine was the same, the pain, sweat and boredom were all the same, but each day the scenery would change. I became quite inventive with my locations and – surprisingly, given that I didn't have much time – I would search out somewhere with the optimum view. In the Etosha National Park I rowed in front of one of the water holes while elephants and lions looked on. I rowed in the Namib Desert and on the Skeleton Coast.

I rowed on the shores of hippo-infested rivers in the Caprivi Strip and in the capital, Windhoek. One morning I set my machine up next to a small football pitch. As always, I was by myself, except for the distant call of Africa's wildlife. Yet as the sun began to rise, I sensed I was no longer alone. Children had appeared to stare at this crazy, sweaty Englishman in a land boat that didn't go anywhere.

It sounds strange, but for a while Namibia and my ergo became an important duo. I really got to know the country during those many hours of pulling. It gave me time to reflect and ingest. It's surprising what you begin to notice when you stare long and hard into one place.

It wasn't just the morning. Each evening, once we'd arrived back at camp I would set it up once again next to my tent, or even in my hotel room, and row for another few hours. It was exhausting and I hated that machine, but it got me fit and it helped me gain a better understanding and knowledge of this strange, sometimes surreal country.

I think what I like about Namibia is its eccentricity. It is a place of huge contrasts. It's not often you go in search of a bull elephant seal on the beach with a man wearing leder-hosen. Namibia has a history as colourful as its landscape.

Located in south-western Africa, it is bordered to the south by South Africa, to the north by Angola and a small part of Zambia, to the east by Botswana and a sliver of Zimbabwe. To the west is the vast rolling South Atlantic, which crashes on to the infamous wreck-strewn Skeleton Coast.

Namibia became a German protectorate in 1884 to fore-stall British encroachment and was known as German South

West Africa; it remained a German colony until the end of the First World War. In 1920 the League of Nations mandated the country to South Africa, which imposed its own laws, including apartheid. Finally, after internal violence, Namibia obtained full independence in 1990, with the exception of Walvis Bay and the Penguin Islands, which remained under South African control until 1994.

Today Namibia is one of the least densely populated countries in the world, with one of the longest-standing and most stable governments in Africa. The country's most prized possession is the diamond and there are still vast areas known as 'forbidden zones', owned by the government, where few people are permitted. According to local lore, diamonds are so prolific in there that you can simply bend down and pick them up off the ground. For more than a hundred years, however, only a few security staff and scientists have been allowed into these areas.

The Skeleton Coast is a harsh environment and the coastal plains of Namibia have an extremely hostile climate. They form a vast desert where it is difficult for anything to live in the hot, dry environment. To survive in such inhospitable conditions, the area's plants and animals have developed strange coping mechanisms. The head-standing beetle, for example, displays amazing acrobatic skills in collecting dew on its back and then tipping it down into its mouth.

None of these adaptations happened overnight. The story for much of the wildlife begins more than 10 million years ago, when the Antarctic split off from the tip of South America, releasing a cold current that stopped hot, moist, rain-producing air rising up over the Karoo and brought the desert conditions that exist there today. That same current was responsible for the presence of the diamonds for which the area became famous. Formed between 3 million and 990 million years ago in so-called kimberlite pipes in South Africa, they were washed down the Orange River then swept up along the Atlantic coast before being spat out on to Namibia's beaches and blown inland. In some places so many of them congregated together that early prospectors told tales of whole valleys of diamonds glowing in the moonlight, and of having to stuff diamonds into their mouths because their hands were too full to carry any more. The lack of a large human population allowed diamond deposits to sit fairly untouched until the beginning of the twentieth century; the dangerous waters off this coast have also protected marine diamond deposits from possible incursion by shipping and the settlement of ports until modern times.

In Namibia today, around 10 per cent of GDP comes from diamonds. The marine diamond deposits are still running strong and are believed to hold somewhere around 1.5 billion to 2 billion carats or more. If this estimate is accurate, they would be the largest on earth.

The Namibian diamond reserves are especially unique because of the calibre of the diamonds found within them. About 95 per cent of the marine diamonds in the waters and along the coastal region of Namibia are of gem quality, a far higher proportion than almost anywhere else on earth.

Today, the diamond-rush settlements that grew to service the prospectors are nothing more than ghost towns, with untended graves, sand-choked entrances and half-peeled-open roofs. This pristine wilderness is full of plants and animals found nowhere else on the planet. Its terrain includes seventeen offshore 'islands' – whose names include Possession and Plum Pudding – home to African penguins and Cape fur seals; a renowned Ramsar site (a wetland area of internationally recognized importance) that hosts around sixty bird species; and the world's most biodiverse desert ecosystem, containing more than a quarter of Namibia's 4,000-plus plant species on less than 3 per cent of the country's total surface area.

Many of these plants are water-retaining species, adapted to making the most of the occasional winter rains, and, because of the shelter and sustenance they provide, whole food chains have anchored themselves in their vicinity, beginning with small insects and branching off through lizards and voles to gemsbok and springbok, birds of prey such as Ludwig's bustard, and a population of ninety or so brown hyenas, which feast on the endless supply of seal pups found along the coast. Together, the whole place is a wonderful stage on which the area's wildlife shows off evolution's ability both to fill environmental niches and to adapt organisms to extraordinarily harsh conditions.

It was here along the rolling South Atlantic surf of the Skeleton Coast, littered with diamonds and shipwrecks, that I went shark fishing off the beach with a slightly eccentric German scientist called Dr Hannes Holtzhausen. The mere mention of the name still makes me shudder. Dr Hannes was responsible for the most filming takes I have ever had to do – thirty, to be precise.

'I'm on the Skeleton Coast shark fishing with Dr Hollus Hanheizer . . .'

'I'm on the Skeleton Coast shark fishing with Dr Hausen Holhannes . . .'

'I'm on the Skeleton Coast shark fishing with Dr Holz Hannheizen . . .'

'I'm on the Skeleton Coast shark fishing with Dr Holthans Himhizer . . .'

'I'm on the Skeleton Coast shark fishing with Dr Haus Hanneshuts . . .'

'I'm on the Skeleton Coast shark fishing with Dr Hans Himhizer . . .'

You get the gist. I'm sure in my frustration I called him Dr Shizer.

Kate Humble once edited them all together and showed them at the Royal Geographical Society in London, for which I received a standing ovation. The only one I have ever received, and I wasn't even there. C'est la vie.

Copper sharks, also known as bronze whaler sharks or narrowtooth sharks, are best known for the bronze appearance of their skin in the sunlight. They live in a number of distinct locations around the world and consequently were previously thought to be a number of different species. It was only with the development of modern taxonomic techniques in the twentieth century that all the communities of copper sharks, from China, to California, to South Africa, were shown to be of the same species.

The sharks, which grow to 3.3 metres in length, feed mainly on squid and smaller fish, and are also known to hunt in schools. Those that live around Africa feed mainly on southern African pilchards. The school of sharks will force the million-strong 'run' of pilchards into a tight ball, then each shark will swim with its mouth open, catching them. The sharks have also been known to hunt much larger prey, such as tuna.

One of the most studied communities of copper sharks lives off the coast of Namibia. Scientists have tracked their migratory movement using satellite technology and have shown that they travel between the shores of Namibia and Angola, and have made the 715km trip in less than three months.

Since the start of Angola's civil conflicts, the bronze shark populations had fallen rapidly and this scientific study aimed to track them to find out what was happening. Some in the conservation community had speculated that the Angolese were fishing them for food, thereby depleting their stocks significantly. To find out, Dr Hannes had to catch the sharks and tag them, and the best way to catch them was with a good old-fashioned fishing rod.

As a child, I had loved fishing in Canada with my grandfather. It was that excitement of the unknown, the exhilaration of dipping my line into the water. As the years have marched on, however, I have become far too sentimental to fish. It's strange how significant the change has been. It's highly hypocritical of me as I still happily eat fish, I just don't like to catch them and kill them. But here on the great expanse of the Skeleton Coast, with huge waves crashing and birds wheeling overhead, I regained that feeling of childhood excitement. We were going shark fishing.

Dr Hannes used a special hook that would limit the

damage done to the shark's mouth. While most hooks have a barb to ensure the fisherman doesn't lose his catch, ours were just simple and barbless. Using enormously long rods, we cast our lines far out into the ocean beyond the wild, crashing surf. It seemed ludicrously surreal to be fishing for something bigger than me while standing on a beach.

We propped several rods up, sat back and waited. Occasionally the rods would give us a false alarm as the line was pulled by the power of a crashing wave. I would leap up from the sand, only to discover a loose, sharkless line. The anticipation was unbearable.

'Shark on!' hollered Dr Hannes at last, handing me the rod.

Suddenly the rod seemed rather insubstantial as I began a mighty battle against the fish. It reminded me of the great Hemingway novel *The Old Man and the Sea*. As a child, that was the first novel I read that really affected me and to this day it remains one of my favourite books. The story of the old fisherman's long battle with a marlin is arguably even more relevant today than when Ernest Hemingway first wrote it, the epic fight symbolic of man's stormy relationship with nature in general.

Now here I was on this wild deserted beach, man against shark. The line was stretched taut. It felt as if it was snagged as I pulled against the elusive shark. I pulled and pulled, but the line simply wouldn't budge, and then the shark began to move, its powerful body surging against the waves and pulling me down the beach towards the crashing waves. Dr Hannes lunged out and grabbed me round the waist to stop me being hauled into the Atlantic.

This was certainly a little larger than the perch I used to catch as a boy. I pulled hard on the rod and managed to steal a little line from the shark, but for every length of line I reeled in, it seemed to pull twice as much back out to sea. For more than an hour I fought against my powerful opponent, until finally it began to tire. Soon I could just make out the coppery colour of its skin, then I could see its full body just 10 feet from me. Now we had to somehow get it from the water up on to the beach. I couldn't begin to fathom how we were going to do this until Dr Hannes rolled up his trousers and strode out into the surf, beckoning me to follow.

There is something rather counter-intuitive about stepping out into the water to pick up a wild shark.

'Be very careful,' he cautioned as he scooped his arms under its tail and dragged it into shallower water.

Soon we had the 2-metre bronze shark beached. It was hard to believe that I had managed to pull this beast from the ocean, but we didn't have time to dwell on our success. We had to race to get a tag on to its body and get it back into the water to minimize the trauma.

Dr Hannes got out one of his little tags and pierced it into the shark's thick skin next to the dorsal. The tag had a code, email address and phone number, and the hope was that if it was caught the researchers would be informed. We weighed it and took its vital measurements before we dragged it back down the beach and into the surf. With one enormous shake of its body, it launched itself into the midst of a wave and disappeared back into the South Atlantic to an unknown fate.

It had certainly been an exciting introduction to Namibia's eclectic wildlife.

From the Skeleton Coast I headed north-east, crossing Namibia's 'Red Line' into the far northern part of the country. The Red Line is a veterinary cordon fence – literally a 2-metre-high stockade fence that runs right across the country, dividing the northern states, where foot-and-mouth and other diseases are prevalent, from the disease-free south. It was originally set up by the German colonial government in the 1890s and has remained in place ever since, preventing the movement of livestock in a bid to control disease. Statistics indicate that there are nearly 1.6 million cattle and as many as 2 million small livestock north of the fence, but farmers from these areas are not allowed to export their cattle to the south or overseas. As a result the Red Line has also become a socio-economic division, hated by northern farmers who regard it as a symbol of apartheid colonialism, dividing the poor from the more affluent, traditional from modern, European-influenced from African. Nowadays, with the spread of more extensive vaccination programmes, the fence is being pushed further back towards the Angolan border and disease-free pockets of land within the northern area are being fenced off as disease protection zones. Nevertheless, crossing the Red Line really is like moving from developed Africa into developing Africa.

North of the veterinary line is a thin tentacle of land known as the Caprivi Strip, a remote region that is vastly different from the rest of Namibia, comparatively green and wet and teeming with wildlife. It has had a colourful history.

It was annexed as part of the Anglo-German Heligoland–Zanzibar Treaty of 1890, in which Germany gave up its interest in Zanzibar in return for the island of Heligoland in the North Sea and a narrow strip of land extending from German South West Africa (modern Namibia) to the Zambezi River, to be known as the Caprivi Strip (named after the German chancellor at that time).

In the Caprivi region lies the lush Mudumu National Park, created in 1990 out of almost 1,010 square kilometres of savannah, mopane woodlands and marsh on the eastern shore of the Cuando River. Many animals can be found in the park, including sitatunga and red lechwe antelopes, as well as elephants, buffalo, kudu, impala, roan antelope and Burchell's zebra. Spotted-necked otters, hippos, tiger fish and crocodiles inhabit its waterways.

On the shores of the Cuando River lies Lianshulu Lodge, nestling under a canopy of shady jackalberry and mangosteen trees, and this was where I stayed while I was in Caprivi. The lodge is run by Ralph Meyer-Rust, who has lived in East Caprivi for over twenty years. His lodge is unique in that it is privately owned but positioned within a national park. Ralph has worked closely with visiting researchers, animal conservationists and biologists for many years and it was while I was staying here and filming for *Wild in Africa* that I caught the crocodile that I humiliatingly called a turtle.

Here too I had one of my first encounters with one of the most dangerous animals in Africa – the hippo. The deadly danger of the hippopotamus is commonly underestimated. While they may seem to be just harmless herbivores, hippos are responsible for around three hundred human deaths a year, which is more than any other African mammal, and are also known to kill crocodiles. They can easily outrun humans, reaching speeds of up to 20 miles per hour; however, there are limits to their agility, as they cannot jump. While the name hippopotamus is derived from the ancient Greek for 'river horse', the hippo's nearest relation is actually the whale and hippos can close their ears and nostrils while submerged and hold their breath under water for up to five minutes. Like their cetaceous cousins, hippos are one of the few animal species to mate and give birth under water. It is unwise to get between a hippo and her child, as mother hippos are famously, fiercely protective of their young, so much so that the Ancient Egyptian goddess of pregnancy and childbirth was depicted with a hippo's head. Hippos can be strongly territorial: they spin their tails while defecating in order to propel their faeces over a wide area, marking out their patch.

Attempts to keep hippos as pets have had tragic conclusions. In November 2011 South African farmer Mauris Els was bitten to death by his six-year-old pet hippo Humphrey, whom he had tenderly raised since the animal was only five months old. US President Calvin Coolidge, famous for his unusual taste in pets, which included wallabies and lion cubs, was presented with a pet pygmy hippo by businessman Harvey Firestone in 1927. Fortunately President Coolidge entrusted hippo Billy to the care of the National Zoo in Washington DC, where he went on to father twenty-three calves and feature in the 1939 New York World's Fair. One of the earliest captive hippos was

Obaysch, who drew great crowds at London Zoo from 1852 to 1878. He was bartered in return for greyhounds as part of an elaborate Anglo-Egyptian exchange and travelled to the UK along with a herd of cows to provide him with milk.

While their grumpiness should not be underestimated, hippos have evolved an ingenious strategy to ensure that they keep themselves comfortable when exposed to the elements. Their pores secrete an oil that protects their bald skin from the sun, acting as a natural sunscreen. Chemical structures in the secretions scatter and deflect UV rays. The natural ooze also helps hippos to regulate their body temperature, fight off bacteria and repel insects. However, sun-worshippers should think again before swapping their Factor 15 for this natural alternative. The substance also causes a gradual reddening effect, leading to the gruesome legend that hippos sweat blood.

So there you have it: hippos may be grumpy, but they have a great natural sunscreen. I actually love hippos and spent hours sitting on a small wooden deck watching a pod of these magnificent creatures argue, snort and fart.

A small farm called Okonjima in central Namibia, near to the town of Otjiwarongo, is the base for a remarkable organization called AfriCat. Once a barren, lifeless region, it has been transformed into a wonderful home to a multitude of Namibia's wildlife and it is a modern-day conservation success story.

AfriCat's history begins in 1970, when the Hansen family settled on Okonjima Farm. Brahman cattle were raised on the land, but every year between twenty and thirty calves were lost to predators, particularly leopards, decimating the herd and causing huge financial losses. As with many farmers at that time, the Hansens embarked on a programme of hunting, trapping and shooting the leopards, and also cheetahs, in an attempt to save their livestock; however, their losses continued at the same rate as before. Other measures were called for and calf-holding pens were built at watering holes where cows could give birth safely. The calves remained in protective custody until they were approximately four months old, their mothers coming in at regular intervals to feed them. Employing these livestock-protection methods reduced losses to about three or four per year.

It was the inevitable conflict with humans on commercial and communal farmland that created the demand for the establishment of the AfriCat Foundation, which began in 1991. Cheetahs were being shot and caught in traps and there were a great number of injured and orphaned cheetahs roaming Namibia. AfriCat's mission is the long-term conservation of Namibia's large carnivores, achieved through education, community support, research and rehabilitation. As well as offering new livestock to farmers who have lost their own to leopards or cheetahs, the charity provides specially trained dogs to protect farmers' livestock from the big cats. It also supplies humane traps to catch the animals alive and allow them to be translocated far from human farming.

Namibia is home to approximately 25 per cent of the world's cheetah population; of these, 90 per cent live on farmland. Cheetahs are unbelievably fast, the fastest land animal in the world (second fastest in Africa would be lion and wildebeest). They can reach speeds of up to 110 km per hour, going from 0 to 84 km per hour in three seconds. An Olympic sprinter covers 200 metres in 19.92 seconds; a cheetah covers the same distance in 6.52 seconds. At top speed, each stride can be up to 7 metres, with four strides per second. There really is something beautiful about a cheetah in full flight, its legs outstretched almost as if it really is flying. You can see how prey doesn't stand a chance.

When I visited, about eighty cheetahs were homed in AfriCat's rehabilitation programme, which was initiated to give some of our captive animals an opportunity to return to their natural habitat by providing a protected environment where previously non-releasable large carnivores can hone their hunting skills and become self-sustaining. Most of these animals have missed out on all that they should have learnt from their mothers – not only hunting skills and techniques, but also the essential 'life skills' needed to survive in the wild – knowing what predators to avoid and when to back off and relinquish hard prey, selecting prey that is the right size and avoiding injuries from horns, tusks or hooves.

The rescue and rehabilitation centre was run by ex-wildlife cameraman Dave Houghton, who came to make a documentary and never left, and his partner Carla Conradie, who first came as a bookkeeper. They gave up life as they knew it to live in the bush, their mission to care for Namibia's largest and most ferocious carnivores.

On the wall of Dave's simple office was one of the most impressive photographs I have ever seen: it showed a huge male lion standing on its hind legs, enveloping a shirtless Dave and biting his neck.

'It was just play,' Dave assured me with a grin, sensing my astonishment. In the early days they regularly got in beside the big cats until a couple of 'incidents' put an end to it.

On my first day at AfriCat we received a newly orphaned cheetah cub whose leg had been damaged in the same trap that had killed its mother. It had been released into one of the quarantine areas, but its wound was infected and Dave needed to get a closer look at the injury. He darted it with an anaesthetic and I was given the task of carrying it to the operating theatre. I will always remember my fear, excitement and joy at carrying a year-old cheetah in my arms. It was surprisingly bony and light. Its head lolled in the midday sun as I raced to get it to the operating theatre.

It was only once I had carefully placed it on the table that I noticed that my arms were covered in red blotches and hives. I had suffered an extreme allergic reaction to the cheetah. I suppose most of us never have the chance to find out all the animals we are allergic to, but I have a pretty comprehensive collection: boxers, rabbits, hamsters, domestic cats. I never thought I would get to add cheetahs, lions and tigers to the list.

Carla had four tame cheetahs, two boys and two girls, which she called the Addams family: Morticia, Gomez, Pugsley and Wednesday. She had hand-reared them and referred to them as her 'babies'. She invited me into the enclosure with them. I would be lying if I didn't admit to some nerves as I walked into the compound – after all, these were predators; but they acted more like domestic moggies, coming up to lick me, purring and behaving generally just like a cat at home. One of my favourite photographs is of

Kate Humble and me posing with Gomez on a termite mound. He looks all regal – until you look a little more closely at his hindquarters and realize that he is pooing on Kate's shoulder.

Carla and Dave had also recently saved a litter of wild dog pups. As with all the animals at AfriCat, the focus was on minimal human interaction to increase the chance of re-integration into the wild. As part of this, the pups were fed an animal carcass. It was like watching piranhas in a feeding frenzy as they tore the carcass apart, stripping it to the bones within minutes.

Most of the large carnivores that come into AfriCat's welfare programme do not require permanent captivity. Almost all of them have been orphaned and are too young to cope on their own at the time of their rescue; they require only temporary care until they are old enough to be re-habilitated and released. As I have seen so many times, habituated cats cannot be released back into the wild as they would almost certainly be shot. The longer the period of time an animal spends in captivity, the greater the degree of habituation, reducing the chance of its successful release.

AfriCat's rehabilitation area works as an interim sanctuary where the animals have a chance to reintegrate back to the wild before they move on to ultimate freedom where they also have to fend for themselves against other predators. While I was there three spotted hyenas that had been in captivity for most of their lives were released into the rehabilitation area. Within weeks all of them were fending for themselves and had become very successful at finding food, whether it was through hunting, stealing kills from the leopards or just plain scavenging.

The released animals are fitted with radio collars so that their welfare, movements, progress and hunting successes can be closely monitored. The objective is that once they have proved that they can hunt for themselves and cope on their own, they can be relocated to private game reserves or released into the wild. In both cases their progress will continue to be monitored in order to assess the long-term success of AfriCat's rehabilitation programme.

Since its foundation, AfriCat has given large carnivores a chance to return to the wild that many had otherwise thought impossible. By the time of our visit, it had been so successful that word had spread across Namibia, with the result that they were receiving predators from across the country and were in danger of running out of space. Even at 100,000 hectares, the enclosure wasn't big enough for the volume of cheetahs, leopards, wild dogs and hyenas. AfriCat needed more space.

Kate and I had heard about a farm bordering the enclosure that was for sale, and for a while we both genuinely considered buying it and handing over the land to AfriCat while retaining a small plot for ourselves. I had spent so much time with others who had dedicated their lives to the natural world that I wanted to do something myself. Helping expand the land for AfriCat seemed a logical step, and both Kate and I had been longing for an opportunity. I got as far as discussions with my bank manager, but there had been worrying reports of a proposed land-reclaim policy from the Namibian government and I didn't feel I was financially stable enough to take such a gamble. In some ways I still regret that I didn't go ahead.

Namibia was the first time I considered investing in animal conservation, but it wouldn't be the last time I looked at buying a conservancy in a faraway land.

Part Four

The Cry

11

California Dreaming

'Can you dive?' asked my agent down the phone. The BBC were looking for a presenter to work alongside Kate Humble as she presented *The Abyss Live* from the depths of the Pacific Ocean.

It was 2003 and I was in Florida finishing off my first book. I had never dived in my life. In fact, I had always been a little scared of diving. There seemed to be something unnatural about strapping on alien equipment and descending into a world in which we don't belong. It had always struck me as too risky. I didn't like its reliance on equipment, and besides, everyone I ever met who did dive seemed to have a story to tell about a diving disaster.

'Yes,' I lied.

It was only a small lie. I didn't, but I would.

Here in Florida, on the Gulf of Mexico surrounded by ocean, it seemed as good a time as any finally to learn. So I found a local dive centre and signed on for an open-water dive course. I was taught about the equipment and we practised in a pool. Most of it was theory, involving tables and conversions. A week later I returned to the UK as a certified open-water diver and before I knew it I was crossing the Atlantic once again, this time to California and Monterey Bay.

The Monterey Bay Aquarium (MBA) was founded in 1984 and is located on the site of a former sardine cannery on Cannery Row, on the Pacific Ocean shoreline. It has 1.8 million visitors annually and holds thousands of plants and animals, with 623 separate named species on display. The aquarium benefits from a high circulation of fresh ocean water which is obtained through pipes that pump it in continuously from Monterey Bay.

I would be diving in the kelp forests in the ocean that surrounds the aquarium, as well as in the specific kelp-forest feature within Monterey itself.

As a child I used to hate swimming anywhere near weeds. There was something terrifying about sub-aquatic plants when they brushed against your feet or legs. I think it was partly the unknown, but also the fear of becoming entangled within the weeds themselves. So plunging into an underwater forest with just a week's worth of diving experience was still a rather daunting prospect.

On the roof of the aquarium was a small pond-like entrance that provided a small window into another world. It was home to tentacles of kelp that grew 12 metres long and swayed in the artificial flow of water within the aquarium.

It seemed strange getting into my drysuit and scuba gear

on the roof of a building. I sat on the side of the small pool, then leapt feet first into the freezing waters and descended into the watery forest below. It really was quite beautiful. Shafts of Californian sunlight filtered down through the pool deep into the water and the kelp swayed dramatically as the light danced around the shadows. Fish skirted in and out of the long tentacles as I plunged deeper and deeper.

As if this environment wasn't surreal enough, all the way down one side was a vast windowpane behind which hundreds of people gawped and stared.

I was in a special diving mask that covered my whole face to allow for a small microphone so that I could talk to the camera and also to the assembled crowd. It was very strange talking to people from 12 metres down while I fed a small Lemon shark from my hand.

I returned to California a few years later with Kate Humble in tow to make a series called *Wild on the West Coast*. It was ten days after my wedding and I ended up spending half my honeymoon with Kate. I told you she was like my second wife. We shared an idyllic little house overlooking the beach in Santa Cruz, south of San Francisco on the California coast. Santa Cruz was the birthplace of surfing, but for the next four weeks it would be our base as we spent time with marine scientists and biologists understanding more about ocean life.

It was 5 a.m. when we arrived at the harbour. A couple of seagulls wheeled overhead while half a dozen fishermen readied their boats. The cityscape of San Francisco broke the darkness with her illuminated skyscrapers.

We had barely had time to recover from the long flight

from the UK when we stepped aboard a very small boat with just a wheelhouse and an open deck. It could have come straight from the set of *Jaws*. She was no more than 8 metres long and smelt of fish. She was a charter boat often used by fishermen, but today she would take us way offshore into the Pacific Ocean to see a phenomenon that few ever get to see and many are too scared to contemplate.

We were setting out for the Farallon Islands, a small chain 20 miles offshore often described as the Red Triangle because of the bloody kills of huge numbers of Great White sharks that hunt here. And that's what we were after.

There is something a little disconcerting about heading off into the wild open ocean in a boat smaller than the creatures we were hoping to see. What's more, Kate Humble has been known to get seasick on the safari boat on the still pond in front of Longleat House, so things didn't bode well as we set out into the surf.

We sat on a rough wooden bench as we made our way out of San Francisco harbour, under the iconic Golden Gate Bridge and then out into the swell of the Pacific Ocean.

'What are our chances of seeing Great White sharks hunting?' I asked the captain hopefully.

'Well, sir,' he began, 'I have been sailing these waters for twenty years and I have seen it just twice.' The odds were certainly against us. I felt rather deflated.

The tiny boat swayed and lurched as the Pacific Shelf disappeared into the deep abyss below and we rocked on the ocean swell, the land disappearing into the horizon. There is a vulnerability about being at sea beyond the sight of land; even after all these years I still find it a little unnerving. I love the ocean and feel incredibly comfortable on it, but I prefer to have sight of land.

The Farallon Islands have designated wilderness status and are entirely uninhabited by humans, except for the scientists who are stationed there to research the wildlife. Due to the large number of seals and sea lions that live on the islands, they are a popular feeding ground for Great White sharks. The sharks here, which are on average significantly larger than other Great Whites found around the world, have been studied by scientists continuously over the last four decades. The first shark attack in the Farallons was witnessed in 1970, and by 2000 the scientists were logging nearly eighty attacks a year. No one really knows why the number has gone up so much. There are theories about fish depletion or the increased activity of man in the oceans, and it is true that the sharks that used to frequent San Francisco harbour have undoubtedly been driven away by pollution, which has changed the size and location of their hunting habitat.

Great White sharks migrate north during the summer, sometimes reaching as far as the Gulf of Alaska, and feed at the islands only during the autumn. Sharks from the Farallon Islands have also been known to travel as far as Hawaii and back again. Interestingly, the smaller male sharks return each year, while the larger females, which grow up to 6 metres long, feed at the islands only once every two years.

Researchers from the Point Reyes Bird Observatory in Marin County, California, have developed ways of tracking the sharks around the islands, recognizing individuals by natural markings and scars, while other researchers have attached radio antennae to them to track their migratory movements. Despite the large amount of research, scientists are still unsure of the total population of sharks that feed at the islands, but believe that it is up to a hundred animals. In more recent years, cage-diving has become a popular attraction in the area, offering tourists the chance to come face to face with the enormous predators.

But I wanted to see these magnificent creatures hunting in the wild and our chances were looking slim.

Soon a small pinnacle of rock appeared far on the horizon; we had arrived at the small island chain. Kate and the crew had turned various shades of green after several hours of Pacific Ocean swell, but soon we were in the relatively sheltered lee of the islands. Flocks of gulls wheeled above as sea lions porpoised in and out of the surf. It had an eerie feel to it.

We pulled the boat alongside the main island with its little lighthouse and Kate stepped ashore to go on lookout while I remained on the boat with our captain. The idea was for Kate to look for the telltale dorsal, or better still a small oil slick. These oil slicks appear when a sea lion or elephant seal has been attacked by a shark under water and the oil from the blubber races to the surface, leaving a highly visible slick.

For several hours we bobbed up and down while Kate scoured the horizon with her binoculars. I had given up hope when I heard her hollering excitedly on the radio: '*Slick!*'

She had spotted a shark.

We raced back to collect her before heading in the

direction of the sighting, then we ploughed through the waters until we reached the huge body of a bull elephant seal. It was floating in the ocean, half submerged, like an iceberg. Nothing looked out of place except for the pool of oil and blood around it. It was only when it turned that I could see the full extent of what had happened. Half its side was missing. Torn away, leaving a massive, gaping wound.

This was a one-ton elephant seal. It was difficult to equate the damage with another creature. We were right alongside it and I stared over the rail at the poor seal, its dark, pleading eyes looking up at me like a Labrador. It looked like Inca.

I was helpless. There was nothing I could do but watch.

As I stared at the injured seal I saw a dark silhouette below and watched in astonishment as it got closer and closer. It was the Great White racing back towards the surface to take another bite from its victim. I could see its razor-sharp teeth pulled back against its gums as it opened its mouth and tore into the defenceless animal.

It was terrifying and beautiful at the same time. I'm not sure if those really are the right words to describe it, but that was how it felt. Death is never lovely, but there was a beauty in the movement, grace and ferocity of the shark.

As we stared open-mouthed, another Great White shark appeared and the two began a mighty battle for the carcass. The ocean had indeed turned red as the huge predators tore it apart, the water bubbling and foaming in the frenzy. All the while we were just a few feet away, right on the front line.

Incredibly, this is where fishermen still dive for abalone (a type of sea snail), plunging down to the ocean floor and harvesting them into a bag by hand. It is still the only way to fish for them and the Farallon Islands remain a popular place to find them. Some fishermen still use tanks and engines on their boats to supply air down a long tube to which they are attached, and I was amazed to hear our captain explain that divers often get into these very waters alone, even while the sharks are about. The divers slip under the hull of the boat, hiding their silhouette until the last minute to avoid looking too much like an elephant seal or sea lion. Peering over the railing at the carnage in the water below I could see why they wanted to avoid any confusion.

I felt privileged to have witnessed this spectacle from such close quarters, but above all it was a reminder of the awesome power of nature and the reality that we wouldn't stand a chance pitted against a predator like this.

Seeing Great White sharks in the wild Pacific was an extraordinary experience, but onshore the Monterey Bay Aquarium, where we would be spending the next month, had just become the first aquarium in the world to keep a Great White in captivity. It was a pioneering experiment and one that had attracted international attention. MBA was at the forefront of developing research on this relatively unknown species.

The main aquarium is one of the largest in the world. In it are huge tuna, barracuda, sea turtles and even the bizarre sunfish that looks like a giant swimming head with no body. A wall of bubbles is occasionally pumped up the window to ensure the inhabitants of the tank don't swim into the clear glass. The theatrics of the lighting cast a deep azure blue across the tank. I could spend hours staring into the abyss. It is like looking at an ever-changing painting.

I was invited to help with the Great White shark's feeding time. I was given a long pole, on the end of which was a large piece of red meat. Carefully I held it over the edge of one of the walkways that cross the top of the aquarium and dipped it into the dark water below. The key to holding the Great White in an aquarium teeming with other fish is to ensure the shark is fed on a regular basis, before it begins to see its neighbours as lunch. I used to watch as the tuna circled the huge aquarium with a slight look of bemusement and fear in their eyes each time they swam past their carnivorous bedfellow.

Of all the surreal experiences I have had over the years, this had to be one of the strangest. It isn't every day that you get to dangle a piece of meat over a giant fish bowl only to have it snatched off by a Great White shark.

Shortly after I left Monterey, the Great White shark from the exhibit was released back into the wild after six months in the aquarium. Nowhere in the world had yet been able to keep a Great White in captivity for more than a year and they didn't want to risk either the health of the fish or their reputation as one of the world's leading marine research facilities.

The studies of the Great White shark that I observed in California were essential on a number of levels. Sharks are an important indicator species that can alert us to climatic and environmental changes in the marine environment, and in terms of conservation it is vital to understand more about their hunting and migration patterns. Another key objective is to reduce human–shark conflict; indeed, the scientists have already been able to glean data that has been essential to reducing attacks. Tips for surfers include to avoid rocky drop-offs beyond the break; to stay in water less than 20 inches deep, as sharks hunt in water depths of 20–90 inches; and my personal favourite – wear a pin-stripe wetsuit.

From the ferocious to the furry. This part of California is synonymous with another creature with an altogether different reputation: the sea otter. I would often watch them swimming in the Pacific surf beyond the aquarium and would occasionally take a kayak out into the bay to get a closer look at them. The sea otters here would use the kelp forests just below the surface as a form of organic anchor while they slept. They would wrap the long weed around their tails before falling asleep, safe in the knowledge that they weren't going to be swept away by the wind or current.

The aquarium's Sea Otter Research and Conservation (SORAC) unit was running a pioneering surrogacy programme for the rescued baby otters brought in. They pair them up with a captive mother, who raises them and teaches them how to be an otter so that they can be released back into the wild having had as little human contact as possible.

This involved another very surreal sight: one of the researchers dressed in a long black cape with a full welder's mask, black gloves and big black hat; it looked exactly like a cheap *Star Wars* fancy-dress costume. The idea was to ensure the otter pups didn't become habituated to people, particularly where food was involved. And such was the keeper's disguise that, unless Darth Vader happened to turn up on the California coast, they would never associate humans with food.

SORAC was started in 1984 when the aquarium received

Toola, a stranded sea otter, who became the first surrogate for the organization. At this point relatively little was known about sea otters, particularly when it came to hand-rearing and rehabilitation. Staff at the aquarium soon found themselves stashing sea otters in bathtubs in a desperate attempt to conserve the species until finally SORAC really got under way and the appropriate housing and care was put in place. However, SORAC is an ever-evolving programme.

There are a number of reasons for this sharp spike in the number of otter orphans. Some of their mothers fall victim to predators, some are killed by motorboats, but 17 per cent die from a brain disease caused by a single-cell parasite, *Toxoplasma gondii*. The parasite is common in humans; in fact I have a particularly virulent variety that has left me hospitalized and bed-bound several times throughout my life. While most humans can live a perfectly normal life with toxoplasmosis, the disease has migrated to the sea with devastating effects, as the immune system of the sea otter is simply unprepared for the assault. The result is a huge number of orphans.

Initially the staff were very hands-on with the pups. They were given names and received the most tactile care. But it soon became apparent that this method had dire consequences for the released pups. Once out in the open they would be unable to keep their distance from members of the public and would often find their way back to the aquarium.

It is the unstinting dedication of the staff and researchers to these vulnerable creatures that will help us understand more about the timeless march of man's effect on the planet and the animal kingdom.

A little further down the coast I met two remarkable creatures, Primo and Puka. They may sound like characters from a children's cartoon, but in reality they were far more exciting than that. They were the two bottlenose dolphins that lived at Long Marine Labs, Santa Cruz. What set these two apart from other dolphins was the fact that they were military dolphins – ex-navy dolphins to be precise. They had been trained by the US Navy to help with their missions around the world. While the precise role of navy dolphins remains a state secret, it is known that they can sniff out ocean mines and it is possible to strap cameras to their backs so that they become remote surveillance. Some have speculated that they can even have remote-control guns fastened to their backs and that they can lay charges and explosives themselves, though I think this might be getting into the realm of video games.

Whatever the truth of Primo and Puka's work during their naval days, once retired it was impossible to release them back into the wild because of their behaviour and training. I couldn't help but wonder whether they couldn't be released for their own protection and welfare, or because they were living, breathing examples of 'modern warfare' that the navy couldn't afford to have fall into foreign hands, like a modern warplane falling from the sky into enemy hands. If captured by the enemy, the dolphins could be used as double agents, turning the spying against their former masters.

So in retirement they had been given to Long Marine Labs to assist with research that may help shed light on fish availability for wild dolphin populations, possible sanctuary sites, and also the effects of military sonar and whether this causes beaching. In recent years, spates of mass beachings of whales and dolphins have been blamed on military sonar. Indeed, many have argued that the dolphin who accidently swam up the Thames may have done so after getting confused by submarine sonar off the British coast.

Interacting with dolphins is a joyful experience; indeed many people rate 'swimming with dolphins' as one of their lifelong ambitions. It has even been used as therapy for people. In recent years, however, particularly after the premiere of *The Cove*, which is about the capture of wild dolphins for aquariums, the idea of swimming or watching dolphins in captivity has become a highly sensitive and emotive issue.

I have always felt uneasy about animals in captivity, but the fact of the matter is that the majority of the population may only ever get the chance to see animals in this way. There are very few of us, like myself, who get the chance to travel the world seeing wildlife in its natural setting. It must also be argued that their captive cousins play an important role in understanding and education.

Long Marine Laboratory (LML), part of the University of California in Santa Cruz (UCSC), is an oceanside research facility located on a site overlooking Monterey Bay National Marine Sanctuary. The lab provides facilities for scientists who require running seawater, large marine mammal pools and seawater labs to conduct their research. The main researcher at the lab was Terrie M. Williams, a professor of biology at the UCSC who has been studying and protecting marine animals for over twenty-five years. She was director of the Valdez Sea Otter Rescue Center following the 1989 *Exxon Valdez* oil spill; she also co-founded the Center for Ocean Health here at Long Marine Lab. Her research expeditions have taken her around the world to study the survival strategies of Weddell seals in Antarctica, Steller sea lions, sea otters and killer whales in Alaska, as well as dolphins in Hawaii and the Bahamas. Her primary question is: how do marine animals survive in the changing world in which we live? With her team, she works with aquariums, research scientists and wild animals across the globe to ensure healthy oceans for both people and the animals that live beneath the waves.

Dolphins are masters at masking any type of illness – an adaptation to avoid predation in the wild. The lab staff therefore carry out very regular and rigorous health checks as a preventative measure, because a dolphin can appear fine one day and be found floating dead the next.

They are extraordinarily intelligent creatures. They have larger brains than humans and communicate using echoes, like bats do. They have even been seen to use tools such as sponges to protect their noses while foraging on the rough seabed. They have no sense of smell and they hunt together, herding fish into bait balls – in which fish are corralled into a dense cloud from which there is no escape – driving them into mud banks, stunning them with sonar, as well as smacking them and stunning them with their flukes.

I spent time with senior trainer Tracy as she carried out some of her routine checks, requesting the animals to perform 'behaviours' by using hand signals and a whistle as a secondary reinforcer, and fish as a primary reinforcer. Primo and Puka, both in their twenties, really were amazing creatures, capable of carrying out up to forty-five 'behaviours' ranging from the simple lifting of fins to more complex and varied behaviours like treading water.

It was astonishing to see the work being undertaken by the facility, but what made it all the more remarkable was spending time with these highly intelligent creatures. What was fundamentally clear was that we should never under-estimate the intelligence of a species. It is so easy for us to assume intelligence belongs only in creatures that look similar to us, that the mere concept of a grey-skinned marine mammal having intelligence is sometimes hard to grasp. Here was a living, breathing example to the contrary. It was also a reminder of man's ongoing and ever-evolving ability to work alongside and train 'wild' animals to do astonishing things.

While in California I was lucky enough to be invited to a secret location on Big Sur on the central Californian coast to help biologists Kelly Sorenson and Joe Burnett and their team from Ventana Wildlife Society (VWS) track, catch and monitor a rare population of the endangered California condor. Under a bright cloudless sky we set off in convoy along this vast coastline. The drive through Big Sur – which gets its name from the Spanish *sur grande*, meaning 'big south' – must be one of the most iconic in the world. The star of a thousand car commercials, it really is impressive as the powerful Pacific Ocean crashes against the cliffs below and the Santa Lucia Mountains rise majestically from the sea.

For the last thirty-five years the VWS has operated as a private, community-based non-profit organization focusing on rehabilitating and releasing wildlife at a 240-acre site in the Ventana wilderness. Their work has included prairie and peregrine falcons, and in the mid-1980s they began a successful bald eagle restoration project which reintroduced this rare bird to the region after an absence of sixty years. Now Kelly and Joe were monitoring condors for lead poisoning. If found, the bird was immediately rushed off to the society's vet for treatment.

With a wingspan of up to 3 metres and weighing in at between 8.2 and 14.1kg, the condor is the largest flying bird in North America. Instead of flapping their wings, they soar in wind currents and can reach speeds of up to 45 miles per hour; they can also climb to altitudes of 15,000 feet (4,600 metres). Other unusual attributes of California condors are that they do not have vocal chords but make only hissing and grunting noises, and it can take up to a week for a condor chick to break out of its egg.

Although condors are generally long-lived birds, they have a slow reproductive rate, which makes it very difficult for a population to recover from any kind of destruction. They mate for life, but usually only once every two years, producing just one egg. Like any species with this reproductive strategy, they cannot withstand persistent high mortality rates. As a result of lead poisoning, in the 1980s condors were estimated to have a lifespan of only six to eight years, whereas under normal conditions they can live for more than fifty years; and because they don't begin to breed until they are six or eight years old the birds couldn't reproduce in time to keep the species alive. In contrast, Turkey vultures and other raptors begin to breed much sooner and can have more than one chick per nesting attempt, so, although they too are dying from lead poisoning, their populations can withstand the mortality rate caused by this toxin, whereas condors cannot.

Condors inadvertently ingest lead from spent ammunition found in the animal carcasses and gut piles on which they feed. Fragments from lead bullets and lead shot have been found within their digestive tracts many times, both in California and Arizona. Lead bullets can fragment into hundreds of pieces before they exit a target such as a deer. Since condors are group feeders and as few as one or two lead fragments or pellets can cause lead toxicity, one animal carcass or gut pile containing lead fragments or lead shot has the potential to poison several condors.

The California condor is currently listed as endangered in North America and they can be found in the wild only in isolated areas where they have been reintroduced: California and Arizona in the United States, and Baja California in Mexico. However, the population in the continent has grown from an all-time low of twenty-two birds in 1989 to a promising 289 today, 135 of which are in the wild. For a time the California condor was thought to have been lost from the Big Sur area for ever, until Kelly and his team successfully reintroduced the species – a sign of hope for the natural history of this beautiful area.

While the condors had been suffering from a man-made affliction, we can't always be blamed for adverse effects on the natural world and the animal kingdom.

Monterey Bay Aquarium had been caught up in a poisoning mystery of their own. At the centre I met one sea lion who had been brought in after suffering a seizure on the beach. I watched him as his head moved involuntarily from side to side, his eyes gazing out in a dream-like state. I had seen the same look on Inca during one of her many epileptic seizures.

Scientists and researchers at MBA had been puzzled by a sudden spike in the number of sea lions developing seizures and abnormal behaviour. The aquarium was receiving new sea lions on a daily basis. The problem had been traced back to algal blooms, which had increased off the coast. The symptoms result from low-dose foetal exposure to domoic acid, a naturally produced neurotoxin in algae that becomes concentrated in the sea lions' food supply. Research had shown that the symptoms comprise a new sea-lion disease.

Domoic acid concentrations rise from time to time due to natural, climatic factors, the scientists point out, although other, man-made, chemicals may have made the sea lions more susceptible. Toxin-producing algal blooms are natural, cyclical events. What I found most surprising was how natural rhythms in the sea could conspire to send a wave of toxins through the food chain.

In the past, domoic acid had been blamed for increased death tolls among sea birds such as pelicans and cormorants, although sea otters, whales and dolphins are also commonly poisoned by it – not only in California, but in nearly all coastal waters off the United States. More rarely, domoic acid has sickened and killed humans. Until now the immune system of sea lions had been able to fend off the toxins, but whether it was a new form of toxin or whether their immune systems had simply been overwhelmed by the toxicity, sea lions were suddenly falling victim.

The poison enters the food chain when sea-lion prey – such as sardines, anchovies and herring – eat the toxin-producing diatomic algae. In pregnant sea lions, domoic acid concentrates in the amniotic fluid, causing prolonged exposure to the foetus.

Scientists are still trying to establish the full impact of harmful algal blooms on marine mammals to determine if similar impacts could affect humans on a larger scale.

My visit to California had been enlightening. Here was a 'wild' environment and rich wildlife habitat in close proximity to millions and millions of people. Here the balance between man and animal has been pushed to the extreme and, though I had witnessed first hand the awful repercussions of the changing environment and effects of pollution, I had also once again seen the best of human nature and its ability to nurture and care.

I loved my time in California. Marina joined me in the last few days and I'm glad I was able to introduce her to some of the people and the animals that had become so much a part of my life. We drove from San Francisco along the Big Sur to Los Angeles, the new Mr and Mrs Fogle, and resolved that one day we would move here for a new life together.

12

Swimming with Monsters

Man has always had a tumultuous relationship with predators. Strained at the best of times, it sits on the boundary between fear and fascination. From the age of cavemen, when we were the hunted and not the hunter, man has struggled to seize and keep the upper hand, but within the animal kingdom there are a number of species that remain as constant reminders of the time that we were prey. We may have been forced to demonstrate our alpha-male credentials to other animals and like to think of ourselves as top of the hierarchy within the natural world, but ultimately we share this planet with many more creatures than ourselves, some of whom, given half a chance, would eat us for lunch. The likes of sharks, polar bears, crocodiles, piranha, tigers, lions, hyena – all of them carnivores – still instil terror in the human race.

Over the millennia we have had to face up to our terror of

predators, often confronting them head-on, and at other times using them to create fear. Look at today's proliferation of young gangs with Staffordshire bull terriers: they use their dogs in much the same way that Nigerian gangs use hyenas on leads, or Colombian drug barons use lions. Dictators like Saddam Hussein kept tigers, to which they allegedly fed humans. Predators can be powerful status symbols; boxer Mike Tyson kept tigers (as well as pigeons, which rather destroys my theory).

Our morbid fascination with predators extends to facing those creatures in the wild. African safaris bring us face to face with big cats. The more fearless among us choose to go cage-diving with Great White sharks. It is man's way of asserting his dominance and arguably hiding his fear. I am no Desmond Morris, but surely that fear is what protects us?

But of course, just occasionally it goes wrong and man is reminded of his place in the pecking order. Sadly, each year a number of high-profile cases hit the headlines in which humans have been killed, eaten or both by predators. A number of Brits have been caught up in the statistics. Look at the case of seventeen-year-old Horatio Chapple, the schoolboy who tragically lost his life to a polar bear in Svalbard in 2011; or Ian Redmond, the newly-wed who was killed by a Great White shark while on his honeymoon in the Seychelles that same year; and Michael Cohen, who just a month later lost his legs after ignoring a shark warning in South Africa. Incidents like this are relatively isolated, but they make international headlines and become the stuff of Hollywood films, from *Grizzly Man* to *Jaws*, serving to provoke and exaggerate our primal fears.

In my travels I have had a few run-ins with wild predators, but only one which provoked me enough to pull out of a filming commitment entirely.

I was in Western Australia in 2011 to make a series called *Year of Adventures* for the BBC. I was preparing for a technical wreck dive, but shortly before I was due to do it another diver, George Thomas from Texas, was killed by a shark at Little Armstrong Bay, where I am as I write this. I had already undertaken some pretty hazardous challenges for the series. I had taken part in a three-day extreme car rally across the Australian outback, done a solo skydive, flown in a MIG fighter jet in the Czech Republic and swum from Alcatraz to San Francisco, all arguably as risky as this dive. So why, for the first time in nearly twelve years of television, did I choose to pull out?

I would argue that no amount of training, safety equipment or experience can ever really save you from nature. A wild animal is just that, and we should never believe that we have superiority over nature's predators.

It all comes down to perceived and actual risk. Besides George Thomas, two other people had been killed in recent weeks, and while the local dive schools, an expert on sharks and even my Australian underwater cameraman all assured me that the attacks had all been freak accidents and that it was safe to go back in the water, it is hard to hide the bare facts. Three attacks in three weeks. Indeed there had been a spate of high-profile shark attacks around the world in 2011, beginning in the Red Sea in Egypt, then the British honeymoon couple in the Seychelles, the man who lost his legs in South Africa and then an attack near Monterey in California.

Experts will reel off the statistics that you are more likely to be killed in a car crash than by a shark, and it's difficult not to agree with the figures, but it is also a fact that there has been a worrying increase in the number of shark attacks in recent years. Are we spending more time in the water? Are shark habits being affected by the change in sea temperature and fish stocks? Or is it, as many argue, pure coincidence?

Which brings me back to the question of why I pulled out of the dive. I was reassured that diving after the recent incident was no different from diving a week earlier or a week later. The ocean remained the same habitat and the sharks have always and will always live there. I have dived in 'shark waters' many times before; why would it be any different now?

But it is. For me, a shark attack, or any animal attack for that matter, is simply a warning, a reminder of the risk, and it all comes down to weighing up that risk. I am often asked why I take risks at all when I have a young family and my answer is that I always take a calculated risk. I train and prepare and, above all, I take local and expert advice. I think that society has become stifled because our children aren't allowed to take enough risks. We live in a mollycoddled world where health and safety reigns supreme. Risks must be taken, because the greatest risk of all is to risk nothing. Without risks you can't learn, feel, grow, love or live. Only a person who risks is free. But those risks must always be calculated and assessed.

My worry was that I would simply add to the scaremongering if I didn't get into the water. Sharks have been demonized ever since *Jaws* bit into every consciousness. I had spent the summer scuba-diving with crocodiles in Botswana and Australia's Northern Territory, so why was this different? What's more, it was only a week since I swam across San Francisco Bay, where Great White sharks were once prolific.

The recent spate of attacks has been dominating the local headlines. Tourism is down and the locals are up in arms. The community seems divided between those who would like sharks to be culled and those who believe we are encroaching on their habitat. The family of George Thomas have called on local authorities to call off their 'hunt' for the killer shark. They, as many locals have pointed out, believe it is impossible to correctly identify the culprit shark. The Fisheries Department, meanwhile, has hired helicopters to patrol the beaches at a cost of nearly £1 million and within days a popular beach was closed after two 5-metre Great Whites were spotted.

I find it fascinating that at once we can support campaigns to save sharks and try to ban shark's-fin soup, while also wanting 'safe' waters in which to bathe. Some would argue it is a basic human right to have a safe environment in which to live, work and play – and they do so because we have become accustomed to being top of the pecking order. Even in England, where we don't have any great man-eating predators, we manage to make a great fuss when a fox attacks a human. It has become built into our psyche. But while safety may be an assumption by those of us in the West, those living in developing countries often see death in the jaws or claws of a predator as just one of the trials and tribulations of life.

I have always been fascinated by sharks; indeed, when I swam in San Francisco Bay I was only a few miles from where I had watched the two Great Whites pull a bull elephant seal apart while I was filming *Wild on the West Coast*. The difference between that swim and my dive now was that the man-made pollution in the bay has simply repelled the sharks from the vicinity. Pedro, my swimming instructor, had swum from Alcatraz eight hundred times without an incident. For me it was worth taking that risk.

I have worked with many of the planet's top predators: polar bears, grizzly bears, lions, tigers, and Nile and saltwater crocodiles. I have a healthy respect for these creatures and I firmly believe that, as an Englishman, I am merely a visitor in their territory, where I play by their rules. But my Australian experience was different. I would describe it as a red alarm bell. Even though my common sense was telling me it was highly unlikely that anything would happen, there was still something nagging – call it human preservation, fight or flight. And I flew.

I think we should continue to enjoy the African savannah, the polar regions and the tropical oceans, but we must accept that we always do so at a risk, and for me, just a week after a young man lost his life, it was not the right time to get back in the water. The recent incidents involving Brits have been tragic reminders that nature is red in tooth and claw. I feel my dive would have been inappropriate for the victims, and arguably unfair on the sharks. It certainly wouldn't have been fair on my family.

Was it the right decision? I think I probably divided opinion. Some will say it shouldn't have even been a debate in the first place, while others will say I am merely propagating the myth of *Jaws* and giving sharks a bad name.

I felt slightly dented by my decision to pull out, but I stand by it. It was self-preservation, risk management and, above all, a healthy respect for our predators.

Which makes the story I am about to tell all the more remarkable.

It was while I was in Botswana with Prince William in 2010 that I learned about an audacious project in the Okavango Delta in Namibia. I heard only rumours, and they sounded too unbelievable to be true. According to local gossip, a husband and wife from a nearby camp had regularly been scuba-diving with wild Nile crocodiles. They had been filming them in their natural habitat without any protection.

Nile crocodiles are one of the most extraordinary creatures on the planet. They have changed little in 65 million years. They are the most intelligent reptiles on the earth and the largest of the four crocodile species found in Africa. They have a maximum length of 6.2 metres from the head to the tip of the tail and usually weigh around 225kg, although they can reach weights of up to 730kg. They have a lifespan of between seventy and a hundred years and their brains and hearts are more advanced than those of any other living reptile. Their broad, long snout ends in nostrils that can close under water and their eyes have a third eyelid, which protects them while they are submerged. Eyes, ears and nostrils are found on the same plane on the top of the head, allowing the crocodile to be completely under the water while still being able to see, smell and hear. They only look slow: Nile crocodiles have been known to 'gallop' at speeds of about 30 miles an hour.

Crocodiles are not solitary predators, as often imagined, but social creatures; they convey messages to other crocodiles through motions, odours, posture, touch and sounds. Nile crocodiles produce at least six different vocal signals. Both cows and bulls maintain territories, especially during the breeding season, when bull crocodiles defend their patch by roaring and constantly patrolling the borders. Nile crocodile bulls also respond to distress calls from their young. Eggs and hatchlings are subject to predation by baboons, marabou storks and monitor lizards by day, and by honey badgers, white-tailed mongooses and other predators at night. Larger, mature Nile crocodiles capture zebras, antelope, warthogs, large domestic animals and human beings. They are thought to kill from 250 to 750 people every year.

The Nile crocodile has been listed as endangered since 1970 and as of 1995 there were only about a thousand of reproductive age in the world. Industrial and agricultural expansion is shrinking and destroying their natural habitat, and the Nile crocodile is also hunted for its body parts. Its meat is eaten by the local people; teeth and claws are sold as souvenirs to tourists. Skeletal bones are used as nutritional supplements in agriculture, while body fat and oil are used to cure skin ulcers, burns and asthma. But the main reason the number of Nile crocodiles is dwindling is because of the high demand for leather. Poachers hunt them for their high-quality skin, which is made into shoes, handbags and belts.

In short, there are few Nile crocodiles left in the wild, but those that do remain are amongst the most dangerous animals on the planet.

When I heard about the couple in Botswana who were swimming with Nile crocs, everyone I asked either shook their head in denial and reiterated that it was not possible or they held their heads in horror at the reckless danger and idiocy. I was fascinated. I wanted to find out more.

My research into the couple paid off and within the year I was heading back to Botswana, this time with my diving gear rather than a royal prince, again to make a film for the BBC.

Brad Bestelink is part of the Okavango fabric. He and his family had grown up in the vast delta and arguably there are few people who know it as well as him. He told me stories of water-skiing on the rivers, until one day a hippo surfaced between his father and the boat, with the result that his dad launched off the back of the unimpressed hippo as if it were a ski ramp and went tumbling head first into the crocodile-infested water.

'He got out pretty smart,' grinned Brad, with typical South African understatement.

As a child Brad and his brothers used to sneak up on dozing crocodiles and jump on their backs, then ride them like rodeo bulls, so perhaps it is not so surprising that it was he who pioneered the art of scuba-diving with crocodiles. But he never meant to do it. As with many things in life, it was an accident. He and his wife Andy had been itching to film the underwater world of the delta but, like so many people, they had been put off by the prevalence of hippos and crocs, both of which compete for the status of most dangerous animal in Africa (after man, that is).

Nile crocodiles are responsible for more fatal attacks on humans than any other crocodiles in the world. Of those victims, the vast majority are wading in water or standing by the water's edge. The most famous attack in Botswana in recent history was the death of Dr Richard Root, an American who specialized in treating HIV and was in Botswana to help combat the epidemic which currently affects a quarter of the country's adult population. On a Sunday afternoon in March 2006 he was canoeing on the Limpopo River when he was snatched by a massive Nile crocodile. The animal was never found, but bits of Dr Root's body were recovered in the following days. Crocodiles in Botswana do not just attack humans: one video of a 3-metre crocodile attacking an elephant in Chobe National Park was circulated on the internet in October 2011 – in this case, the elephant fought off the reptile and survived.

Before deciding to go ahead with their film, Brad and Andy spent many months making a recce of the river, looking for a suitable spot that was deep, clear and, most importantly, croc and hippo free. They picked a secluded part in which they felt pretty sure they were safe. It was far from any known hippo or croc habitat and it was still winter, which meant the water was cold enough to suppress the crocs' appetites. Apprehensively, they put on their dive gear and slipped into the surprisingly clear water.

They were overwhelmed by the beauty of the aquatic world they found – a world that Brad had never seen, despite having lived in the delta all his life. They began to film, but, as they worked their way along the bank, they watched in horror as an enormous saltwater crocodile slipped into the water above them and descended to the sandy surface below. It settled right in front of them.

'We thought that was it,' recalled Brad.

But it wasn't. The crocodile didn't seem to mind these two aliens who had suddenly invaded its habitat. Whether it was because it had never seen anything like them before, or whether it was scared, or whether it was simply too cold is anyone's guess, but crucially it allowed Brad and Andy to film it for nearly half an hour.

But then they had a dilemma. They didn't know how to get out of the water without arousing the croc's interest.

'Getting back to the boat was pretty scary,' commented Andy, with more understatement. 'I thought it would attack us as soon as we got to the surface.'

The croc may have put up with them in the water, but as soon as they broke the surface they would look like the prey that they were and they risked being attacked.

Slowly Brad ascended until he was under the bottom of the boat, where he hid in her shadow to avoid breaking the shape. Andy soon followed. They were just a foot from the surface, but they still had to get out – no easy task with 50kg of diving bottles and equipment on your back. Somehow they had to get to the side of the boat and haul themselves out of the water as discreetly as possible.

Andy came up with a plan. She pumped some air into her buoyancy compensator, or BC as they are known, and slipped it off her shoulders, keeping the regulator in her mouth. She handed it to Brad, took a deep breath and pulled the tube from her mouth. With one deft movement she slipped along the bottom of the boat until she reached the engine at the back, where she shot out of the water like a penguin, landing with a thud in the bottom of the boat. Slowly Brad pushed her BC to the side of the boat and she lifted it carefully on board. Now it was Brad's turn. He did the same, and before they knew it they were both safely back on the boat with the crocodile none the wiser.

'It was quite a rush,' smiled Brad.

They couldn't understand why he didn't attack them. No one believed them until they showed the footage, which unsurprisingly became an internet phenomenon. It's still there – take a look for yourself. It really is something.

It is rare in this day and age to do something truly pioneering, but Brad and Andy had just become the first people in the world to dive with a wild Nile crocodile and they were hooked.

It was this pioneering spirit that got me involved, and before I knew it I was in a tiny aircraft bouncing above the African plains on my way to their remote camp in the Okavango Delta.

For a hopeful naturalist, the Okavango must be one of the most exciting places on earth. Water from the highlands of Angola travels for 1,000 miles along the Okavango River, through Namibia and into Botswana, before forming into the Okavango Delta in the Kalahari Desert. Unlike most deltas, which form as a river flows out to sea, the Okavango simply runs into the desert, where the water either evaporates or is taken up by plants. The delta is home to an extremely wide range of wildlife, including leopards, cheetahs, lions, zebras, hippopotamus and elephants, as well as over four hundred species of birds and many fish. The size of the delta changes with the season, covering less than 9,000 square kilometres in the dry season and over 16,000 square kilometres in the wet season, making this the world's largest inland delta. With these fluctuations come the movement and migration of many of the animals that live in the area.

The great diversity of wildlife is due, in part, to the purity of the water that passes into the delta, as the course of the Okavango River is sparsely populated. None the less, 660,000 tons of sediment, formed of mud and foliage, is deposited by the river across the delta each year. With such a diversity of wildlife, the delta has become a tourism hotspot, and today water-based tourism is the second-largest source of foreign currency for Botswana's economy.

The landscape of the delta is a result of long-term geographical changes. Originally the Okavango River flowed into the massive Lake Makgadikgadi, which covered 80,000 square kilometres 20,000 years ago. As the lake dried up, the delta formed, and today it includes many islands, the largest of which is Chief's Island, whose formation was the result of tectonic movements. Yet within the delta there are a lot of smaller islands, composed more simply of soil. It is thought that many of them started as termite mounds which then became places where trees could begin to grow.

The delta is under threat from a number of human technological developments. Perhaps the most significant of these is a plan presented by the Namibian government for a hydropower station that would restrict the flow of water to the delta. Meanwhile the development of infrastructure for oil production in Angola is also likely to result in high demands for water, which would otherwise pass eventually into the delta. In 1994 the governments of Angola, Namibia and Botswana signed an agreement to promote sustainable water resources in the region, setting up the Permanent River Basin Commission (OKACOM).

A tiny runway had been constructed on a small island in the middle of the swamp and when I arrived a large, towering man met me off the plane.

'Hello, Mr Ben, I am Mr P,' he said, holding out his enormous hand.

We walked to a small panga boat and cruised through the shallow waters, past cattle and farmers, waist deep in the water, until we reached the main tributary. Tall grasses lined the river like a fence. Soon we reached Brad and Andy's lodge.

Before I could go in with the 'big boys', I had to prove I was capable and confident diving in the complex river system. Strong currents, tree roots and submerged trees are all obstacles for the novice diver like myself. The river snaked and twisted through the delta and the riverbed dipped and troughed, so the depth could go from 20 metres to just 1 metre before you even realized it.

We packed up the dive boat and headed out. It was a cool winter's morning. It can get surprisingly cold in the delta and frosts are not uncommon. I wrapped myself in a thick fleece and scarf against the chill.

Brad took us to a remote corner of the delta where two rivers meet. It was full of clear water and largely croc free – 'Although we can't guarantee that,' smiled Brad mischievously.

I pulled on my thick wetsuit, followed by another shorty

for added warmth around my core. The water temperature was about 8 degrees, which is pretty chilly when you're submerged for any length of time. I pulled on my booties and my hat, then slipped on my regulator with my air bottles. As it would be so dangerous, insurance insisted I dive with two bottles as opposed to the standard single bottle. The second was a 'bail out' bottle in case things went wrong.

Diving is a dangerous pursuit at the best of times, but here in the crocodile- and hippo-filled rivers of Africa it was a whole new game.

Shortly before leaving the UK I had to go on a special diving course to teach me the intricacies of diving in a fast-flowing river. The key to a safe croc dive is what is known as a 'rapid negative buoyancy entry'. On normal dives, you will fill your BC with a little air before stepping or falling back into the water. You then have time floating on the surface to ensure you are happy before purging the air from the BC and slowly descending. Here in Africa it was all about speed. A slow entry could mean the difference between life and death.

I sat on the side of the boat. The water was crystal clear and I could easily see the sandy bottom 5 metres below. There are many different kinds of dive masks, but I would be using a special type called an MK20 so that I could communicate with Brad under water. He needed to be able to direct me to, or from, a crocodile. This mask is a little more complex than a regular one and needs to be fitted over the whole head, then tightened with six straps; it is time-consuming and often requires help. Ingrid was my designated dive buddy above the water; once immersed I would be in Brad's hands.

Fully kitted, I perched on the side of the boat waiting for my signal to fall back into the water. Was I scared? To be honest, no. There was too much to think about and I felt I was in safe hands. This was just a practice dive after all.

What I was about to discover was that a practice dive in Chiswick is a million miles from one in the Okavango Delta.

Three, two, one . . . Ingrid used her hands to signal. On the final count I fell backwards into the freezing water. Without any air I tumbled through the water and plonked head first on to the riverbed, and then it all went wrong.

I had completely underestimated the power of the current which ripped at my body. I dug my hands into the sand, but it was impossible to remain upright and I flipped upside down. I felt a hand grab for my wrist to steady me, but the water was too strong. It was tugging at my mask, which was beginning to flood. I hadn't tightened it enough and it began to fill with water. I had cleared my mask under water a thousand times before, but suddenly in the pressure of the moment I forgot how and did it the wrong way, further flooding the mask.

It was chaos. I couldn't find my neutral buoyancy and the current tumbled me around like a sock in a washing machine. I gestured with my thumb that I needed to head to the surface. I had been in the water less than five minutes and already I was in trouble.

And then things went from bad to worse. I miscalculated the air in my BC and went shooting to the surface several metres from the boat. So much for the carefully orchestrated exit. If Brad and Andy were concerned, they had every right to be. I had assured them that I was a competent diver, but I had just cocked up spectacularly.

I caught them deep in conversation. They were worried. Really worried. If I couldn't cope with the diving conditions, which were tough enough on their own, there was no way I could be introduced to a 5-metre croc.

'The problem is,' said Andy diplomatically, 'you need full control under water. If you tumble uncontrollably, you could end up bumping into a crocodile.'

She didn't need to elaborate. I already knew the risks, but suddenly it felt as if I had bitten off a little too much. This was a pioneering project and I wasn't about to jeopardize their work. The Botswanan government was already twitchy about people diving with crocs. One bad encounter would lead to a media frenzy and a whole heap of negative publicity for Botswanan tourism. I had to up my game if I was going to have a chance of diving with crocodiles.

Joining me in Botswana was Adam Britton, a world crocodile expert who had moved from Yorkshire where there aren't many crocodiles to Australia's Northern Territory where there are lots. Over the years he has built up a wealth of experience and knowledge about crocodiles and he had agreed to join us in our groundbreaking project.

Adam is in the middle of a pioneering study which could well catapult him to scientific stardom. He is leading a project to collect blood from crocodiles in the hope of developing a powerful antibiotic for humans after initial tests showed that the reptiles' immune system was powerful enough to kill the HIV virus.

A crocodile's immune system works differently from that of a human and is much more powerful. It directly attacks bacteria as soon as they enter the body, so preventing life-threatening infections after savage territorial fights which often leave the animals with gaping wounds and missing limbs. Initial studies in 1998 found that several proteins (antibodies) in the reptile's blood killed bacteria that were resistant to penicillin, such as *Staphylococcus aureus*, or golden staph, which can cause a range of conditions in humans, from boils to life-threatening illnesses.

Adam had spent time collecting blood from wild and captive crocodiles, both saltwater and freshwater species, and hoped to isolate the powerful antibodies and eventually develop an antibiotic for use by humans, but the main worry was that the crocodile's immune system may be too power-ful for humans and may need to be synthesized for our consumption.

Adam also wanted to make sense of a crocodile's life under water. A staggering 90 per cent of what is known about crocs is based on their land habitat. Human–crocodile conflict has become a real issue in many parts of the world. Here in Botswana, as in so many regions, the density of people scratching a living close to croc habitat had invariably led to an increase in attacks. The number of incidents had risen dramatically as crocodile numbers had increased after the hunting ban, and the result was man and species at loggerheads. Much of the Okavango Delta region is swamp-land and the farmers move their cattle through waist-deep water, both cattle and farmer becoming easy prey and fair game. The result has been disastrous. Adam theorized that the more we could learn about their aquatic behaviour, the more we could do to reduce that conflict and the number of attacks or deaths by making changes so that we are better adapted to the environment and, more specifically, to the crocs' hunting habitat.

After my practice dive, I visited a local village in which Nile crocodiles had attacked many of the women. Women tend to be the most vulnerable in Africa, as they are the ones who use the shallows of the river to wash clothes or collect water. The most common injury occurs when they have their arms in the river and the croc attacks them. I saw far too many women, most of them mothers, with missing arms and I met one mother and daughter who had been attacked.

The daughter was washing the clothes when a Nile crocodile struck, grabbing her arm. She started to scream. Her mother rushed to her aid and fought to prize the crocodile's jaws off her daughter. She succeeded, but not before it had snatched both of her own arms, leaving her with a double amputation above the elbow. Her daughter escaped with just one arm, but the psychological scars can last a lifetime. It was a sobering reminder of the brutal reality of life out here.

People flock from across the world to go on safaris and gawp at these predators, but the average African actually has to live alongside these beasts. They share the same land, same habitat and often the same food. Nature can be a bloody battle and here in the Okavango Delta I was on the front line.

Brad and Andy suggested another practice dive. I had

learnt from my mistakes and was now more prepared for the difficult conditions. The difference this time round was that there was no guarantee that we wouldn't come across a crocodile. It was a different location with deeper, cleaner water and a slightly slower current, but also closer to known croc habitat.

'Well, it is what you're here for,' said Brad. 'This time you'll need one of these.' He handed me a heavy metal spike. 'It's a croc spike – just in case.'

I didn't like the sound of this.

Once again I perched on the edge of the boat, sweating under the powerful African sun before plummeting to the depths of the mighty river. I used the spike to anchor myself to the sandy bottom and turned myself into the current. 'Breathe deeply,' I repeated to myself, 'calmly.' I have discovered the importance and power of mind control over the years and have worked out ways of conquering my fears through breathing and, often, talking to myself. I have found I need to make myself concentrate in order to overcome fear. As soon as my mind is elsewhere I lose it and that is when panic sets in.

I settled myself. My diving watch registered 8 metres. I cleared my ears and gave Brad the thumbs-up. Slowly I pulled my stick from the sand and we were off.

It really is a little like being in a washing machine as the currents propel you through the water. Every few metres I would use my stick as a break and anchor myself back to the bed. Soon we reached what could only be described as a submerged forest. Whole trees, their branches dancing in the current, were silhouetted like some surrealist painting. It was ethereal and otherworldly. It was one of the most beautiful places I have ever seen.

Soon we were able to use branches and roots as anchor points. A couple of nosy fish came to investigate these intruders in their world. Brad gave me the thumbs-up and then I heard him crackle through my earpiece.

'I think we have company.'

My heart began to race. Until now, swimming with crocodiles had always been an abstract idea, but suddenly it was a reality. I had only just got used to the diving. A crocodile seemed too quick. But time waits for no man.

'Move very slowly,' Brad crackled. Underwater comms occasionally break up; it sounds a little like spacemen talking to one another. Sentences don't begin clearly, or end with a full stop. There are breaths and pauses and beeps and squelches. Think of the immortal line 'One small step for man . . .' and you'll get an idea of what it sounds like under water when you're looking for a crocodile.

Visibility at this time of year is about 8 metres, but as you follow the current downstream you end up swimming in your own disturbed water. Make too much mess with your fins in the sand and you find yourself in your own cloud.

'He's here somewhere,' repeated Brad. 'Stick close to me.' I could hear my heart beating in my ears. My adrenaline was pumping. This was scary. Really scary. I felt like an actor in *Alien* when they are watching the alien close in on them with the flashing light. The difference here was that Brad was no Sigourney Weaver and this was real life.

'Very slowly, Ben. No sudden movements.'

I crept along the riverbed using the stick as an anchor. I

couldn't see any crocodiles, just the silhouette of palm trees above.

'OK, I've found our croc,' crackled Brad through my earpiece. 'Follow me very slowly.'

Slowly, slowly, I crept along the bed until I reached what looked like a fallen tree. I could make out a greeny-black silhouette against the light sand.

'Do you see him?' asked Brad.

I stared long and hard. Nothing. I had disturbed some silt and the water was still clouded. All I could see was a dazzlingly white object shining like some jewel. I crept closer.

Suddenly I realized that the white object was in fact a large shiny tooth. Then I saw another and another.

They were so clean, white and shining that they looked fake. Soon I could make out the green gums and before I knew it I was just a few feet away from a very large Nile crocodile.

'He's about three metres,' said Brad, remaining close to my side.

Adam had explained that although not the biggest by far, 3-metre male crocs are the most troublesome. The larger crocs tend to gain status through sheer size and age, but 3 metres signifies a male coming of age and still trying to assert his authority. Most attacks are made by crocs exactly like this one.

'Come in a little closer,' said Brad, beckoning me.

It was astonishing. I could make out every marking on its face. I could see the individual markings of each scute, or scale, on its long tail.

Suddenly the croc turned its head and started moving towards me. 'Oh shit, oh shit, oh shit,' I began mumbling under my breath. It came to within just a few inches of my face and then turned away.

My heart was racing and I froze rigid, watching as its long body moved past my face. I saw its claws flicking at the sand and then stared as it disappeared into the gloom.

I had had my first crocodile encounter.

Carefully I executed my exit strategy, clinging to the bottom of the boat. It was better than my last attempt, but it was still clumsy and if I was going to have another encounter I needed to get quicker.

Next it was Adam's turn.

Adam reminded me of a slightly mad scientist. His glasses were held together with tape and his toe stuck out of one of his shoes. His wetsuit was covered in gaffer tape stuck over holes and he had brought a whole bag of home-made instruments to use in experiments. My favourite was the small extendable fishing rod with a polystyrene ball attached to the end. 'To test reactions,' he explained. He had brought a little box of multicoloured food dyes to analyse the currents and a tape measure, to measure the thing.

Adam was going down with our cameraman, Mike Pitts. Mike is a seasoned professional and we had worked together before. Along with Doug Allan, he is one of the top underwater cameramen in the world. With thousands of highly technical dives under his belt, many of them with sharks, Mike was undoubtedly the best man for the job.

To dive with a crocodile, first you need to find one. We sped along the river in our flat-bottomed boat until we saw the familiar splash of a croc slipping into the water. All those memories of watching Tarzan came flooding back.

'He's a big boy!' said Brad.

'How big?' I asked. 'Let's find out.'

Mike would buddy with Brad and I watched as the two of them effortlessly and fearlessly fell off the boat and tumbled to the bottom of the river.

Next it was Adam. The key to getting in with the crocodiles is speed. But there was a problem with Adam's mask; the seconds ticked by while we attempted to fix it. A minute later, Adam went into the water with Andy. I would be in charge of the communications box on the boat while Mr P followed their bubbles on the surface to ensure we were never too far when they resurfaced. With the currents it was easy to travel several kilometres under water.

It was like being in a control room as I listened to their underwater conversation. I could hear their laboured breathing and the clicks and crackles as they worked their way along the underside of the river overhang.

'Whoa!' I clearly heard. Then more clicks and crackles.

'Over here.'

'*F***ING HELL!*'

And then nothing.

My heart started to pound again. Something was wrong. Mr P had been following the bubbles and they had all moved into the middle of the river, a sign that they were ready to come up.

'Coming back, coming back,' repeated Brad on the intercom.

Something was wrong. Mr P looked worried.

Mike was the first back to the boat.

'Get me out!' he said as his head broke the surface and with that Mr P lifted him and his bottles clean out of the water in one movement, dumping him on the floor of the boat.

'It tried to bite me!' he spluttered. He was ashen white.

Next Andy came up. She was still clutching her croc spike. Silently she slipped from the water and pulled off her mask. She looked shocked.

'I don't know what happened.' She shook her head. 'I've never seen that before.'

'It tried to have me,' continued Mike. 'You saved my life, Andy – you saved my life.'

It was confusing and terrifying. We didn't understand what had gone on, but we still had two divers in the water and we had to get them out sharp.

In a few moments Adam appeared. Mr P wasn't taking any chances and, as with Mike, he hauled him out in one. Brad soon followed. Everyone was in shock as they explained what had happened.

Brad and Mike had been waiting on the bottom of the river. There was no sign of the large croc, but they were waiting for Adam and Andy. After the delay over Adam's mask, they watched the two divers descend.

As they landed, Andy spotted what Brad and Mike hadn't. Between the two of them was a 5-metre crocodile. Unbelievably, neither of them had noticed because they were concentrating on the boat. It was far too close for comfort and, in Andy's eyes, an outward act of aggression on the part of the crocodile. She raised her spike.

To Mike and Brad this must have looked utterly ridiculous, like some pantomime act in front of them – but it made them look behind.

Brad remained calm, but – naturally, I think you'll agree – Mike panicked. He still had his camera and he recoiled, holding the camera in front of him for protection. The croc swung its head around, opened its enormous jaws and struck. Luckily for Mike, he had his camera as a shield and he was able to stuff it into the croc's mouth. It crunched down on the hard metal, its teeth cutting it like butter, and then shook it furiously.

'I thought I was a goner,' explained a still shocked Mike.

The divers scrambled to get out of the way, but the croc hadn't finished and it made another lunge. Again the camera acted as a barrier. Feeling something hard and metallic rather than something soft, fleshy and edible, the croc gave up and disappeared into the gloom. They had had a very near miss.

'In all our years of diving, that has never happened before,' said Andy. Whatever the explanation, it looked as though our pioneering project had come crashing down. How could we get back into the water after that?

We examined Mike's chewed camera. It was rather sobering to see the teethmarks. Mike just sat there shaking his head. 'Andy saved my life,' he repeated. 'I never thought I'd say that, but Andy saved my life.'

That evening we decided to visit a witch doctor. The locals, who fear and loathe the crocodiles, undergo a special crocodile ceremony to give them protection, and both Mike and I needed all the protection we could get if we were going to get back in the water.

I have been to a witch doctor once before, in Zambia. It was my first visit to Africa and I went with my friend Ken Lennox. We had both been rather spooked by the accuracy of his diagnosis of ailments he couldn't possibly have known about, and, in Ken's case, an ailment even Ken didn't know about. It was only when he returned to England to get a second opinion from his doctor that the witch doctor's assessment was clinically confirmed. I have been fascinated by witch doctors ever since.

Mr P drove us in one of the pangas through the darkened water. We could hear the old-man laugh of a pod of hippos grazing in the shallows. Half an hour later we reached Mr P's village. A large fire had been set and the entire village had come out for the ceremony. There is something rather exciting about Africa at night. It touches every one of your senses – the smells, the sounds, the light, the feel. You've never really met Africa until you've experienced the night.

The croc ceremony was slightly maniacal with its frenzied dancing and chanting. For three hours I watched dozens of women stomping their feet and rocking, trance-like, while river water was applied to my head with a horsehair whip. It was bizarre and at the time a little scary, but it was also deeply special. Over the years I have found myself in some pretty unusual situations, but this had to be one of the strangest.

It was deep into the night when the ceremony finished. The fire was mere ashes and even the dogs were curled up against the night chill. We made our way back to the lodge where I would have to make the decision I was dreading: whether to get back in the water.

Next morning over breakfast, Adam tried to explain why he thought the crocodile had attacked. He reasoned that because there was a gap between the entry of the divers, the croc had had time to swim to the bottom of the river and then watch the second pair descend. It had watched them and then moved in for a closer inspection. Until now, Brad and Andy had relied on a principle of being the stalkers rather than the stalked, but this break in the diving 'protocol' had changed the dynamic and the croc had become the stalker.

It sounded a simple enough theory, but while I wanted to believe it was a freak accident I had to think about my family. Was it worth getting back into the water when I had two young children and a wife depending on me back at home? As a family man I had my responsibilities.

This is where you have to rely on your trust in those around you and your own gut feeling. I was here in Botswana to dive with crocodiles and I had entrusted my safety to Brad, Andy and Adam. I would like to think that, at thirty-eight, I am a pretty good judge of character. I've met enough people over the years to identify the bullshitters and the mavericks.

I trusted this team implicitly and had to believe their reasoning. I would get back into the water.

I have known fear in my life. I have met it more times than I care to remember. I have confronted it head-on and lived to tell the tale. Contrary to popular belief, I don't thrive on fear, but I've learnt how to control it.

Fear has the power to awaken a primal feeling in man. It takes us back to those early complexes we had as cavemen. It comes in many guises. There is the sheer physical fear of a situation, or the perceived mental fear of a threat. For me, humans have always scared me the most. Sadly, in many parts of the world human life is cheap. Drugs, alcohol or sheer indifference can make man the most dangerous animal on earth. But apart from that, I have always found the un-predictability of animals scary. In many of the things I've done, there has been an element of control; to a great extent I have been in charge of my own destiny. But throw an animal into the equation and things become very different indeed. I have lost count of the number of people I have met in the world who have ultimately met a tragic end by the savage tooth of nature and now, here, perched on the edge of a boat in the heart of Africa, I was scared. Really scared.

In fact, if I extract that single moment in time, I can categorically say it was the most fearful sixty seconds of my life. I could feel bile rising in my throat. I was dizzy and sweating.

So why was I still there? What was driving me on? Trust. Absolute trust in those around me and a deep need to confront those primal fears.

Was it a wanton risk to go back in? You can decide. I've already told you that I do have the ability to say no. But here I was, less than twenty-four hours after our cameraman nearly got eaten, diving back into the crocodile's lair.

Three, two . . .

I gripped my steel croc spike tightly in my hand and held it aloft, ready to strike.

. . . one . . .

I tumbled back, out of the blindingly bright African sun, into a murky world of greens and browns. It really was like stepping into another world. I almost had an out-of-body experience as I tumbled through the water. Falling, falling, falling, like some aquatic skydiver. I watched as the boat above became smaller. I could make out Mr P, his face distorted by the water.

My body flipped and I watched as the bottom of the river raced towards me. I didn't even have time to equalize my ears. I was terrified that I would land on a crocodile. As has happened before.

'Whatever you do, don't drift on to a crocodile,' Andy had reiterated before we dived.

Andy really was an enigma to me. She is one of the best divers I have ever seen. She looked like a water fairy. She is one of the only people I have ever met who genuinely looks more comfortable and at ease under water than above. She has perfect neutral buoyancy and quite literally dances around under water, fearless and confident. I envied her right now as I dug my spike into the sandy bed.

One of Adam's theories was that the underwater communications may have attracted the croc, so in order to minimize the risk of another close encounter we had abandoned the comms, which meant we were now down to hand signals.

Andy was my dive buddy as, once again, we worked our way along the bottom of the river. Now that I was in the water, my fear had started to subside and I relaxed into the task in hand. To find our croc.

It wasn't long before Brad made a snapping gesture with his hands and pointed to a cave entrance hidden in the bank.

The hippos that infest the river create huge underwater cave systems through which they can take shortcuts from river to river. They form something of an underwater rabbit warren of tunnels that the crocs also use.

A croc's underwater lair is a pretty creepy place. Before I left England, my father-in-law, who is a doctor, told me the tale of one of his patients who was in Africa and had been snatched by a crocodile while taking a swim. He had fallen unconscious and had woken sometime later, badly mauled but alive, to find that he was in a half-submerged cave, lying on a ledge surrounded by bones and skeletons.

Brad pointed to my eyes with his two fingers and then gestured to a submerged trunk. He then made a 'very large' gesture by holding his hands wide apart, the way one would describe the size of a fish.

There in the murk was an enormous tail. It really was the largest tail I had ever seen. I crept around, keeping my distance. I watched in astonishment as Brad went to touch it. He then gestured for me to do the same.

Remember, this was a wild Nile crocodile that could kill me with one bite. It could knock me out with a single swish of its tail and here I was reaching out like ET to touch it. My finger made contact with its scaly tail. It was astonishing and unreal.

Adam had brought his vision-testing kit down, but first we had to measure the creature. I fished the tape measure out of my pocket and slowly started to pull the tape from its reel, then gently pushed the metal tape along the riverbed next to the croc's body, making sure I didn't accidentally spook him. Five metres. He was BIG.

Next Adam began to extend his fishing rod with the white polystyrene ball. He held it in front of the crocodile's snout. Nothing. He waved it gently in the current as I looked on in astonishment. He was a braver man than me.

I stared intently at the crocodile's eyes. Still nothing. They were staring into the middle distance. Adam moved the ball a little closer, at which point something rather unexpected happened. The crocodile shifted its head slightly – which was enough to make me jump out of my skin – and then it slowly opened its mouth like some clockwork toy and snapped it down gently on the ball.

At this point you might expect Adam to drop the rod and flee, but not our fearless croc expert. He wasn't about to lose his scientific instrument to some croc, not even a 5-metre one.

The crocodile – now clutching the ball, which was still attached to the rod, which was firmly clenched in Adam's hands – began to swim off . . . trailing Adam with him. It was like a dog on a lead bolting and dragging its owner with it, only this was a mighty wild crocodile.

It's funny how life twists and turns, and how fear can morph into absolute joy in just a few seconds, but that was what I was experiencing. I was doubled up with laughter, as were Andy and Brad. Tears streamed from my eyes. It was one of the funniest sights I have ever seen. Gary Larson couldn't have made it up for *The Far Side*.

Fortunately for Adam, the line snapped and the croc disappeared.

'Well, I think that worked,' he beamed as we clambered back on to the boat.

Over the next few days we did dozens of dives with these mighty creatures, building up a profile of several crocs and their behaviour. But as if the crocodiles weren't enough cause for worry, we also had to plan for the risk of an encounter with a hippo.

On our penultimate day we had returned to one of the best diving spots on the 'Filipo' river. The area got its nickname when the locals warned Brad that it was 'fullofhippos'. It also happened to be one of the perfect places for crocodile encounters.

We watched a large crocodile slide into the water, then pulled on our masks and diving gear. We were just about to go in when someone spotted something. It was a giant boulder near the shore.

'I don't remember that,' said Brad, quizzically.

We pulled our masks off and slowly approached. As we got closer we realized that it wasn't a boulder at all, but the back of what appeared to be a dead hippo. It was motionless, in an awkward position. Half submerged, it must have been dead.

Mr P splashed the water with a paddle. Nothing. We hollered and shouted. Still nothing. Finally Mr P threw a piece of wood at it and still nothing. It was dead.

We pulled the boat close to its back for a closer look. Hippos have magnificent skin. We decided to use a stick to turn it over for a better look. Brad got the stick and poked it hard against the animal's back, at which point all hell let loose. The hippo wasn't dead after all, but in a deep sleep, and we had just disturbed it. Hell hath no fury like a pissed-off hippo, and this one was mightily unimpressed. He was furious.

Mr P ran to the engine and threw it into reverse. We all fell to the floor as we accelerated away, with the hippo charging at us. It kept up with us for a surprisingly long time before it finally gave up.

It was a sobering reminder not to become complacent when diving in an African river.

All good things must come to an end and my time was up in the Okavango Delta. I was genuinely sad to leave. I had enjoyed the company of Brad, Andy and Adam and we had all become firm friends. I had been part of a pioneering project that could genuinely open the door to the understanding of crocodiles, as well as have the power to save lives. Also, I had learnt about a species of which I had known very little before.

Shortly before I left, Brad appeared from the river with a souvenir.

'Don't tell anyone,' he said as he handed me a shiny white crocodile tooth. 'For your son, Ludo,' he said.

It made me quite emotional. Not just that Brad had been so considerate, but that he understood what this project meant to me. I have become so used to jumping from project to project or adventure to adventure that sometimes I don't have a chance to savour the experience, but my time here in the Okavango Delta had been so raw and intense that it had affected me more than I realized.

'I have an idea,' said Adam with a smile before I set off in the panga with Mr P to catch my small plane and join my family for the summer in Austria. 'I think we could do this with saltwater crocodiles in Australia. There's only one catch: I need you to come with me.'

He didn't even need to wait for a reply. He knew I would say yes. I didn't want my crocodile adventure to end. But, as I would soon discover, it was only just beginning.

13

Crocodile Daddy

One of the most famous crocodile-attack stories is that of Ramree Island, off the coast of Burma, during the Second World War. An amphibious assault by the British Royal Marines to capture a Japanese stronghold in the north of the island led to the nine hundred defenders within it abandoning the base and marching across the island to join a larger battalion. The route crossed 16 kilometres of mangrove swamps and, as the Japanese struggled through the thick forests, the British forces encircled the swamps, trapping the enemy in deep, mud-filled land. Despite British calls for them to surrender, the Japanese refused and remained for days in the swamp. The marines shot any enemy soldiers attempting to escape and many of the Japanese were quickly afflicted with tropical diseases or died for lack of food and drinking water, but it was the saltwater crocodiles that led to what the *The Guinness Book of Records* lists as 'The Greatest Disaster Suffered from Animals'. According to the naturalist Bruce Wright, many of the soldiers were attacked and eaten by the crocodiles:

> That night [of 19 February 1945] was the most horrible that any member of the M.L. [motor launch] crews ever experienced. The scattered rifle shots in the pitch black swamp punctured by the screams of wounded men crushed in the jaws of huge reptiles, and the blurred worrying sound of spinning crocodiles made a cacophony of hell that has rarely been duplicated on earth. At dawn the vultures arrived to clean up what the crocodiles had left ... Of about 1,000 Japanese soldiers that entered the swamps of Ramree, only about 20 were found alive.

The story has never been authenticated, but when the stand-off was over, of the nine hundred troops that originally fled into the swamp only around twenty seriously wounded and weakened Japanese soldiers remained to be captured by the British. It is a startling reminder of the ferocity and power of the saltwater crocodile, a species with which I was about to attempt to dive.

An area as large as France, Italy and Spain combined, the Northern Territory is Australia's least populated area. It has been home to aboriginal communities for about forty thousand years and is the site of one of Australia's most famous spiritual landmarks, Uluru (Ayers Rock). One aboriginal Dreamtime legend claims that the sandstone monolith was formed by two boys playing with mounds of mud, who themselves transformed into boulders upon its surface. There have been tensions between Uluru's status as

Left: In Namibia filming *Wild in Africa* with a cheetah.

Below: AfriCat's Dave Houghton with a coalition of cheetahs.

Bottom: With Kate Humble and Gomez perching on a termite mound. Look a little closer and you'll see why we're both laughing so hysterically.

In Libya before the war and the fall of Gaddafi. I love working with camels, sometimes described as 'ships of the desert'. They're grumpy and cantankerous but very useful.

Above: With Prince William at the Predator Conservation Trust, working for TUSK in the Okavango Delta, Botswana.

Below: Assessing a bronze whaler shark, filming *Wild on the West Coast* in Namibia. Sharks can be rather scary, even though this one was just a pup.

Above: Saltwater crocodiles are a big problem in Australia's Northern Territory. One estimate is that there are 100,000 warning signs like this one. One per croc.

Below: The morning after my infamous confusion between turtles and crocs during my first crocodile encounter in Namibia's Caprivi Strip.

Top: Diving near Darwin, Australia, with a saltwater croc.

Above: On a blustery coastline in Arnhem Land, northern Australia, where we released Ludo the salty. He had a tracking beacon on his head that was covered in a white waterproof paste. I thought it made him look like a chef.

Left: A crocodile jumping from the Adelaide River. They propel themselves out of the water using their tails.

Above and left: On Carcass Island in the Falklands with one of the impressive bull elephant seals.

Below: Some of the elephant seal's Californian cousins near Monterey in the United States.

Above: A kiss from a sea lion at a marine facility in California.

Left: Kate Humble and me filming *Wild on the West Coast* for the BBC with Primo and Puka, the remarkable ex-navy dolphins.

Above: Just a small sample of the plastic, rope, fishing line and rubbish that I collected from the Indian Ocean while working with the Plastic Oceans Foundation.

Right: Diving into the ocean while working off the Sri Lankan coast for the project. The water may look beautifully clear, but hidden within it is a toxic mix of microscopic plastic particles creating a 'plastic soup'.

a spiritual site and its appeal as a major tourist destination. Aboriginal owners of the site have previously threatened to ban all tourist access to it in protest at the Australian government's interventions in indigenous community life. The World Heritage Site is also subject to a number of thefts, although it seems many thieves soon suffer a guilty conscience; the national park currently receives an average one fragment of the rock returned by post each day, along with apologies from visitors and tales of the illnesses, break-ups and other bad luck they have been cursed with since the theft.

The Northern Territory's capital, Darwin, is named after the pioneering biologist because HMS *Beagle*, the vessel used in the third British attempt to settle the coast, had previously carried Charles Darwin on his historic voyage to the Galapagos. Commander John Clements Wickham of the *Beagle* named the initial port settlement in honour of the naturalist, his former crewmate. Attempts were made in the early twentieth century to give the Northern Territory a more distinctive name, with 'Kingsland', 'Centralia' and 'Territoria' all possible contenders, but the original British appellation stuck. Due to its sparsely populated nature, the Northern Territory was also considered as a possible location for a new Jewish homeland during and after the Second World War.

Territorians, as the Northern Territory's residents are known, seem proud to celebrate their croc neighbours, as the town of Jabiru is home to the Gagudju Crocodile Inn, a 110-bedroom hotel in the shape of a gigantic crocodile. Guests enter through the massive jaws and can indulge themselves in the swimming-pool heart of the beast. In short, the Northern Territories is the saltwater crocodile capital of the world.

I flew to Darwin via Singapore and touched down early in the morning. Adam had described his home to me when we were in Botswana, but it's amazing how things can get lost in translation. He had talked about his house and his street and his neighbours, so I hadn't expected to find a rambling estate hidden in the jungle.

Adam was married and had several dogs and cats, but the real star of the family was Smaug. He had often spoken about Smaug, but nothing prepared me for my first encounter.

Over the years I have met dozens of people with unusual pets. I have seen people walking their ferrets in Hyde Park and there was the man who walked around Notting Hill with an iguana on his head. Of course there was Christian the lion who stalked up and down the King's Road, but when it comes to unusual pets, Smaug had to take the biscuit.

You won't be surprised to hear that Smaug was a saltwater crocodile. What I hadn't anticipated was just how big he was.

Adam led me through the thick foliage to what looked like a water plant. It was a little like the set from the series *Lost*. A tall wire fence had been erected with large yellow 'Danger' signs, and an electric fence had been rigged for added safety. We walked through the gate to what looked like an oversized garden pond. It was covered in lily pads and a couple of newts skittered across its surface, but there was no sign of Smaug.

'He's waiting to be fed,' explained Adam with a smile.

Next to the pond was another wire fence which had been submerged into the water to create an aquatic barrier; on the other side was a small hole in which a diver could be submerged in order to meet Smaug.

It all looked very creepy, like something from a low-budget sci-fi film. Hollywood designers couldn't have created a more realistic set for a mad professor who lives in the jungle with his crocodile.

Once again I found myself climbing into my dive gear in the unnatural surroundings of the Australian rainforest.

'Whatever you do, don't stick your fingers through the wire,' warned Adam as I slipped into the chilly water.

It was very murky and it took me some time to adjust my eyes. I could clearly make out the fence, but there was no sign of Smaug. I strained my eyes into the gloom and moved a little closer to the fence.

BAM!

I nearly jumped out of my skin. Smaug rocketed out of the murk and skirted along the side of the fence. The water pressure from his movement sent me flying backwards.

I regained my composure and returned to the fence, where Smaug had settled. He was *huge.* I had never seen a crocodile as large in all my life. I stared at his enormous teeth as he drifted up and down the fence, watching in astonishment as Adam threw him a whole chicken which he swallowed in one like a piece of popcorn.

It was a sobering reminder of the dangers of what we were about to attempt. No one had ever tried to dive with salt-water crocodiles, without doubt one of the most temperamental and aggressive of all the crocodile species. But if we were going to achieve our goal then we had to find somewhere with clear water in which to do it.

We had decided to keep our project a secret. With the Nile crocodiles in Botswana we had been able to glean important information about water temperature, hunting habitat and vision, and Adam was desperate to do the same with the salt-water crocs. But he felt sure his research would be closed down if the Australian authorities got a sense of what we were doing. The people of the Northern Territory were at war with the salty, as they call the crocodiles, and we were about to discover the full emotional force of that conflict.

Adam had flown in from Botswana a week earlier to begin a recce of the local rivers. He had already clocked up more than 2,000 kilometres in his pursuit of a clear river in which we could dive safely. Clarity was key; our lives would depend on it.

In the meantime, I went out with the Darwin Harbour patrol who lay traps for any crocs that come close to human habitation. Darwin Harbour authorities have a one-strike rule. If a croc strays into a populated area, then it is caught and sent to the croc farm, where it is turned into a belt. It may sound harsh, but the realities of a salty attacking a human in a populated area are even harsher.

To catch the crocs they use enormous traps not dissimilar to those used by rat-catchers. A huge metal cage is half submerged in the water with the use of floats. At one end, a large metal door is opened on a spring trap that is connected by means of a cable to a large hunk of decaying meat. Like a mousetrap with cheese, the crocodile smells the meat and when it enters the cage and grabs it the cable releases the spring and the door closes. They have been known to catch 5-metre crocs in these traps.

Of course the traps need to be checked once a day and I went out to check for any asbo crocs that had strayed into the wrong area. Even in the harbour, next to the million-dollar yachts, crocodile traps had been set – a reminder of the ever-present danger posed by salties.

The saltwater crocodile, one of Australia's two crocodile species, is the largest and one of the most dangerous types of crocodile in the world. Their average length is around 5 metres, but they can reach up to 7 metres and weigh up to 1,000kg. There are between 200,000 and 300,000 saltwater crocodiles worldwide, with the majority living on the northern coast of Australia.

Due to its third eyelid, the saltwater crocodile has impeccable underwater vision, giving it a distinct advantage when hunting its prey. Saltwater crocodiles are at the top of the food chain, and also have been known to attack humans, killing on average one or two people a year. In April 2007 a saltwater crocodile bit the forearm off a vet in a Taiwanese zoo; the limb was subsequently reattached successfully after seven hours of surgery. Occasionally they have also attacked other fearsome predators; for example, in August 2011 a Bengal tiger was eaten by a 5-metre saltwater croc.

The number of their victims may seem small compared to the many hundreds killed in Africa each year by Nile crocodiles, but there is no difference in the danger of the two; indeed, many crocodile experts like Adam will tell you the saltwater croc is the more ferocious. The danger doesn't come with the species but the environment. Here in Australia essentially the only human–croc conflict happens in recreational areas, so they have strict guidelines on where you can fish, paddle and bathe. The government has done everything it can to reduce the number of attacks. In resource-poor Africa, however, where man and croc are forced to share the same living and working space, the number of encounters, and hence of attacks, is far greater.

Despite their name, saltwater crocodiles spend only part of each year in the salt water of the sea. During the wet season, between March and November, the female crocodiles swim upstream to freshwater rivers and will lay between forty and sixty eggs on the riverbank. They guard their eggs for up to three months, making sure that they stay moist by splashing the nest with water. Perhaps one of the most interesting biological facts about the saltwater crocodile is that the temperature at which its eggs are incubated can control the sex of its offspring. If the eggs are kept below 30°C the young will all be female, while if they are kept above 32°C they will all be male. During the dry season some crocodiles will swim far out to sea, and indeed some have been found thousands of miles from their natural habitat.

Australians seem to have a love–hate relationship with their crocodiles. Some may argue that the crocodiles came first, but the general sentiment is that they are a pest. Indeed, there is a large movement campaigning for an outright cull.

Saltwater crocodiles have been responsible for twelve human deaths in Australia over the past two decades. During the 1970s the Northern Territory played host to one of Australia's most persistently ferocious predators, Sweetheart the Crocodile. This ironically named reptile dwelt in a billabong in the Finniss River and attacked at least fifteen boats, the motors and propellers taking the brunt of his attacks while the passengers narrowly escaped. Sweetheart was finally caught and put to rest by local authorities in 1979 and his body is now on display at the Darwin Museum. Reportedly, upon autopsy a bullet was found lodged in Sweetheart's spine, perhaps explaining his lust for vengeance against humankind. The story of Sweetheart has since been exaggerated and immortalized in the 2007 croc horror film *Rogue*.

A number of solo canoeists have had the surprise of their lives when bumping into innocuous-looking floating logs that turn out to be giant hungry crocodiles. Crocodiles have an indelicate approach to their prey: they shake their victims, tearing off their limbs until they are small enough to consume. These attacks have also resolved a number of missing people cases, such as that of a missing schoolgirl in 1933 whose body was eventually discovered in the belly of a crocodile.

'Sometimes we find crocs in the cages with no heads,' described one of the wardens rather morbidly. 'People come to the cages and kill them, then cut their heads off out of pure hatred.'

What would drive people to such a hideous act? To decapitate a wild creature?

While many Australians will complain about their native salties, there is no doubt that they have harnessed and exploited their reputation as one of the crocodile centres of the world. The Northern Territory is chock-a-block with crocodile-themed attractions. Crocodile cage-diving, crocodile parks, crocodile farms, crocodile safaris, and even a jumping crocodile boat trip.

Jumping crocodiles are a rather contentious attraction. With saltwater crocs, you're not even safe if you stay on dry land. They are capable of launching themselves the full length of their bodies out of the water in order to snatch prey from the banks of rivers. Hunting was made illegal in 1961 because by the late 1950s humans had decimated the crocodile population in northern Australia. Given the lack of crocodiles and the new laws, some of the old crocodile hunters began offering tourist cruises along the Adelaide River in 1985. These tour-guides would dangle pieces of meat from their boats and the wild crocodiles learnt to grab the food by jumping high out of the water. The sight of this has, over the last few decades, become a major tourist attraction. Of the jumping crocodiles of the Adelaide, the most famous is the 6-metre long Brutus, who lacks one of his front legs. In 2011 a photograph of him jumping from the water next to a boat full of tourists as he lunged for a piece of buffalo meat caused a sensation in the international press.

In much the same way that cage-diving has been blamed for undermining sharks' fear of man by associating us with food, some argue that encouraging crocodiles to come to boats for food and then to leap out of the water to grab it is merely creating a Darwinian Frankenstein's monster. Once again there seems to be a cruel irony and contradiction in our relationship with wildlife, and with predators in particular. It's a little like teasing a dog with food. Taunt her for long enough and even my lovely Labrador, Inca, will take my fingers off if I'm not careful. It's all about consistency and respect.

Adam was struggling to find clear water. The massive flooding that had affected most of Australia in the summer of 2010/11 had left the entire country with heavily silted water. According to locals, the only place where there was still clear water and crocodiles was a remote island to the far north of Australia called the Cobourg Peninsula, deep in the native Arnhem Land.

The Cobourg Peninsula, a piece of land jutting out of the north of Australia 220 miles east of Darwin, is today nearly completely uninhabited. But this has not always been the case: in 1837 the British government attempted to settle one of the peninsula's many inlets, Port Essington. The settlement lasted only eleven years, and it functioned not as a town but merely as a military outpost with a small population. Today it is just ruins. A second important building project on the peninsula was the 28-metre-high Cape Don Lighthouse, which was built between 1915 and 1917. It continues to work to this day, but is again unpopulated, as it became electrified and unmanned in 1983.

The whole of the peninsula now forms part of the Garig Gunak Barlu National Park. It is surprisingly varied in its terrain, ranging from mangroves, to rainforests, to sandy beaches, to grassy fields. But today's tourism trade values the peninsula mainly for its fishing sites, both lagoons and coral reefs. An extraordinary range of fish lives in the area, and it is also home to marine mammals such as dolphins and dugongs. But perhaps the most interesting wildlife on the peninsula are the banteng. These are a breed of wild cattle which were first introduced by the British through the base at Port Essington in 1849. Today, whilst being considered endangered in the wild, the largest population of banteng exists on the peninsula, numbering approximately ten thousand.

The prospect of the Cobourg Peninsula presented us with a number of problems: first and foremost, getting permission from the aboriginal landowners; and second, how to get ourselves and all our heavy equipment there. To attempt our dive we would need Adam's research boat with all of our dive equipment on board, but Cobourg was a long, long way away from Darwin.

That wasn't all. Cobourg was also famed for being in one of the most dangerous bodies of water in the world, not for its storms, waves or even rip currents, but because, according to locals, 'there were more poisonous creatures in that water per cubic metre than anywhere else on earth'.

If the crocodiles didn't have us, then the sharks would; and if the sharks didn't have us, then the sea snakes would; and if they didn't have us, then the stone fish would, or the Portuguese Man-of-War jellyfish, or the fingernail-sized irukandji jellyfish that can kill instantly, or perhaps the cone shells that would kill with a single barb; and if that wasn't enough then you might be as unlucky as the late Steve Irwin and die by the barb of a ray.

It was a huge gamble, but Adam's wife Erin agreed to drive the boat the long journey up while we took a small Cessna to begin the recce.

We landed at a remote sandy airstrip from which we were ferried to the hotel by open-topped Land Rovers of the kind you'd normally find in Africa. The vast herds of water buffalo and camels only added to my confusion of where in the world I was.

The original hotel had been destroyed by a hurricane and had spent several years falling into disrepair. It hadn't taken long for the rainforest to encroach and soon it was like a Mayan ruin, until some Darwinian entrepreneurs decided to intervene and re-open it as a luxury hotel. Built on the Timor Sea, it has everything you need from a luxury resort with its white sandy beaches and warm turquoise waters, except that you couldn't go anywhere near the water or the beach because of the danger of sharks and crocodiles. Quite a combination, I think you'll agree.

One of the guides told us that crocodiles had been seen in an area a few hours down the coast where a tidal estuary pumps clean water through the mangrove swamps. He had seen plenty of crocodiles basking on the beaches and it had clear water.

We set out in Adam's flat-bottomed boat, which wasn't really made for open-water journeys. The bilge didn't work and it floated dangerously close to the water with us all on board. But we set out anyway.

For several hours we motored along the beautiful coast-line, passing sunfish and sea turtles, pods of dolphins and leaping sail fish. In fact, I don't think I had ever seen so much marine life in one place.

Soon we reached the large bay from which we would start our search. The coral had infiltrated the entire swamp, which meant there were deep-water channels with coral surrounded by mangrove trees. If we were going to succeed anywhere, this was our best hope.

Before we entered the bay and came across any crocodiles, however, we wanted to test our dive gear in a controlled environment. If diving in Botswana had been a worry, this was a whole new ball game. It was like going to war. Despite the warm water, I had to wear a full wetsuit to protect me against the potentially fatal stings of the Box jellyfish and the tiny irukandji; someone had been killed the day we arrived by a single sting. I had to wear toughened booties to protect against any stone fish and thick work gloves for the cone shells.

And then there were the sharks. They were everywhere. We had seen them circling our boat as we were loading it up at the pontoon by the hotel. To protect me I wore a shark repeller. As ridiculous as this sounds, they are becoming quite common among surfers and divers. They consist of a small bracelet worn around the ankle which drags a short stretch of line. The device emits a short, sharp electric field that sends out a shock to any approaching shark. The shock is pretty minimal, but apparently it is enough to put them off.

And last but by no means least there was the croc stick. Adam had had them made up by the local blacksmith but he hadn't explained what they were in case the blacksmith told the authorities.

Like some commando, I stepped off the side of the boat and into the Timor Sea. It felt good to be back in the water, but I was horrified by the poor visibility. We were still in the open water but the plankton and sediment meant it was hard to see my hand in front of my face. It was a reality check.

Safety dive over, we began to enter the bay. Tiger sharks circled our tiny boat and I watched as the silhouette of a giant bull shark swam past.

'Crocodile!' hollered Adam.

I couldn't see anything but turquoise water. It was still only early morning but already it was mind-bakingly hot. Sweat dripped from my brow into my eyes. The mixture of insect repellent and salt stung at my eyes.

'Do you see its snout?' he asked.

I could see what looked like a stick.

'I reckon it's a four-metre, maybe five, judging by the distance between its snout and eyes,' Adam went on.

It was astonishing to see a crocodile out at sea like this. Researchers have found them travelling hundreds of miles in search of food or a mate, but nothing prepares you for the bizarre sight of a crocodile at sea, and this one was a whopper.

Jumpy and elusive, it disappeared before we could get any nearer, but not before we watched its mighty silhouette vanish under our boat.

We carried on into the mangrove swamp. It was a very strange place. The beaches were covered in the now familiar 'slide marks' of crocs. Sharks darted beneath the boat as we motored deeper into the seawater swamp. The water was crystal clear and we saw every kind of fish imaginable. It was like our very own aquarium, the water smooth enough to act as a window into this aquatic world.

It was hard to tell the depth, but Adam estimated it to be

a couple of metres. We would have to wait for high tide to get a better chance to dive.

The sun beat down on us, frying our heads and melting our brains. It felt like stepping into a Dali painting, a surreal world unlike anything I have seen before. I have never been anywhere that felt quite so remote. Perhaps it had something to do with the fact that it was native land and no one permanently lived there, but I felt like an early explorer. It seemed like a genuine expedition into the unknown, and it was exciting.

We spent hours wending our way through the meandering swamp, but there were no more crocodile sightings. By now it was high tide and Adam decided that it was our last chance to dive. It would be nightfall soon and we had a long open-water journey back in a distinctly unseaworthy vessel.

It was pretty dangerous. We knew the area was infested with sharks and we had seen plenty of slide marks. Adam slipped into the water with a local dive buddy called Che. Che had seen it all. He was the son of a diver master and they had both just returned from the set of the *Life of Pi* where they had been filming dive sequences with real live tigers. Che wasn't scared of anything, although he looked a little worried.

They strode into the clear water and began to explore the coral below. With the high tide, sediment had been filtered through the isthmus and clouded the water. The poor visibility made it too dangerous, so they returned to the boat.

We spent several days working our way up and down the coast, seeing plenty of crocodiles but never getting the chance to swim with them. In the end we flew back to Darwin with our spirits slightly dampened, but still determined to have our salty diving experience.

Shortly after we left we heard some astonishing news from the Cobourg lodge. A water buffalo had been taken by a large crocodile close to the small airstrip and dragged into the water, where it had then been joined by another croc and a shark. A fight had ensued between the two mighty predators. We never found out who won, but I'd like to hedge my bets on the 200-million-year-old crocodile.

If there is one film that marks my childhood, it is *Crocodile Dundee*. I don't know what it was about Australian culture, but as children my generation were obsessed with it. *Neighbours* and *Home and Away* were both 'must watch' programmes. Our boarding-school timetable worked around the broadcast of both. *Crocodile Dundee* propelled Paul Hogan to stardom and taught my generation all sorts of previously unknown words, like 'G'day', but it also did for crocodiles what *Jaws* had done for sharks.

One of the most iconic settings from the Australian part of the film was in the Kakadu National Park. It was here that not long ago a young German tourist had been taken by a crocodile while skinny-dipping and, shortly before I arrived, a fisherman had narrowly avoided being dragged from his boat while he dozed. So Kakadu was on the front line of human–crocodile conflict and Adam took me there to learn more about the divisiveness of the crocodile issue.

Kakadu is a popular tourist destination that plays on its crocodile heritage, but it is also a very popular destination for fishermen who use the tidal fords as fishing grounds. We travelled to one of the most popular, where the road passes directly through the river. At low tide, there is just a small trickle across the tarmac and into the deeper channel beyond, but at high tide, as the water rushes up from the ocean, it floods the road. With this tidal surge come all sorts of fish, swept upstream from the open water, and with this fish feast comes a crocodile feeding frenzy. What astonished me most was not the number of crocodiles that suddenly appeared on cue, but the number of fishermen who continued to fish, often calf- or waist-deep in the water.

It was here that several years ago another man was taken by a crocodile in front of a horrified crowd of onlookers. The tide had turned, but he thought he could make it if he ran. He began to wade through the water up to his neck. The onlookers watched helplessly as a crocodile slipped into the water and disappeared beneath the surface, their warning cries drowned out by the noise of the water. The croc surfaced just next to the helpless man and launched itself at him, grabbing him between its jaws. Somehow he was able to get away, but not in time to avoid being swept downstream, where he grabbed a tree and climbed from the water. But the tree snapped, sending him back into the jaws of the waiting croc. His body was later recovered decapitated.

One of the first on the scene had been Paul, my aboriginal guide, who was also a park warden. He had been horrified by the discovery and it had deeply affected him. As an aborigine he had been taught to love and respect the crocodile, but he found it hard to forgive. Over the years he became the mediator between the opposing views in the croc–fishermen conflict and set upon his own way of reducing the number of incidents.

His theory was simple. The high density of visitors to the park had meant that crocodiles had lost their inhibitions and their fear of man. The regular sight of wading Aussies had merely acted as a magnet rather than a repellent. Somehow, Paul needed to reverse it and de-evolve the crocodiles' habit. He had to make them fearful of humans and that was how he started his 'hazing' programme.

If this sounds like something boys do to one another at boarding school, then I am glad it didn't happen to me, because quite frankly it isn't very pleasant.

Paul invited me out one night with three fellow rangers for some 'hazing'. Using a powerful lamp, we cruised up and down the river looking for the white reflection of crocodile eyes. They give a very distinct glow and, with experience, it is possible to estimate the size of a crocodile from the width between the eyes, as I had seen Adam do.

Once we had settled on a croc, my job was to hold the lamp as still as possible, angling it down towards the creature as we approached. As we got closer to the crocodile, the lamp turned from 'finder' to 'blinder'. The croc stayed frozen to the spot, like a rabbit in the headlights, because most crucially it couldn't see us coming.

Meanwhile Paul stood at the front of the boat with a barbed spear. As the croc loomed into view, he launched the spear into its back. The barbs pierced the skin and the hook was released, attaching the croc to the boat with a long nylon rope. There then ensued a mighty battle between 'protector' and 'protectee'. The crocodile was eventually bound and its mouth taped closed with gaffer tape (borrowed from our rather surprised soundman, Callum) and then blindfolded.

It sounds pretty barbaric, but then that is the point. Paul's theory is to re-associate man with pain and danger rather than drunkenness and prey. He explained that the barb feels like little more than a needle to a crocodile's thick skin, but it didn't make it any less disturbing to watch. Once aboard, the croc was weighed, measured and marked for future identification.

The final test was to sex the croc, which involves placing a finger up its anus. Paul volunteered me for this cheery task, which to date remains one of the most absurd things I have had to do. It was a male.

Finally, it was time to release it. It was too dangerous to do that from the boat, so we carried the still bound croc ashore on to the boat ramp and untied it, standing back while Paul untied its mouth and removed the blindfold. At this point the crocodile went absolutely mad. I don't blame it, and I suppose really that was the point. It growled like a dinosaur and hissed as it reared its head. In all my time working with crocodiles I had never seen one quite so angry. And all that anger seemed to be directed, rightly or wrongly, at Paul.

I had heard that a crocodile is capable of running as fast as a human, but until now I had never believed it. Trust me, they can and do.

Like hysterical schoolgirls we ran from side to side while the angry croc vented its fury. A local police car had come to see why we were making such a racket; it only added to the surreal quality of the night to have a flashing blue light illuminating the chase. Eventually Paul managed to entice the beast on to the jetty. The croc made one final lunge, missed and fell back into the river.

'I think it worked,' said Paul.

Once again it was a reminder that sometimes you have to be cruel to be kind. Paul and his team target specific problem crocs that have been loitering around the pontoon or bothering fishermen. It was a sobering reminder of the conflict to pass so many fishing boats laden with drunken Aussies. The potential for disaster was all too clear and it was Paul's job to protect both people and crocodiles.

We spent several days exploring Kakadu, but shortly before we were due to leave we got a call from Paul. He told us to meet him at an agreed point along the highway. When we pulled alongside his pick-up truck, before I could even say hello, my senses were overcome by a toxic, stomach-turning stench. It was foul. It smelled like decaying meat, which is what it was.

In the back of his truck was the most enormous crocodile head I had ever seen.

'Terrible, isn't it?' lamented Paul. He explained that this was one of the biggest crocodiles from the area. He had been nearly 6 metres long and he'd been murdered.

'His owner is furious,' he added.

Murdered? Owner? This was not the vocab normally used when referring to a saltwater crocodile.

The crocodile had been shot between the eyes. 'A single bullet,' explained Paul. 'They knew exactly where to point the gun. He was assassinated.'

Paul had heard reports of the murdered croc and had

gone down to remove it for evidence. Weighing several tons, it was simply too heavy to move, so he and his brother cut off the head, which weighed 200kg alone, and took it away to try to find the bullet.

It was a shocking sight. I can still see it. He was a majestic crocodile. What senseless individual would do such a thing? It wasn't sport. It wasn't hunting. This was, as Paul had described it, murder.

I was still perplexed as to how a wild 6-metre crocodile could have an owner, but Paul explained that for her entire life his aunt had gone down to the water where this crocodile lived and talked to him. To all intents and purposes, he was hers. And now she was distraught.

Paul arranged for us to meet his aunt, known to everyone as Aunty.

'How could someone do that to such a magnificent creature?' she asked. 'Why would they do such a thing?' She broke down in tears. It was raw grief, the likes of which I had seen only when people lost their dogs, not their crocodiles. I was amazed that her feelings for a wild creature could run so deep.

She told me how she would sing to it and dream about it.

'What was his name?' I asked.

'He didn't have a name, he didn't need a name. He was a wild crocodile. The biggest crocodile in all the land.' She broke down again. 'It is no different to them killing my brother or my son,' she wept. 'He was my family.'

In the meantime, the Darwin Port authorities had trapped a 3-metre crocodile in the harbour. They had removed it from the trap and sent it to Adam's holding pen for the weekend until they could relocate it to the crocodile farms for its belty fate.

'I've had an idea,' said Adam. 'If we can't dive with the crocodiles, we could always find a crocodile to dive with us.'

He explained that he knew of a deep, clear water hole, or billabong, where crocs had often been found. If we took the captured crocodile into the billabong with us, then we could dive with it. It wasn't perfect, but it was as close as we were going to get to fulfilling our dream.

So the crocodile was transported to the billabong and a small muzzle of fishing line was wrapped around its mouth before it was released into the water. The combined agitation of being caught in a trap and then transported and man-handled into the water had made it understandably angry, and it didn't seem like a good time to lose a limb.

We all put on our diving gear and descended into the clear saline water. It was beautiful, full of fish and submerged trees, and there was our saltwater crocodile. To be honest, it never felt like a real encounter because it was an artificial situation. It's amazing how something as simple as a thin twist of fishing line can boost your confidence.

If only I had known then what we found out later – that the line had broken.

We spent several hours following the young crocodile around the billabong until it was time to leave.

'How on earth are we going to get it out of here?' I asked, genuinely puzzled. How do you catch a crocodile?

Adam revealed what looked like a shepherd's crook with a circle of rope at the top. He would dive down to the crocodile and loop it over its head while we held on to the end of the line from the shore and hauled it in. Sounds simple? Hmmmm.

He descended under water and returned several minutes later.

'He just opened his mouth,' he said matter-of-factly.

'But what about the fishing line?' I asked, a little puzzled.

'It was broken.'

Whoa! So we had dived with a fully operating saltwater crocodile after all. I'm not sure I would have crept so close had I known.

Whatever the case, we now had a situation where we had to capture the croc before the authorities found us. Fishing line or no fishing line, it didn't change Adam's mode of capture and he returned with his shepherd's crook as if he were after a sheep rather than a creature fully capable of killing him.

Thirty minutes later and we were hauling on the line of a very, very angry crocodile. I was astonished at its strength as it performed the death roll, which is great for the croc if it has an animal in its mouth but not so great when it is attached to a rope. The death roll simply coiled the rope around its body like cotton on a spool, delivering it to us like a pre-packaged sausage roll ready to be taken off to the croc farm.

The croc farm? Such an awful place. I had visited one in Botswana and another here in Australia. Dreadful places that house crocodiles like battery hens. Tens of thousands of them share greenhouses full of water until they have grown large enough for their skin to be harvested.

Now I am all for farms if they stop people hunting wild

crocs for their skins, but the industrial scale left an uneasy taste in my mouth. This croc had helped with our study. He had become an unwitting protagonist in our pioneering science. I couldn't allow him to become a shoe or a bag. Surely he was worth more than that?

'I have an idea.' I looked at Adam.

'Hello, is that Aunty?' I said down the phone. 'How'd you like a new crocodile?'

And with that his fate was sealed. We carefully blindfolded him and placed him into the boot of the car before beginning the long journey back to Kakadu National Park.

But our crocodile hadn't finished helping us with our studies. Adam had been itching to tag one and follow its navigation. Some people believe that crocodiles are like homing pigeons, always going back to where they were first captured; it is one of the reasons that the Harbour authorities never translocate and release a captured croc. Adam had a theory that if the crocodile had a magnet on its head during its translocation, that would destabilize and confuse its natural compass and prevent it from returning to human habitation.

With that in mind, he strapped an enormous magnet on its head for the journey back to Kakadu, where Aunty had agreed to allow us to release him out to sea in a remote corner of the park. As a native landowner, Aunty had the final say, even if the authorities weren't so sure.

We met Aunty and her family at the river crossing that marks the boundary between the national park and Arnhem Land and began the bumpy journey across country to the shore. Several hours later, shortly before dusk, we arrived at the windswept beach where Adam set about fitting the tracking device. In true Caractacus Potts fashion, he had converted a rudimentary tracking device into a sub-aquatic croc beacon capable of working for up to a year.

Strapping a tracking beacon to a croc is no easy task and the result was a little crude. Although it did make him look like he was wearing a chef's hat. It was actually quite funny. Adam reassured me that it wouldn't affect his swimming. After all, anything was better than the farm.

'Can I name him?' I asked Aunty, unsure of what she would say.

'Sure,' she smiled.

'I shall call him Ludo, after my son.'

'Great name – my best friend is called Ludo. Now there will be two of them living in Arnhem Land,' replied Paul.

I took a marker pen and scrawled the name on to Ludo's chef's hat. It made me smile. My son Ludo had become captivated by crocodiles after I gave him his lucky tooth and now he had a crocodile named after him.

The sun was beginning to dip as we carried Ludo down to the water and began to unbind him. We removed the ties and I sat on his back until all that remained was some gaffer tape on his snout and the blindfold . . . and his chef's hat. Adam collected his shepherd's crook and put the noose tightly around Ludo's mouth before removing the tape and then the blindfold.

We all stood back as he loosed the noose.

Ludo lifted his head. He could smell the salty air and taste freedom. He looked around at all of us as if to say thank you and then slowly made his way down the beach towards the ocean.

The sun had turned the beach orange. Slowly we followed Ludo towards the water as he swam through the crashing waves. I could just make out the white of his little chef's hat as he disappeared out to sea.

I looked around at Aunty and Adam. They both had a tear in their eye. It was a deeply moving moment. Who'd have thought that crocodiles had the power to elicit such emotions? I felt deeply humbled to have been part of such an incredible journey.

Never judge a book by its cover. What Ludo and his friends had taught me was that the more you understand about nature, the more it will give back to you.

Every creature has its place on this planet and sometimes we need a little reminder to make us respect it, whatever its reputation.

14

Elephant Slugs

Australia provides an environment for its wildlife unlike anywhere else in the world, but if you head further south still, you'll reach another remote corner of the world with an ecosystem even more unique. The Falkland Islands are not normally highlighted for their wildlife; it is often overshadowed by the region's geopolitics. War and oil tend to be mentioned more than penguins and orcas, but in fact the islands are a naturalist's playground. Rich in flora and fauna, the Falklands were my first insight into the nature of the Southern Ocean.

The Falkland Islands comprise two main islands and seven hundred smaller ones. It is a beautiful archipelago, but at 51 degrees south it is battered by strong winds and gales. A little like their Hebridean cousins, the islands have endless deserted white sandy beaches and a hardy people who work the land.

During my first visit in 2001, a number of scientists had been sent out after worrying reports of 'falling' penguins. Several helicopter pilots had reported that penguins had become so mesmerized by their helicopters that they had fallen over backwards and been unable to get up. The story had been picked up by the world's press, who were enchanted and horrified by the story. Scientists had been dispatched to investigate this potential environmental problem (and pick up any floundering penguins) and soon reported back that the phenomenon had been limited and infrequent, and that low-flying helicopters and jets posed no great problems to the penguin rookeries.

I have always loved penguins. A little like puppies and seals, they have a cuteness that makes you want to scoop them up and hug them. They are also tremendous fun – they have great comedic value with their distinctive little waddle. *March of the Penguins* and *Pingu* have cemented them in our psyches as lovable creatures, and they endear themselves further to us by the fact that they take mates for life. I'm sure that somewhere there is a psychologist who has studied why we humans are attracted to them.

For me the greatest penguin tale of all is that of Bruno Zehnder, an adventurous Swiss photographer best known for his striking images of penguins. In 1997 he was spending the southern hemisphere winter at Mirny Station on the Antarctic coast south of the Indian Ocean in cooperation with the Russian Antarctic Research Agency. His primary goal was to study and photograph the breeding activities of emperor penguins, the only Antarctic creatures that breed on open sea ice in the continuous darkness and at winter temperatures of minus 56°C. It was the last days of summer in Antarctica and he had been warned that he had just a few days to get out of his remote posting before the winter weather set in. Zehnder, however, who adored penguins so much that he had changed his name by deed poll to Pinguin, had lovingly spent the best part of the year with the emperors and he wanted to complete the cycle. He insisted that he remain until the bitter end. Unfortunately, winter came thick and fast and he missed the window to leave. Suddenly he was faced with a full polar winter with few supplies and just a tent. When a search party finally arrived four months later, they found his icy remains in his tent. A little like Scott and his men, he had perished in his sleeping bag, having succumbed to the ferocious weather of Antarctica.

His body was recovered and, in accordance with his will, he was buried in Antarctica. The Russian Mirny crew gathered for his funeral on the tiny Buromsky Island, where those who die at or near the base are buried. The ground was too frozen for burial so Zehnder's coffin was left atop a boulder and surrounded by rocks. Suddenly, so the story goes, from nowhere, thirty penguins arrived and joined the congregation. Penguins had not been living on Buromsky. The birds stood in silence, their heads bowed, as the world's greatest penguin-lover was laid to rest.

I love that story. Whether you believe it or not, I love the sentiments of loyalty on both sides, between man and penguin and penguin and man. The thing is, I want to believe it.

I have been lucky enough to see penguins all around the world – the Galapagos, South Africa, Antarctica and Chile –

and I never tire of them. The more I understand them, the more obsessed I find myself. In fact, when my son was born I went on a strong campaign to persuade my wife to call him Penguin, or Pen for short. I thought, and still think, it would be a wonderful name. Unfortunately – or fortunately, depending on what you think of the suggestion – Marina thought it was ridiculous and vetoed it outright.

One of the best days I have ever had with my son Ludo so far was the day I was finally able to take him to meet penguins. His godmother, Kate Humble, had arranged for us to go and feed the penguins at London Zoo.

It was a chilly November day as we walked into the out-side enclosure and on to their sandy beach. A little rockhopper penguin called Ricky waddled up to Ludo, who stared in amazement.

I say amazement, but I sometimes wonder whether amazement is something reserved for adults. Amazement requires reference and comparison that a two-and-a-half-year-old simply doesn't have. Introduce a toddler to an alien and he will probably smile and want to give it a hug. Do the same to an adult and they'll either run screaming or take a photo and sell it to the newspapers.

Ludo stared in wonder at this little penguin. I could hear a squeal of delight as he looked at Ricky's feathered crown. He bent down to get a closer look at the little creature, who stared back at him. It really was a fantastic sight. It makes me quite emotional just thinking about it, because here were two things about which I care deeply. I don't want to over-sentimentalize it, but I felt sure there was a connection between the two of them. I have never known Ludo be so quiet or focused for such a long period of time, but he was transfixed, as was Ricky.

I hope that Ludo will have the same fascination and passion for nature as I do and that that first meeting between him and Ricky the penguin was a seminal moment in his young life. He may never remember it, but I hope that deep in his subconscious it has done something that will leave a lasting impression.

At the time of my first visit to the Falklands, the news was not of Argentina's ongoing claim to the islands but that of a murderer terrorizing Port Stanley, the capital. The locals were divided between those who wanted to pursue him and those who wanted to leave matters to nature. The murderer was, of course, not some crazed local, but a bloodthirsty sea lion that was preying on unsuspecting penguins down at Gypsy Cove, a popular beauty spot. According to the *Penguin News*, the Falklands weekly newspaper, the sea lion had been waiting for locals and tourists to gather before sneaking up on sunbathing magellanic penguins and decapitating them, then horrifying the assembled crowd by playing catch with the headless body for hours on end before tossing it back into the surf.

It was an interesting debate and one I would experience many more times over the ensuing years: when is it right to intervene? Are we supposed to interfere with nature? It is a huge ethical question and it divides people firmly between those who think nature should be left to its own devices and those who feel the responsible thing to do is to exercise our power to intervene.

I have found myself in plenty of situations where I have had the power to alter nature's cycle. A quick warning call or a loud noise could have done it, but I have never interfered, even though I have found myself desperate to do so. The reality is that nature is harsh and can seem cruel. It is a dirty, bloody business and sometimes emotions and sentimentality can overwhelm sensible decision-making.

The sea lion was undoubtedly causing distress to those onshore, but was it right to remove him from Gypsy Cove?

In many parts of the globe they have strict animal enforcement laws that aim to prevent such a conflict between wild animals and humans. In northern Canada and Alaska they have polar bear teams whose job description involves relocating any bears that have strayed too close to human habitation; the same goes for saltwater crocodiles in Australia. The difference here, of course, is that these are two predators that pose a very real danger to humans. Here in Gypsy Cove, the sea lion was merely causing distress by needlessly killing off Pingu.

In the end the sea lion continued its killing spree for several weeks until a passing orca picked it off. That's the cycle of life.

In the Falklands I spent hours sitting in the middle of penguin rookeries, watching as hundreds of the birds bustled to and fro. I found it incredibly cathartic to be amidst this great natural wonder, but there was another encounter that completely blew me away. The Falklands are also home to what is arguably one of the strangest creatures in the world: the elephant seal. I had heard wild tales of these enormous creatures but had never seen one for myself.

Carcass Island, in West Falkland, is a wild, weathered, remote island on which there is just one house, owned by Rob and Lorraine McGill. With his ruddy, weather-hardened features, Rob met me at the tiny airstrip in his ancient Land Rover. Its door was held closed with some twine.

Their little settlement was green and lush, giving it the feeling of a small English farm estate. The house, Valley Cottage, was built in 1870. A green Aga heated the kitchen while Rob's VHF radio crackled in the background. VHF radio is the main lifeline of the Falkland Islands. It doubled as a telephone and radio, supplying information to the furthest corners of the archipelago.

Perhaps the biggest surprise in Rob's small farmhouse kitchen was the neatly stacked pile of five hundred mugs.

'Take a look in the larder,' he invited.

It was like peering into a French patisserie, with every type of cake, gateau and pastry imaginable. Scones, Danish pastries, flapjacks . . . Rob explained that his small house had become a big hit with passing cruise ships, which regularly stopped by, disgorging their entire complement of passengers to have tea and cake with Rob.

Rob had lived on Carcass Island for thirty years and had become largely self-sufficient. During the war in 1982 he had stuck it out on the remote island, cut off from the rest of the world and removed from the heavy fighting. He recounted one story of how, several weeks into the war with Argentina, he had been sitting at his little kitchen table when he heard a knock at the door. Not particularly unusual if you live in London, but here Rob was miles from anywhere on a bleak, windswept island. He cautiously opened the door to discover several men dressed from head to toe in full scuba-diving gear with their faces painted black.

'I don't suppose you have a bed for the night?' they asked in familiar English accents. They were soldiers from the Special Boat Squadron.

After the war, the SBS sent Rob a plaque thanking him for his war effort. It stood in prime position next to the mountain of cups.

Carcass Island must be one of the best places in the world to see wildlife. Its shoreline is teeming with gentoo and magellanic penguins and with seals, and I wasn't the only person visiting. A team of Italian scientists had been living on the island for several weeks as part of a study project involving the vocals of elephant seals. I set off to find out more about their project and to see for myself these extra-ordinary creatures.

Elephant seals must be one of the strangest-looking animals on earth and nothing prepared me for my first encounter. They look more ludicrous than they do menacing. Mate an elephant with a slug and you get an idea of what these creatures look like. They get their name from their trunk-like proboscis, which is inflatable. They are also huge, weighing up to 5 tons. They look like giant beached whales as they sunbathe on the shore.

Just behind the beach was an area of dunes protected by tall grasses. As with everything in the Falklands, it all looked a little oversized and weathered. As I wandered gingerly through high marron grass, twice as tall as me, I could smell the elephant seals before I could see them.

A number of smaller females were lying on the beach, but I was in search of the daddy, the bull elephant seal that ruled this beach. I could hear him sniffing and snorting somewhere in the dunes. Carefully I picked my way between the tall tufts of grass.

When elephant seals lift their heads they can be upwards of 12 feet tall, and as I rounded the grass I suddenly caught a glimpse of an enormous dark eye looking down at me. It was terrifying and mesmerizing at the same time. I could just make out the shape of a huge head before the animal came crashing out of the grass with a loud roar. I was overpowered by a rotting smell of fish as the bull elephant seal opened its vast pink mouth and bellowed from deep within its belly.

They can look pretty intimidating and aggressive as they rear up, but they are actually quite lazy and, a little like a balloon that has lost its air, they seem to deflate as they collapse to the ground like a tired slug in a wheezing splatter of blubber and fat.

I soon found the two Italian scientists, Mario and Luca, who were studying the cries of these huge beasts. They were recording the phonetics for analysis, which involved holding tiny microphones on long sticks as close to the creatures as possible. It was one of the funniest sights I have seen to date as the two scientists crept up behind an unsuspecting elephant seal. Slowly they would work their way along its side, making sure that they didn't startle it, then when they had the microphone sufficiently close to the mouth one of them would make a sound or movement to get the animal's attention. The mighty beast would lift its head, then rear up and 'holler' at the microphone. I could practically watch the hair on the scientists' heads blowing in the roar. They told me that they sometimes had to remove bits of fishy residue that had been blown on to them.

The South Atlantic is often considered a bleak, lifeless place, but what I have discovered in the Falklands and on subsequent visits to Antarctica is that it is in fact a rich, vibrant environment, teeming with life, a magnificent testament to the adaptability and durability of nature.

15

Man vs Wild

During my encounters with marine life in California, with crocodiles in Botswana and Australia, and with the unique creatures of the Falkland Islands, I had seen at first hand the ways in which man is affecting the environment are in turn affecting wildlife. But there was another important example of the human–environmental debate which, for me, would bring a whole new perspective to an already emotive subject.

Halfway between Africa and Indonesia lie the British Indian Ocean Territories (BIOT), a small island chain also known as the Chagos Islands. They are still a British protectorate, described by the Foreign Office as an Overseas Dependency; however, they have a terrible history that ends in Crawley, West Sussex, and it is my ten-year campaign for this little-known cause that has brought me some of my deepest soul-searching in the world of conservation.

Crawley holds a sad, dark secret. Hidden within its terraced streets lies a story that has embarrassed the British government – a story of deceit and tragedy that has been described by some as the darkest day of British overseas policy and has landed the UK government in court. It has transfixed me for over a decade and shaken my very principles on conservation, ecology and the environment movement. It is a story of deceit that has left thousands of 'British refugees' living in misery for the last forty years, exiled from their island home by a conniving and unrepentant government.

The British Indian Ocean Territories are an island chain consisting of fifty islands spread out hundreds of miles along the Chagos atoll. They were dependencies of Mauritius, which was part of the British Empire until 1964, when independence was granted on the understanding that the Chagos Islands would be excluded from the deal as they were deemed of 'significant' geographical interest to Britain. Thus a new overseas territory was born.

But in 1964 a secret British–American conference was held in London. The US needed a mid-Indian Ocean military base for access to the Middle East and Africa. In the chilling words of official jargon, the islands were 'closed' in a secret agreement between the British and US governments. In an exchange of letters never shown to either parliament or senate, a 'defence' agreement was signed, leasing the Chagos to the US for fifty years, with the option of an extra twenty-year extension. The deal was struck on the understanding that the entire island chain was 'fully sanitized' and 'cleansed' of life, and the islands were handed over in exchange for a discount on the US-manufactured Polaris nuclear submarine. Humans for arms?

There was one problem: the British had overlooked the existence of the native population of Chagossian people. The descendants of slaves, the population of about a thousand had lived on the islands since 1793, working the copra (coconut) plantation. As members of an overseas territory, they were British nationals.

In the summer of 1971 a group of officials arrived in the islands from Whitehall with an eviction order and informed the islanders that they were now illegal squatters. The 'British' islanders were deported to Mauritius and the Seychelles; some people say that they believed that they would be gassed if they refused. One man, Christian Simon, drowned himself as their boat, the MV *Nordvaer*, left their island home for ever. Old people, working men and women, and little children were dumped on the quaysides in Mauritius and in the Seychelles Islands. In Mauritius they were sent to a derelict housing estate where they made little shelters for themselves in the stables and pigsties; in the Seychelles they were housed in the prison. It was a nightmare, but it was only the beginning.

Soon they learned that they would never get home again. Families had been forcibly split between islands in the hasty removal and their British citizenship revoked. The governments of Mauritius and the Seychelles were paid off for these 'refugees' and the people themselves were offered money – £325 per person – as compensation for their home, their livelihood, their history and their plans for the future. The Organization of African Unity demanded their restoration.

Before the islands could be handed over to the Americans, the British Army had one last task to complete. They rounded up the eight hundred pet dogs that had been left on the island and gassed them in a temporary 'gas chamber'. 'I first made the building secure, and then introduced into it pipes attached to the exhaust pipes of US vehicles,' admitted Mr Moulinie, the former UK-appointed official who had been ordered by BIOT commissioner Sir Bruce Greatbatch to complete the 'cleansing'.

I think you can tell a great deal about someone by how they treat dogs! The islanders had been removed, their dogs gassed and the transformation of the largest island, Diego Garcia, could begin.

I have been involved with the plight of the Chagos islanders since 2002, when I was writing my book *The Teatime Islands* about Britain's overseas territories and became one of a handful of people to visit illegally some of the islands within the atoll. It was eerie walking through the ghost towns. They were frozen in time. Vegetation had smothered many of the buildings and choked the stones in the graveyard. Sunlight still streaked through the stained-glass windows of the church and the small copra factory remained largely intact. I was horrified to find dozens of international 'travellers' living among the ruins while the islanders themselves remained pariahs, exiled by their own government.

For years the islanders fought for their right to go home and in 2000 they went to the High Court and won. They celebrated their victory and prepared to return. The government, advised by Foreign Secretary Robin Cook, ruled that the Chagos people could be rehomed on the outer islands of the archipelago and their British passports were given back. Four hundred and fifty exiled islanders flew to the UK, settling in Crawley, the nearest town to Gatwick airport, in anticipation of their return home. But nothing happened, and then on Cook's death in 2005 Jack Straw reneged on his predecessor's promise and took the matter to an Order in Council and got the decision he wanted: that the Chagos people could not go home. The case is currently waiting to be heard in the European Court of Human Rights and should come up in 2013.

In late 2011 I went to a cultural day held in Crawley library. Hundreds of Chagossians attended with photos, paintings, diaries and food that represented their dying culture. 'I have one dying wish,' whispered an elderly lady, still traumatized by her enforced exile, 'to set foot on my island and clear my husband's grave. Then I can die happy.'

It seems a simple wish, but one which has been thwarted by the powerful environmental lobby, to which I am obviously a subscriber. In 2010 the islands were declared a marine sanctuary. The 250,000 square mile conservancy was greeted with delight by environmentalists but was condemned by human rights groups. Conservationists and scientists have since voiced their concerns that the Chagos reserve was rushed through without consensus in order to ensure Gordon Brown an environmental legacy to outdo that won by George W. Bush's end-of-term decision to protect vast tracts of the western Pacific.

Mauritius was furious at the unilateral decision. In 1965 it had been told by Britain that the Chagos Islands would be given to it when they were no longer needed for defence purposes. Foreign and Commonwealth Office officials privately admit that they cannot foresee a time when this would be the case.

'This has nothing to do with the environment,' said the Mauritian High Commissioner to London. 'They want to prevent islanders from going back and keep these islands for ever. But we are not going to let this go. They will face the consequences of this.'

Their concerns seem to have been confirmed by WikiLeak revelations that cast doubts on the environmental debate. According to the leaks, the Foreign Office had no regrets over the illegal action of expelling the Chagossians from the islands and had been planning for some time to destroy their campaign to return home by making their former homes a marine reserve in which no people would be allowed to live. Colin Roberts, director of the Foreign and Commonwealth Office, told the US political councillor that there would be no 'Man Fridays' on the uninhabited islands. In a section of the WikiLeaks document headed 'Je Ne Regrette Rien', Mr Roberts said, 'We do not regret the removal of the population' and told a meeting that establishing a marine park would, 'in effect, put paid to resettlement claims of the archipelago's former residents'. When it was pointed out to him by the US officials that the Chagos people continue to demand a return to their homes, he replied that the UK's 'environmental lobby is far more powerful than the Chagossians' advocates'. It was also asserted that the Conservatives, if in power after the next general election, would not support a Chagossian right of return.

Whatever your feelings on the ethics of WikiLeaks, I was horrified by the revelations.

In 2011 Mauritian Prime Minister Navinchandra Ramgoolam announced that his government has filed a case before the International Tribunal for the Law of the Sea in Hamburg: 'By creating the protected marine area, Great Britain did not take into account Mauritius' rights and those of the Chagossians it shamefully evicted from Chagos.'

Opponents have said that the islands lack the resources for a return, but, having visited myself, I found clean freshwater bore holes and many of the houses could be repaired. With small subsistence fishing, they could rebuild their community with minimal impact. Most of the islanders want to return to the outer islands, more than 100 miles from the high security of Diego Garcia. There is nothing stopping their return except for mean-spirited political meddling.

Indeed, today Diego Garcia is home to four thousand American troops and civilian contractors who use it as a base for the wars in Iraq and Afghanistan. It is, unsurprisingly, a much-coveted posting. Take a look on Google maps and you'll see swimming pools, tennis courts and warships. Not particularly green credentials for the new marine sanctuary! Perhaps some of those contractors could be exiled native Diego Garcian islanders themselves.

As a keen conservationist and environmentalist I had been asked to support the creation of the marine sanctuary within the Chagos Island group. At the time I was assured that the protectorate would include a clause that would allow the Chagossians to return home, but it appeared that once again the government had used environmental black-mail to get their way. I was duped into supporting a scheme in violation of basic human rights, and I have since spoken to a number of scientists who agree that they too were misled.

Financing the new marine reserve is a big concern. The area is patrolled by the *Pacific Marlin*, a small vessel that costs £1.7 million a year to operate. Before the reserve was founded licences sold to French, Spanish, Korean and Taiwanese tuna-fishing vessels contributed about £1 million a year to the cost. A faster patrol ship will probably be necessary to prevent illegal fishing in the new reserve, but who will foot the bill? All this at a time when the government is selling off its own forests and cutting back on national park spending. It simply doesn't add up. After all, wouldn't the islanders themselves make the best wardens?

It seems to me that governments are increasingly using environmental causes to 'greenwash' issues. I remain a passionate advocate for the environmental movement, but we must not allow ourselves to be dazzled by 'green' policy, blinding us to the bigger picture.

I teamed up with the historian Philippa Gregory to help spearhead a campaign with the islanders. We organized a large conference for islanders and environmental groups, including Blue, PEW, WWF and RSPB. Coincidentally, the conference was held in May 2011, on the same day that Selfridges department store in London launched their big Blue Ocean campaign, part of which was a celebration of the new marine sanctuary. So while my friend Kate Humble, who was staying with us, went off to celebrate the Chagos sanctuary, I was a few miles down the road arguing against it. It is one of very few things that we have been divided over.

I went on a very public platform revoking my support for the marine sanctuary and effectively going against a number of organizations for whom I was either an ambassador or to whom I had previously pledged support. I tried to argue for the creation of a working model where people and the natural world could live in harmony. We fight tooth and nail to avoid animals becoming extinct; surely we owe the same to an island people? Do fish and coral really have a higher value than basic human rights? We all share the guilt over the treatment of these islanders, but we also have the power to change history. We owe it to the Chagos people to ensure that they have access to the most basic of democratic rights: the right to go home.

All of this put me at loggerheads with a number of environmental organizations and created larger questions about the balance between conservation and habitation. As the population on this planet continues to expand, so will the conflict between man and nature.

I am deeply ashamed of the way Britain has treated the people of this paradise. Once again it has highlighted the fragile equilibrium between man and planet. Ultimately, it is our own ceaseless consumption and greed that has created the need for marine-protected areas in the first place. If we weren't busy emptying our oceans of marine life at such a rate then we wouldn't be forced to look at ways of protecting areas that in turn can devastate those who need the environment and its fruits the most.

The reality is that those of us with the greatest power to

make a change live in big urban cities, often completely removed and detached from the earth's fragile environment. We take for granted our ability to walk into a supermarket and buy a fillet of beef or fish. It is a cruel irony that those that need the oceans most should be the ones whose lives are affected by the way we live.

But of course problems don't arise just through our over-use of the environment in which we live, but through our misuse of it too, as I would soon find out on the other side of the Indian Ocean in Sri Lanka.

16

Plastic Oceans

*B*UMP! The whole boat jolted and shuddered.

I was 2,000 miles out to sea in a tiny 22-foot rowing boat made of plywood and glue when I felt a great thud under the vessel. It was as if I had run aground.

It stopped me in my tracks. I was in the middle of the Atlantic Ocean where the water was hundreds, if not thousands, of metres deep. I was puzzled but, after many weeks at sea, sleep deprivation, hunger and thirst had all muddled my brain and I simply couldn't think coherently.

'We've run aground!' I shouted to my rowing partner, James Cracknell.

It was 2005 and we were in the middle of the Atlantic rowing race. I surveyed the miles of nothingness around us and concluded that we had indeed run aground.

BUMP! It happened again, followed by a scraping sound.

I was astonished. I was also too tired to think straight. We had already begun to hallucinate, so I simply carried on rowing into the abyss.

Ocean rowing is one of the most boring pursuits on earth and for many weeks my brain had been numbed into a sort of mushy chaos. We had been on our own since we left land and had seen neither ship nor animal. Not a bird had broken the horizon, nor a dolphin the ocean. I longed for some animal interaction. A creature to remind me that life continued.

I can remember my excitement when I first saw a crocodile in the middle of the Atlantic.

'A crocodile!' I hollered. 'A crocodile!'

It turned out to be an inflatable crocodile lilo that had escaped some young child's clutches and made it halfway across the ocean.

I used to stare at the large swell behind the boat as I rowed. It gave me a point of reference and I would gaze into the heart of the waves as they helped propel our little vessel along. I learnt to distinguish the minutiae of colour and hue within the wave. Each shade of blue and green and grey and white.

Now as I gazed at the wave I noticed a large grey shape appearing beneath the surface. I hadn't seen anything like it before and I struggled to make sense of it. It was vast.

We were being followed by a submarine! My heart began to pound. James and I had been plagued by paranoia ever since we set off.

I stared at the vast, elongated shape surfing in the wave. What was it? My brain simply couldn't compute.

'Whale!' I mouthed in awe as I finally realized what I was looking at. I stared in disbelief as it surfed in the vast swell behind our boat, dwarfing the little vessel. It was one of the most beautiful sights I had ever seen. I was watching a Fin whale surfing.

I dropped the oars and called for James, who was resting in the cabin. He came tumbling out and we both watched in amazement as it glided slowly under the boat, jerking us slightly with its body as it tracked beneath us. We would later learn that it was using the small barnacles that formed on the bottom of our boat as a sort of scratching post.

Surprisingly, it wasn't scary. Even though it was more than twice the length of our boat and could have tipped us with one sweep of its tail, neither of us felt any fear. On the contrary, I felt a deep sense of calm. For the first time in weeks I felt peaceful and at ease. It was as if the white noise and chaos had been switched off. Whales have long been credited with having a calming influence, but I was surprised how powerful its presence was.

The next few days seemed to fly by in the company of the whale, which I named Rufus. I'm not really sure where that name came from. It certainly didn't look like a Rufus. I don't know anyone called Rufus. I couldn't even be sure it was a male, but for some reason I called it Rufus.

During the day, the whale would take up its favourite position surfing in the waves behind the boat. At night it used to make me jump as it broke the absolute silence of the ocean when it came up for air. I used to leap out of my seat as it made a sharp inhalation with its blowhole, followed by a sharp exhalation. You'd be amazed at how loud it can be, and even more surprised at how smelly it is. If the wind was in the right direction I used to get a waft of fishy breath that clung to the boat and would linger even once the whale had disappeared back beneath the surface.

Then one day the whale disappeared as quickly as it had appeared. I was devastated. I don't think James even noticed, but that solitary whale had had a powerful effect on me and I felt de-energized and low for days after it left us.

The day we crossed the finish line in Antigua was the same day that a lone whale appeared in the Thames in London. I remember thinking how strange it was that a whale should turn up for the first time in the middle of London, just a mile from my home, on the day I arrived in Antigua. Of course it was impossible that this was the same whale. It was a different species, and it couldn't possibly have covered that distance since it had left us, but in my muddled world of deprivations and hallucinations I was convinced that it was Rufus coming to find me.

From that encounter I became a fully paid-up whale-head.

Ocean rowers have had a long history of interactions with marine life. As well as the flying fish that plague night-time rowers with heart-attack-inducing slaps in the face through their kamikaze flying, there are tales of dolphins leaping over boats; but one of the most extraordinary encounters by far was that of a boat called *Sun Latte*, crewed by a Kiwi couple. They had been traversing the ocean in the same race as us when they too had been brushed by a large marine mammal. Thinking it was a whale, they carried on – until the huge object returned, this time with greater force.

Peering over the side of the boat, they realized to their horror that it was a Great White shark. Contrary to a shark's normal behaviour, it kept smashing at the side of the boat with ever-increasing ferocity, forcing the two rowers to seek safety inside the cabin. The shark continued to attack the flimsy plywood vessel and soon water began flooding into it. The beast wouldn't relent and by now had caused such structural damage that *Sun Latte* began to sink.

Fortunately for the rowers, the *Aurora* support yacht wasn't far away and after a frantic satellite call they were rescued from their deluged boat. *Sun Latte* sank as they stepped aboard the support vessel. It had been a sobering reminder of the dangers of ocean rowing.

From the terrifying to the surreal, there is another extraordinary tale of a four-man crew who were also halfway across the ocean when they too felt a juddering thump under their boat. They peered over the edge into the deep water below. There were no silhouettes, no whales and no sharks. They were puzzled, until one of their crew, who had been sleeping in the tiny cabin, appeared looking ashen-faced. He beckoned the others to peer through the little hatch.

Inside, piercing the cabin in two from floor to ceiling, was the unmistakable blade of a sawfish. Somehow it had managed to propel itself with such force at the bottom of the boat that it had cut through the entire vessel, leaving the poor fish dragging helplessly underneath.

They were left with a conundrum: whether to remove the blade and risk opening up a gaping hole in their boat, or to leave it in. They wouldn't be able to row with the giant fish attached to the bottom of the hull. It would be like rowing with a giant anchor at sea.

Fortunately, after a struggle the fish escaped, leaving them with its blade as a memento. They decided to leave it in place rather than worsen the damage and for the rest of the crossing had to sleep around the enormous blade.

Whales have always been emotive creatures. There is something about these graceful giants that instils wonder in us. Whaling has long been a rich part of many nations' heritage and to this day it provokes extraordinary reactions in people.

When I was thirteen, my father took my two sisters, Emily and Tamara, and me on a 'father's holiday'. My mother was performing in the West End and he saw it as a way of spending some time with us in his native Canada. He hired an enormous Winnebago and we set off into the Rocky Mountains on a Fogle Family Adventure.

For me the most memorable part was the first time I went whale watching – the first time I saw a whale.

We set out in a rigid inflatable boat, or RIB – the first time I had ever been in such a vessel – and headed into the Pacific Ocean. Salty water crashed over the front of the little red boat as we bounded over the swell in search of these ocean giants.

I can still remember my surprise that a creature so large could be so elusive, but after an hour of searching we finally found our first one. I caught a brief glimpse of it on the horizon and then suddenly, without warning, an enormous whale surfaced right next to our little boat. I could see the mottled colour of its skin and the barnacles that grew on its snout. It was mind-blowing. Here I was next to the largest creature on earth. That encounter has stayed with me ever since.

In later years I have had brief encounters with whales in South Africa, New Zealand and during the Atlantic row. But I was to get a whole new insight into the secret, hidden life of the Blue whale when in 2010 I joined a unique and pioneering project called Plastic Oceans, which was trying to help us understand more about the state of our oceans and the effects the rubbish and plastics thrown into them are having on our marine life. I had been invited to join a team of marine scientists and experts on an expedition deep into the Indian Ocean to study the Blue whale, the largest creature on earth. We would attempt to dive with these ocean giants, with the aim of getting close enough to them to take a biopsy of their blubber to see if the plastic is getting into their systems.

It was a bold, exciting experiment and I soon found myself setting off again for a faraway land in search of one of the planet's most mysterious and beautiful creatures.

I flew to Colombo in Sri Lanka, from where I would travel cross-country by bus to Galle to join our vessel.

Colombo is a colourful and energetic city. The country was just emerging from the trauma of civil war. The Tamil Tigers had been corralled into a tiny spit of sand in the north of the country and effectively exterminated. It had been a bloody end to a long and bloody war. In addition, Sri Lanka was still struggling to recover from the effects of the Boxing Day tsunami of 2004 that caused so much damage and death.

I have visited the country several times over the years and have found the Sri Lankans a tough, resilient people, blessed with a beautiful land. Indeed, it was here that I bottle-fed my first baby elephant.

I had been surprised by the number of ex-British soldiers on my flight from London and in the lobby of my Colombo hotel, but Sri Lanka and the Indian Ocean are presenting great post-army career opportunities for British soldiers. The country is in the middle of one of the world's busiest shipping routes, which also has to pass through one of the most deadly and dangerous bodies of water on earth, the Sea of Aden. Here the ocean narrows as it passes the Horn of Africa and Somalia – pirate country. There have been so many incidents in which ships have been hijacked and their crews held to ransom that most shipping insurance companies now insist that armed guards escort their vessels through the 'danger zone' to ensure the safety of the crew, cargo and ship.

Shipping is a multi-billion-pound industry that has been threatened by a few struggling Somali fishermen, and the conflict has created a booming micro-industry in private armies of soldiers to escort the flotilla. Colombo and Galle are a gateway to the shipping, so ex-soldiers arrive into Sri Lanka and are airlifted on to the ships offshore where their weapons await them.

As our bus pulled into Galle, the harbour was a hive of activity as vessels both great and small prepared themselves for the pirate-infested waters. Vast rolls of razor wire and barbed wire were being unravelled along the sides of the ships while metal cages were being fitted around the sterns.

High fences had been erected in front of the wheelhouses while the windows had been given extra protection too. They looked like riot vehicles about to enter the fray and reminded me of the Land Rovers in Northern Ireland during the Troubles, but this was the Indian Ocean.

It made our defenceless boat look all the more vulnerable as we boarded. We weren't heading into pirate territory so we wouldn't need the protection our sister ships required, but it was still a little disconcerting, especially given that the pirates' range has been getting wider and wider as more and more ships have bolstered their defences.

We would be at sea for ten days. I was joining a unique band of ocean warriors, many of whom have become legends within their industry. Perhaps the most famous of all was the award-winning cameraman Doug Allan. I have long been a fan of Doug, who has been responsible for some of the most iconic wildlife filming ever made and in 2012 was awarded a Polar Medal by the Queen for all his services to the polar regions. I must admit that I was a little star-struck on meeting him.

Also in our team was Mike Pitts, another underwater legend who has dived all over the world and with whom I would later go diving with crocodiles in Botswana. The rest of the team was made up of crews from Hong Kong and two former BBC Natural History unit executives.

As we pulled out of Galle naval base under a blistering Sri Lankan sun, I suddenly felt a rush of excitement. For the first time I was working on a project that combined conservation with environmentalism.

* * *

There is a great misconception that plastic pollutes. That's wrong. People pollute. We make the plastic and abandon the plastic.

The Great Pacific Garbage Patch, also described as the Pacific Trash Vortex, is a gyre of marine litter in the North Pacific Ocean. Because the prevailing wind systems and currents come together here from both directions, it stays in more or less the same place and draws in rubbish from both sides of the ocean. While many refer to it as a plastic patch, it would be better described as a plastic soup made up of plastic and chemical sludge. Despite its size and density, it is not visible in satellite photographs as the plastic has broken down to suspended particles and polymers.

The patch first hit the headlines when marine scientist Charles Moore was returning across the Pacific from a sailing race and passed through an enormous stretch of floating debris. The story of the 'plastic island' made international headlines, but the absence of photographs or film meant the world soon lost interest. Why were there no photographs? And why had no one noticed it before? The answer was simple. It wasn't an island but a nearly invisible soup of plastic. From above it looked like a 'plastic slick', but a sample of the water revealed the reality of the situation. It was a symptom of our visually obsessed society that the story waned without any sensational photographs to accompany it.

Contrary to popular belief, the North Pacific Gyre isn't the only one. There are similar patches of floating plastic debris to be found in the Atlantic Ocean, the Indian Ocean and the South Pacific Ocean. In fact, research has shown that this plastic marine debris affects at least 267 species world-wide and only a few of those reside in the North Pacific Gyre.

Some of these long-lasting plastics end up in the stomachs of marine birds and animals and their young, including sea turtles. I have seen photographs of turtles whose growth has been restricted by plastic hoops, their shell hideously disfigured as the plastic has remained in place while the turtle has grown. I have also seen the stomach contents of black-footed albatross that include everything from plastic lighters to plastic pen lids.

On a macroscopic level, the physical size of the plastic kills birds and turtles as the animals' digestion cannot break it down, while on a microscopic level this 'soup' or marine sludge is being absorbed into the bodies of various marine mammals and fish. A further consequence is that many of these fish are then consumed by humans, resulting in our ingestion of toxic chemicals. Marine plastics also facilitate the spread of invasive micro-organisms such as bacteria that attach to floating plastic in one region and drift long distances to colonize other ecosystems to which they do not naturally belong.

We had been at sea for three days when we came across a vast rubbish patch. It began with a few bottles and bags, but soon the whole boat was surrounded. As our eyes adjusted we could make out flotsam and jetsam all around. We weren't in the Indian Oceans Gyre itself, but we had hit one of the many common 'patches' of plastic that litter the seas, and this one would eventually be swept into the main gyre.

I put on a snorkel and mask and leapt into the litter-strewn waters. It was like diving into a rubbish dump. Once in the sea, the volume and density of the plastics became apparent. What surprised me most was the marine ecosystem that had evolved and created a micro-environment within the trash. Crabs had hitchhiked on bottles and discarded flip-flops, while small barnacles and molluscs had attached themselves to lighters and plastic bags. These in turn had attracted jellyfish and turtles, as well as schools of fish that followed the patch.

It was deeply unpleasant swimming through this plastic soup. The surface was littered with everything imaginable, as well as with dozens of dead fish, jellyfish and even sea birds. When I got out of the water I had to use antibacterial gel to cleanse my body of the man-made chemicals that were seeping from the rubbish. The next morning I woke up with slightly orange hair. I don't know how or why it changed colour, but I feel sure it was a sign. And that sign certainly wasn't green.

For several days we worked a pattern up and down the deep channels that tumble off the Sri Lankan Shelf several miles offshore. The whales were proving more elusive than we'd hoped. It was swelteringly hot and after a third day of roasting under the Indian Ocean sun we decided to have a quick swim. The captain stopped the boat and we all dived into the deep waters around the boat. There was quite a swell, so we tried to stay relatively near the stern where a small ladder had been placed to help us back up on to the deck.

We all snorkelled around the clear waters and noticed several large remora fish. One of the Sri Lankan crew, a very cheery fellow called Mohammad, had taken out a surfboard and was busy paddle-boarding when I heard a shout. In the distance I could just make out Mohammad on the board. He was paddling furiously.

'SHARK!' he hollered.

It's amazing the power of a single word. I didn't need any persuading as I sped back towards the boat. The only thing was, everyone else remained in the water. They were all busy snorkelling and chatting as if nothing had happened, and I began to doubt my own hearing.

'*SHARK!*' I heard him scream again. Still there was no reaction from anyone else.

'These are some very cool cucumbers,' I thought to myself as I watched the BBC Natural History Unit's finest paddling without a care in the world.

Lizzy, our producer, was standing on the steps down from the boat, chatting to Doug Allan. My heart was pounding and part of me wanted to clamber over her to get out of the water, but she was my producer and therefore my boss, and whatever happened to male chivalry?

I put one foot on a step and beckoned for her to get out – but she carried on chatting. Now this was awkward. I *really* wanted to get away from the shark; instinctively I wanted to run as fast as I could, trampling over her head if need be. But there was a strange calmness that brought rationality to my thought process. I thought about the *Titanic*: 'Women and children first.'

'EVERYONE OUT OF THE WATER!' bellowed the captain from the deck. 'THERE'S A SHARK!'

It was like someone turning on a light switch. I have never seen people move so fast as the crew clambered on top of one another to get out of the water.

We stood on the deck watching the dorsal fin of the shark circling the water around our ship. Suddenly the presence of the remora made sense, as these strange fish use sharks to hitchhike around the ocean, treating them like a number 92 bus, hopping on and off at will.

It was a reminder that even seasoned experts can sometimes get it wrong.

For ten days we sailed up and down the deep-water channel as a vast convoy of ocean traffic streamed past us. Some ships were stacked with containers fifteen storeys high. They looked ridiculously top heavy as they powered past at great speed. There was something strange about looking for the largest mammal on earth in the middle of a busy shipping lane.

Each morning, long before sunrise, we would slip out of the harbour and towards an unseen horizon, dotted with the lights of dozens of fishing boats already out there. If we'd carried on, the next land we would have seen would have been Antarctica, 6,500 miles away. A dozen of us would scour the horizon for the telltale signs of a whale. Below us the deep blue disappeared thousands of metres, its swell shadowing whatever might lie below. It was eye-wateringly hot.

'Whale!' shouted Doug.

I stared into the horizon. Nothing.

'There she blows!' he hollered again, a smile stretched across his face. I looked and still saw nothing.

'Beautiful!' said Lizzy, peering through her binoculars.

Was I blind? Why couldn't I see what they were seeing? We were talking about the biggest living creature on the planet, not a tadpole.

I stared into the horizon until I saw what looked like smoke. Or was it steam? Why was the ocean smoking?

We altered course and headed towards the head of steam.

I was about to have my first encounter with an animal as big as an aeroplane and just as loud.

It is hard to comprehend the scale and enormity of a Blue whale until it is next to your boat.

'Oh my God!' It quite literally took my breath away as its giant head broke the surface of the water, its massive blowhole venting a long, noisy bellow of air. It was like a steam train blowing its whistle. That familiar fishy air I had experienced on the Atlantic filled my nostrils.

These are the largest animals ever known to have lived on earth. These magnificent marine mammals rule the oceans at up to 30 metres long and upwards of 181 metric tons. Their tongue can weigh as much as an elephant and their heart as much as a car. What has always seemed most incredible to me is that the Blue whale reaches this astonishing size on a diet composed nearly exclusively of tiny shrimp-like krill. During certain times of the year, a single adult consumes about 3.6 metric tons of krill a day.

Blue whales are baleen whales, which means they have fringed plates of fingernail-like material, called baleen, attached to their upper jaws. The giant animals feed by first gulping an enormous mouthful of water, expanding the pleated skin of their throat and belly to take it in. Then the whale's massive tongue forces the water out through the thin, overlapping baleen plates. Thousands of krill are left behind – and then swallowed.

Occasionally swimming in small groups but usually alone or in pairs, Blue whales live in all the world's oceans. They often spend summers feeding in polar waters and undertake lengthy migrations towards the Equator as winter arrives. They are graceful swimmers, cruising the ocean at more than 5 miles an hour, but can accelerate to more than 20 miles an hour when they are agitated. Blue whales are also among the loudest animals on the planet. They emit a series of pulses, groans and moans, and it is thought that, in good conditions, they can hear each other up to 1,000 miles away. Scientists think they use these vocalizations not only to communicate, but, along with their excellent hearing, to sonar-navigate the lightless ocean depths.

The Blue whale looks true blue only under water, but on the surface its colouring is more a mottled blue-grey, like a camouflage against the sea and sky. Suddenly I could understand how a whale could remain hidden for so long. It is their breathing that gives them away. I wondered why evolution hadn't created a small cap at the top of the hole to dampen down the cloud of fine mist they emit, a little like a flare? This highly visible jet would have condemned whales to a certain death from the whalers that used to patrol these waters.

The whale's underbelly takes on a yellowish hue from the millions of micro-organisms that take up residence in its skin, and its broad, flat head and long, tapered body end in wide, triangular fins or flukes.

Blue whales are among the earth's longest-lived animals. Scientists have discovered that by counting the layers of a deceased whale's wax-like earplugs they can get a close estimate of its age. Using this method, the oldest Blue whale found was determined to be around 110 years old. Average lifespan is estimated at around eighty to ninety years.

I was completely transfixed as I stared at this graceful creature.

'Calf!' I heard someone shout.

As I turned, I noticed a much smaller head breach the water. I use the word 'smaller' in a comparative sense. Indeed Blue whale calves enter the world already ranking among the planet's largest creatures. After about a year inside its mother's womb, a baby Blue whale emerges weighing up to 2.7 metric tons and stretching to 8 metres. It gorges on nothing but its mother's milk and gains about 91kg every day for its first year. Every fact about the Blue whale seems impossible.

Blue whales converge here in Sri Lanka because of the meeting of the warmer coastal waters with the colder waters of the continental shelf which creates a cycle of rising nutrients called 'upwellings'. The rich, rotting matter from the ocean bed feeds the krill, and the krill feed the whales. It's an efficient exchange, a marker of oceanic fertility.

That the whales choose to feed between the island and the world's busiest shipping lane seems symbolic of the effects humans have upon them.

Despite their size, these whales remain incredibly vulnerable and they are at the mercy of us humans and our actions. Between 10,000 and 25,000 Blue whales are believed still to swim the world's oceans. Aggressive hunting in the first part of the twentieth century by whalers seeking whale oil drove them to the brink of extinction. Between 1900 and the mid-

1960s, some 360,000 Blue whales were slaughtered. They finally came under protection with the 1966 International Whaling Commission, but they have managed only a minor recovery since then.

They have few predators, but they are known to fall victim to attacks by sharks and killer whales, and many are injured or die each year from impacts with large ships. Blue whales are currently classified as endangered on the World Conservation Union (IUCN) Red List.

Before I even had time to register that there were in fact two whales alongside us, Doug Allan and Mike Pitts, our underwater cameramen, were tumbling into the ocean with their waterproof housing. While spotting a whale in the water is hard enough, filming them under water is virtually impossible. They have been known to dive up to 100 metres to feed and can spend anything from ten to twenty minutes under water. In this time they can travel huge distances and for those following it becomes a guessing game of where they are going to surface next.

For an hour we tried to second-guess the whale and her calf as Doug and Mike yo-yoed in and out of the water from their little dinghy. It was important that we didn't scare the whales, so we held back on the mother ship. Sometimes it looked as if the whale blew or breached right next to their tiny boat.

We were lucky to have had so much time with these incredible creatures, and although we hadn't got a biopsy we had managed to scoop up some whale poo – a surprisingly rare catch for a scientist.

Nothing remains a secret for long, and our location had

been spotted by the army of whale-watching boats, who descended on us like a flock of sheep. They could tell from our movements that we were on to a whale and before we knew it we and the whales were surrounded by a dozen boats. While whale watching can have enormous benefits to the species, showcasing these majestic creatures to the public, it can also have negative repercussions. It has become a huge business around the world and Sri Lanka's fledgling whale-watching industry is already experiencing problems. Unregulated and unscrupulous operators can stress the whales, chase them and even drive them away. Scientists are asking for strict guidelines to be enforced, limiting how many boats can be allowed to approach whales, and how close they are allowed to come.

I was horrified to see so many boats corralling the whale and its calf in a man-made pen. Even more shocking was the presence of a Sri Lankan naval vessel, *Jetliner*, which was not there to patrol or guard, but had jumped on the whale-watching bandwagon and was supplementing her upkeep by taking paying passengers out to sea. I felt physically sick as I watched her chase after the whale and her calf at high speed.

Conservation is like a seesaw. In the Chagos Islands I had seen how man has tipped the balance in favour of wildlife in the creation of the marine sanctuary to the detriment of the people that belong there; but here in Sri Lanka I was seeing how easy it is to tip the balance the other way – even if the sentiments were good-hearted.

Here was another example of man's exploitation of nature, a case of us tipping the balance. What my experience in Sri Lanka reminded me of was the need to find a harmony between our fascination with the natural world and our urge to trample all over it for a short, quick fix.

Conclusion

'Breathe deeply.' I keep repeating it to myself as fear and panic begin to well up within me. I feel physically sick. 'Breathe deeply, Ben.'

The postscript to a book should be happy and uplifting. Mine is neither of those. If the page of a book or a computer screen could be tear-stained, then these pages are soaked.

You can probably guess where this is going.

Time waits for neither man nor dog, and one of the brutal truths of the natural order is that man outlives most other species. I always knew it would happen, but nothing really prepares you for the sudden shock.

I was in the Isle of Wight with the children and the dogs on our first family holiday together in July 2012. Inca's deterioration had been rapid. She had lost full control of her back legs and even walking had become difficult. She would often collapse while eating or, worse, while she was squatting to pee or poo; frequently I found myself holding her while she did her business. I had to carry her in and out of the car and soon she couldn't even get up from her bed.

I called Dad and told him about her decline.

'What do you think?' he asked.

There was a pause. Not because I was thinking, but because I couldn't bring myself to say it.

'Then we know the answer,' he said.

I burst into uncontrollable tears.

In many ways this is the last piece of the jigsaw puzzle in our relationship with animals. Not slaughter, poaching, culling or loving, but euthanasia. Is it possible to love someone or something so much that you would choose to let them go? It must be one of life's most unbearable decisions, but one which is afforded to animals and not to humans. However hard it is, you owe your best friend the favour that is denied to us humans.

Much is made in the press of the arguments both for and against euthanasia in humans and to be honest I have always shied away from the debate, mainly because it is an unbearable confrontation of our immortality. I can say here and now that if ever my life is reduced to existence by machine, I would prefer to leave this beautiful planet of ours. It may bring untold pain to those left behind, but to keep someone alive on a machine for the sake of it could arguably be construed as selfish. Are we keeping them alive for themselves or for us, their loved ones?

And herein lies the burning question that faces all dog-owners and animal-lovers. Do you keep a dog alive through medical intervention for their sake or for yours? When does it become unfair on the animal?

I can honestly say that the twenty-four hours that followed that phone call were probably the most painful of my life. The *knowing*. Inca, my beloved Inca, who had loyally trusted me all her life. Was this the ultimate act of love or of betrayal?

'Breathe deeply.' I am beginning to panic again just thinking about it. Tears are streaming down my cheeks as I write this because it is so raw. I don't want to do this but I need to do it. I want to try to express the complex tangle of love between man and dog.

It was time for Inca to go.

Before we left the Isle of Wight for the agonizing journey back to London, we took Maggi and Inca to the beach one last time. I carried Inca from the car down the steep steps to the sandy beach and took her to the edge of the sea so she could lie there with her paws in the water. Here we were on a beach by the ocean again, just as we were on Taransay when her life was beginning. She had loved the beaches, the sand and the water so much. I had always felt guilty about taking all that away from her and bringing her back to London.

Now I sat on the sand with her while the children and Maggi frolicked in the sea. I watched as her ears flapped in the wind and she lifted her nose to smell the sea air. Then, her belly covered in sand and sea water, I carried her back to the car and we began that torturous journey to London. I couldn't look anyone in the eyes. In the rearview mirror I could see her snout on Maggi's back.

'Breathe deeply.' Panic is surging in again.

It was 9 p.m. when we got home. Dad was waiting.

I lay on the floor and sobbed uncontrollably into Inca's fur.

'One more night.'

I carried her up to our bedroom, put her bed next to mine and lay there listening to her deep snoring. I didn't sleep. I felt sick with panic and in the morning my pillow was stained with tears.

At 6 a.m. I carried her downstairs and fed her, then picked her up and took her into the garden.

'Give Inca a big hug,' I said to Ludo, who threw his arms around her.

'Where's she going, Daddy?' he asked.

'Up into the sky,' I said, turning away to hide the tears that tumbled down my cheeks.

We were worried about the effect on the children, so at 7.30 a.m. I carried Inca to the car, taking Maggi with us too, and drove ten minutes up the road to my parents' house. I don't remember much about that journey except that I cried uncontrollably all the way.

I'm not sure what would be worse – knowing or not knowing. Is sudden death better than planned death? The bottom line is that they are both unbearable. But I had made the decision.

'Thank you, Inca,' I sobbed as we drove through the empty streets of Notting Hill. 'Thank you for being my best friend. I owe everything to you.'

It may sound stupid talking to your dog like this, but then it's all true. Inca changed my life and I owe everything to her.

I carried her from the car into the house, burying my face

into her fur, and laid her on the kitchen floor. Mum, Dad and my sister were all there. If ever there was family unity and bonding, this was it.

I lay on the floor hugging Inca while Dad injected her. Her breathing became heavy. I could feel her heart pounding and the warm blood beneath her skin. I breathed the familiar scent of her fur as I nuzzled into her thick coat. I have never sobbed like that in my life. It was a primal, uncontrollable, guttural sob as I felt her heart stop beating.

I lay there on the kitchen floor clutching my best friend, unable to move. Wishing, hoping it was a dream, I held her lifeless body to me.

I can't tell you how hard it is to write these words, because they are so painful. It is as if my heart has been wrenched from me. I have lost my best friend, my shadow, a limb, a part of my being.

What is it about a dog that can elicit these kinds of emotions? To be honest, I think you have to have had one of your own to understand the bond fully. Each of us forges a unique relationship with our dog that no one else will ever really understand and my twelve-year bond with Inca created something so unique.

It seemed like yesterday that I brought Inca the puppy into this very home when I was still living with my parents. It was here that she spent the first few months of her life before we packed our bags for Taransay. And this is where it ended.

'Breathe deeply.' The panic is overtaking my whole body again. The emotion I feel now is so raw and unbearable that I don't know what to do. I keep having flashbacks of that journey back to London and then to my parents' house. The knowing. Inca was my best friend. She relied on me and trusted me, and yet it was me who knowingly and decisively sent her on her way. I proactively chose to end her life. It wasn't my father, the vet. It was me, her best friend. How could I do that?

As Marina said, we lost Inca many years ago. Her enjoyment of life ended long before her actual life did. In many ways I was lucky to have had her for as long as I did. She lived for more than six years with her epilepsy. She could no longer go to the park and she sat all day staring at the wall. To keep her alive any longer would have been a selfish act on my part. If you love someone enough you will let them go, and I have. But it hasn't made it any easier. It has had the opposite effect and made me panic. I took the final decision. It was me. I, who so often default to other people for answers, had to make the final, hardest, most painful decision.

As I lay on the floor with her, Dad told me that if I hadn't made it he would have made it for me. The way my family handled those few hours on that rainy Wednesday morning will stay with me for ever and I love them dearly for it.

Maggi came and sniffed Inca's lifeless body. I wanted her to sense that her friend had gone.

'Where's Inca?' asked Ludo as I returned home with Maggi.

'Stay strong, Ben,' I said to myself.

'She's gone up into the sky,' I explained.

'Where?' he asked inquisitively.

I pointed to the sky.

'Can we fly up to see her?' he asked.

'Hello, Inca,' he says, waving to the sky each time we leave the house.

Her loss is like a big, yawning chasm in my very soul. The pain I feel as I recount this tale is still so raw, but I don't want to end with my tears. You see, Inca's life was a metaphor for the natural world itself and our complex relationship with the animals within it.

I like to think that one day, when my time comes, I will be greeted by all my long-lost friends who have been loyally waiting for me up in the sky.

This book is the celebration of a remarkable dog.

My best friend, Inca.

In 1992, when I was nineteen years old, I had been in Ecuador helping in an orphanage for a year when my father crossed the world to join me in Quito, the capital. We spent a week driving up and down the Andes, visiting Incan ruins and eating guinea pig together. It was a happy time, and one of the few times it was just Dad and me. I loved spending time with him. After a week we boarded a flight for the Galapagos, where we spent ten days sailing around some of the most important, environmentally rich islands in the world. It was here that Darwin developed his theory of evolution.

For zoologists, vets and budding naturalists, the Galapagos Islands are the holy grail of destinations and the days spent sailing between islands, meeting marine iguanas and blue-footed boobies with my father remain some of my happiest memories. We snorkelled with sharks, went swimming with spotted manta ray and sunbathed with penguins. We had a naturalist on board who explained the intricacies of the species and subspecies that were endemic to each individual island and so had helped Darwin establish his theory of evolution.

In some ways our journey through the Galapagos islands was a kind of father–son pilgrimage. Where some families may choose to walk the religious road to Santiago de Compostela in Spain, we chose the evolutionary road to the Galapagos in the Pacific Ocean. It was a way of Dad sharing the joy and wonder of the natural world with me.

There were too many animal encounters to remember (although I still have a small scar on my foot from the bloodied wound inflicted by a blue-footed booby). But there was one meeting that stood out above all others. Lonesome George. A giant tortoise, Lonesome George was estimated to have been more than a hundred years old and was the last of the Pinta subspecies. He was being homed at the Charles Darwin research facility and meeting him was like meeting a living legend. I couldn't quite grasp the fact that this magnificent creature had been around these islands for a hundred years. He had come face to face with history. He had outlived some of the great early explorers. Lonesome George soon became not only an icon for the Galapagos but a beacon for natural history and science.

Not long ago, in June 2012, Lonesome George passed away. With his death came extinction – he was the last of his subspecies. And it had happened in my lifetime. Scientists had spent many years trying unsuccessfully to help him find a mate and reproduce. He had become a symbol of the

Galapagos and it was the differences between these sub-species that had helped Darwin establish his theory of evolution. In some ways his death is like a metaphor for everything I have been trying to say in this book. A story of science, greed, hope, devotion and loss.

Which brings me back to the nature of this book. The Accidental Naturalist? Am I? I still feel slightly uneasy using the term. The dictionary describes a naturalist as 'a student of natural history . . . someone who cares for the environment'. I will happily attribute both of those to myself.

In writing this book I hoped I would understand more about man's relationship with animals, but in reality it has created more questions than it has answered. What it has done is to highlight the complex and fragile relationship that we have with the world around us. Our own relationship with nature and the natural world is so key to the future of mankind that, if we don't stop to think about what we are doing and what we have done, we stand to lose it before we realize we have it.

The world has become obsessed with materialism and consumption, but there is still a place for selfless acts of altruism. I have met people prepared to put their own lives on the line in the pursuit of conservation. Environmental philanthropy is rife.

I have been incredibly fortunate in being able to travel to the places to which I have been and to have spent time with some of nature's most extraordinary flora and fauna. I hope that by sharing some of those experiences and encounters with you, I am performing my own small act of environmental philanthropy.

Not long ago I was sitting outside one of my favourite pizza restaurants in Notting Hill Gate, London. It was a sunny day and I was with some friends enjoying the spring weather.

A man strode by, doing a double-take as he walked past my table. I caught him out of the corner of my eye as he stopped and stared at me.

'Excuse me,' he said, 'are you Mr Fogle?'

I nodded sheepishly, as I always do. Isn't it strange how someone who stands in front of the camera for a living can still get embarrassed? I always go red when people stop me on the street. I'm not sure why. It's as though I am apologizing for being me. It's a silly habit and I try to hide it, but I don't like standing out on a busy street. It's the one time I still crave anonymity.

'One minute,' he said, holding a finger in the air before disappearing back down the street.

I carried on eating, assuming that he would return with a camera or a piece of paper and a pen, so you can imagine my surprise when he came back about ten minutes later with an enormous white, fluffy cat.

Without hesitation he handed me the moggy.

'He fell out of the window the other day,' explained the stranger. 'It wasn't far, but he seems to have a limp.'

'And?' I thought to myself, waiting for the rest. Why was he telling me this?

'I was wondering whether you could have a look at him and give your medical diagnosis?' he finished.

He actually thought I was a vet? My friends smiled with delight. I didn't know whether to be flattered or embarrassed. Had he mistaken me for my father? Or had I somehow actually taken on the persona of a TV vet after more than a decade of wildlife filmmaking?

In 2007 I was awarded an honorary degree from my old university, Portsmouth, for my services to sport and adventure, becoming a Doctor of Letters and therefore a second-generation Dr Fogle. To be fair, mine is a complete cheat and I would never use it, but it gives me a slight feeling of satisfaction whenever I receive correspondence from the university addressed to Dr Fogle.

What I have discovered is that we often forget to thank or even value those around us. Like a comfortable piece of furniture, we become complacent, often neglecting to appreciate what we have. Sometimes the answer is right in front of us. What has become obvious to me is that the real Dr Fogle, my father, really is my hero. He has spent his entire life dedicated to animals. He has given himself to veterinary medicine and science. He and so many other people I have encountered over the years, from Africa to Wiltshire, have selflessly bequeathed themselves to the animal kingdom.

Where there is environmental hopelessness and despair there is human hope and inspiration – a small army of scientists, zoologists, wardens, keepers, vets, naturalists and animal lovers who will continue to police, protect and care for our environment and the flora and fauna within it. There will always be a conflict between man and nature – the volume of people living on the planet will ensure that – BUT, we can find a balance. We must find that balance.

And as for me? The truth of the matter is that I am neither a doctor nor a naturalist. I'm just a bloke with a dog who has developed a deep love for and fascination with the animal kingdom and the world in which we live. We can learn so much from the wildlife around us if only we try. We may think that we are the superior species, but we're not. If we were we wouldn't be in the mess we're in today.

My life has taken a meandering path, ebbing and flowing, waxing and waning. I often describe it as being like a river. For thirty-nine years I have been following the flow downstream towards the sea. It has taken many twists and turns, but soon it will empty into the mighty ocean.

I have always felt at home on the ocean. I wonder whether it is something to do with the fact that we are 70 per cent water? I feel calmer and happier when I am near to or on the sea. And now the Atlantic Ocean is calling me back. The Atlantic, where my meandering career began on the windswept island of Taransay in the Outer Hebrides; the ocean on which I toiled for forty-nine days as I rowed from east to west.

In 2013, I hope to swim 3,000 miles from the USA to England, becoming a human scientific instrument, recording first hand the effects we are having on our oceans. Man working with the natural world, not against it.

Acknowledgements

To Dad, my hero, for helping me find my inner animal. I am proud beyond words of everything you have done for veterinary medicine, science and the animal world over the years.

To Mum, Tamara, Emily, Grandma Aileen, my late Grandma Jean, Grandpa Dick and Grandpa Morris.

To Marina, Ludo and Iona, my beautiful family.

To Inca, Liberty, Lexington, Honey, Humphrey, Jaws, Milly, Bejo, Russett, Lola, Marni, Macy, Luca, Maggi, Beca, and all the other animals I have known and loved.

A great many people worked on *Animal Park* over the years. Particular thanks to Chris Powell, Annette Clarke, Annie Rigby, Lucy Bing, Alexis Giradet.

Thanks too to all those at Longleat Safari Park: Andy Hayton, Mark Tye, Ian Turner, Ryan Hockley, Tim Yeo, Darren Beasley, Lord Bath and everyone at Longleat.

Thanks to Kate Humble and Ludo Graham.

To Jess Farrish and Hannah Fair for their research.

To Adam Britton, Brad Bestelink, Ingrid Kvale, Ted Oates,

Mike Pitts and everyone who worked on *Swimming with Crocodiles.*

To TUSK, Charlie Mayhew, the Duke of Cambridge, Ian Craig and the Craig family, and everyone at Lewa.

To Rebecca Jones for helping pull this all together, Doug Young and Alison Barrow.

To Sarah Brumwin and all at WWF.

To Julian Alexander and everyone at LAW.

Many, many other people helped make *Animal Park* such a success over the years: Nick Aarons, Andrea Arnold, Jake Auerbach, Matt Baker, Anna Ball, Claire Bamford, Dominic Bekes, Cassie Belham, Nick Bell, Sarah Binns, Adam Birley, John Blystone, Jason Boxall, Lindsay Bradbury, Danielle Brigham, Sarah Brooks, Stephen Brown, Luke Burwood, Nigel Burwood, Carrie Bush, Brian Campbell, Graham Carr, Naomi Carter, Suzy Carter, Jonathan Challis, Mark Chan, Rob Chandler, Nikki Cheetham, Nick Cleave, Emily Commens, Kate Cotter, Paul Coueslant, Pete Coventry, Adam Craig, Nonie Creagh-Brown, Susanne Curran, Helen Dakin, Hong Dan, Hannah Dawes, Naomi Dennison, Mark Dolan, Jill Dunham, Sophie Dunn, Gavin Dutton, Catrine Ericsson, Barbara Evans, Ruby Evans, Patrice Fentiman, Charlotte Fitzpatrick, Dave Gaisford, Mark Goldie, Tanya Gottlieb, Sam Grace, Julian Green, Nicky Hammond, Peter Harvey, Rob Hawthorne, Marie Howarth, Mike Howarth, Jeannot Hutcheson, Vari Innes, Saffron Jackson, Clair Jardella, Cindy Kasfikis, George Kidson, Sue King, Marcia Kirby, John Kirk, Karen Loader, Andy Loftus, Jo MacGregor, Zazie Mackintosh, George McMillan, James Mair, Hitesh Makan, Richard Malone, Ros Malthouse, Sean Millar, Gary

Moore, Richard Nash, Clive North, Fay Pain, Jessica Parrish, Karen Partridge, Monica Patel, Elaine Paterson, Richard Perry, Claire Pickering, Hannah Pocock, Tony Pound, Katie Rawcliffe, Matthew Reinders, Sarah Richards, Simon Richards, Spencer Richley, Francis Robertson, Mark Robinson, Laurie Rose, Jacqui Rubin, Gareth Sacala, Owen Scurfield, Stewart Shape, Matthew Skilton, Alistair Smith, Barry Smith, Hayley Smith, Louise Smith, Andew Snowball, James Snowden, Adam Souter, Imogen Sparks, Genevieve Taylor, Sarah Taylor, Blythe Tinker, Paula Tonks, Camilla Turner, Dominic Vallely, Amanda Walker, Lorraine Want, Will West, Claire Wheeler, Graham Whittaker, Simon Whittaker, Mike Williams, Joff Wilson, Steph Withey, Katy Woods, Paul Zanders.

To all the scientists, naturalists, zoologists, vets, wardens, keepers, conservationists and environmentalists I've ever had the pleasure of working with.

To the London Veterinary Clinic (formerly the Portman Veterinary Clinic) and all the veterinary nurses I have known over the years: Jenny Ward, Ashley McManus, Arin Collins, Letty Lean, Hester Small, Angela Bettinson, Suzy Gray, Maxine Clark, Manda Hackett, Hilary Hayward.

To all at Endemol, Lion TV, Gill Wilson and Nick Bullen at Spungold, and the BBC for giving me the opportunity to explore the planet's wild side.

To Hilary Murray and everyone at Arlington, Alison Griffin, Bovey Castle and the Plastic Oceans team.

Information about the following charities can be found at:

TUSK Trust – www.tusk.org

WWF – www.wwf.org.uk
Plastic Oceans Foundation – www.plasticoceans.net
Cheetah Conservation Fund (CCF) – www.cheetah.org
AfriCat – www.africat.org
Born Free Foundation – www.bornfree.org.uk
British Hedgehog Preservation Society –
   www.britishhedgehogs.org.uk
Hearing Dogs for Deaf People – www.hearingdogs.org.uk
Save the Rhino – www.savetherhino.org

Picture Acknowledgments

Every effort has been made to contact the copyright holders. We apologize for any omissions in this respect and will be pleased to make the appropriate acknowledgments in any future edition. All images have been supplied courtesy of the author unless otherwise stated.

Section one

Page 6: BF and his father at Buckingham Palace © Anwar Hussein/EMPICS Entertainment. Page 7: The Fogle Family, 2011 © Jane Mingay. Page 8: BF with a lamb © Ben Curtis/PA Archive/Press Association Images; BF with Inca and Angel the cow © Leila Angus.

Section two

Page 9: Filming *One Man and His Dog*, both photos © Andrew Crowley/Telegraph Media Group Limited 2005. Page 10: BF with the Duchess of Cornwall © Adrian Sherratt/PA Archive/Press Association Images. Page 11:

Filming *Escape in Time* at Acton Scott © Lion Television 2009. Page 12: Filming *Animal Park* © Longleat Safari & Adventure Park. Page 13: BF with Max the Rhino © Endemol; BF with Nepalese park wardens © Ken Lennox. Page 14 and 15: All photos © Ken Lennox. Page 16: BF with baby albatross © Ken Lennox; BF carrying Pixie the caracal and BF with a wild warthog, both photos © Endemol.

Section three

Page 17: BF and Kate Humble with Gomez the cheetah © Endemol. Page 18: BF in the Libyan desert with a camel © Ricochet Ltd 2007. Page 19: BF in Botswana with Prince William © Chris Jackson/Getty Images; BF assessing a bronze whaler shark in Namibia © Endemol. Page 20: BF beside a Crocodile Safety sign © Ingrid Kvale; BF holding a baby croc © Endemol. Page 21: BF diving with a crocodile © Brad Bestelink/Natural History Film Unit; BF releasing Ludo the crocodile © Ingrid Kvale; Jumping croc © Graham MacFarlane. Page 22: BF on Carcas Island © Ken Lennox; Page 24: Both photos courtesy of Plastic Oceans Foundation.

Index

The Accidental Adventurer
My Wilderness Years

Ben Fogle

Ben Fogle's life has been packed with action and adventure. He has rowed across the Atlantic, walked to the South Pole, run the Sahara and ice-skated across Sweden. He has encountered isolated tribes in deepest Papua New Guinea, caused a Boeing 747 to dump £100k of fuel before making an emergency landing in Sao Paulo, and frequently been mistaken for Prince William along the way.

So how did a cripplingly shy, geeky, perennially homesick boy end up doing all this? Ben's still not entirely sure himself, but this wonderful book tells his story and will strike a chord with anyone puzzling about life, and how to live it differently.

This is a book about defying expectations, conquering fears, battling laziness and, just occasionally, winning.

'Ben Fogle is never one to turn down a challenge'
TELEGRAPH